Custody/Access Assessments

A Practical Guide for Lawyers and Assessors

Barbara A. Chisholm
B.A., M.S.W., C.S.W., A.C.S.W.

H. Christina MacNaughton
B.A., LL.B., MEMBER OF THE ONTARIO BAR

CARSWELL
Toronto • Calgary • Vancouver
1990

Canadian Cataloguing in Publication Data

Chisholm, Barbara A.
Custody/access assessments

Includes bibliographical references.
ISBN 0-459-34203-7 (bound). — ISBN 0-459-34213-4 (pbk.)

1. Custody of children — Canada. 2. Custody of children — Canada — Psychological aspects. 3. Mental health consultation — Canada. I. MacNaughton, H. Christina, 1948- . II. Title.

KE600.C48 1990 346.7101′7 C90-093196-5
KF547.C48 1990

To my Mother and Father, in gratitude.

B.A.C.

- and -

To Helen M. VanDusen and Marion G. Fry,
my earliest mentors.

H.C.M.

Foreword

The determination of a contested custody dispute has long been one of the most feared and difficult tasks a judge can be asked to undertake. Recently, assistance arrived with the widespread acceptance and use of mediation and independent custody assessment. Of the two, almost all of the available literature has been focused on mediation. Although equally important, little attention seems to have been directed towards professional assessment reports. Now with the publication of this book, *Custody/Access Assessments: A Practical Guide for Lawyers and Assessors*, the authors (one a social worker, the other a lawyer) have truly rectified that serious omission.

The reader will soon realize that this book's strength lies in its detailed explanations of the necessary functions required of both the family law lawyer and the assessor in the custody/access assessment process. These are carefully presented in chronological order against the background of their actual occurrence in the process.

For the lawyer these begin with how to choose between assessment and mediation and proceed to the selection, appointment, and payment of an assessor, with assistance as to strategies to reduce client anxiety, receiving and understanding the report, dealing with the upset client, the use of the assessment at the pre-trial conference, as well as how to examine and cross-examine the assessor at trial.

For the mental health professional they range from the preliminary contact with the lawyer through acceptance or non-acceptance of the referral, to conducting the necessary interviews and visits, including detailed guidelines for writing the report and framing its recommendations, as well as how to cope with being cross-examined upon it.

Add to all of this a reliable collection of precedents, a comprehensive table of contents and index, and you have a book which will surely prove to be a most useful and practical addition to the library of any psychiatrist, psychologist, social worker or family law lawyer.

George T. Walsh
High Court of Justice
Supreme Court of Ontario
Osgoode Hall
Toronto, Ontario
October, 1989

Table of Contents

Table of Cases

Preface

When families rearrange themselves through separation or divorce, one unavoidable task facing parents is planning for and arranging the details of the ongoing care and raising of their children. Such decisions must be made at a time of stress and often high emotion, when the details of the adults' lives may be far from clear for themselves. Yet many parents make these arrangements, the restructured family adjusts to the new situation, and the children settle into the pattern provided by their parents.

For other families, however, arriving at such arrangements by themselves proves impossible. Whatever the reason, the emotions and attitudes associated with the separation or divorce extend to the question of the children, and a struggle ensues over matters of custody and visitation. If not already on the scene, lawyers now enter the picture. Each parent seeks and expects a favourable solution to emerge, as the power of the legal system is brought to bear on the dispute.

Experience has demonstrated, however, that so-called blind justice may not resolve the dispute at all. In matters so sensitive as the relationship of parents and children, the legal system, necessary though it is, may be an awkward tool at best. Litigation will lead to a court order, but may leave the litigants still angry and ill disposed to cooperate; the case may be over, but the quarrel is not. In such instances, it is difficult or next to impossible for children to settle into the court-ordered pattern. They remain both the focus and the victims of a continuing guerilla warfare.

The legal system is necessary and has a valuable role to play in the formal reordering of the family and its critical responsibility for children. To facilitate the exercise of that role, the last decade-plus has witnessed the development of new services whose aim is to enhance reliable decision-making by parents and more fully-informed judgments by the courts. The new services, mediation and assessment, have brought together the legal profession and the mental health professions in new, previously uncharted working relationships. The filter of experience has clarified much about how those relationships can and should work. Much has been written about mediation, describing process and suggesting structure for inter-professional cooperation. Organizations have emerged across the continent, addressing essential matters of qualifications, ethics and standards of practice for mediators. Much less has been undertaken with respect to the use of assessment as a mechanism to assist in resolving custody and access disputes. This book is a step toward remedying that deficiency.

Cross professional contact in custody/access disputes is not always easy. Misconceptions about each other's role are not uncommon. Case sharing calls for professional maturity and efforts to understand the boundaries such sharing sets on each profession's activities. The skills used remain the same but the context changes. While lawyers in such cases continue to represent a parent as their client, they are acting within the shadow of the children's futures. When contracting to undertake an assessment, mental health professionals, geared to providing helpful support for problem solving, now must direct that imperative toward assisting the legal system, rather than "owning" the matter themselves. Both roles have called for practice adjustments not anticipated at first.

The development of the use of custody/access assessments, sometimes referred to as custody evaluations or custody home studies, has been rapid but uneven. Standards of practice are only just emerging and there is as yet no widely-held consensus on what constitutes a reliable and thorough assessment. We hope with this book to provide a guideline for both the legal and the mental health professions which will assist in the search for that consensus.

The structure of this book was designed to model the integration of the legal and mental health roles in custody/access cases. It sets out the assessment process chronologically from the lawyer's initial consideration of whether an assessment might be useful, through the pre-assessment stages, the conduct of the assessment itself, and concludes with the use of the assessment report in negotiation or litigation.

Although specific chapters are addressed to assessors and others to lawyers, each profession will find the entire text relevant — assessors to understand the context and limitations of the role they are asked to fulfill; lawyers to understand how the assessor carries out that role.

For the legal profession, assistance is provided in the following areas:

- Deciding on seeking an assessment (as against mediation), with an explanation of the similarities and differences between the two.
- Choosing an assessor and obtaining an agreement or order appointing the assessor.
- Making the referral.
- Preparing the client.
- The lawyer's role while the assessment is being conducted.
- Receiving the assessment report and dealing with the client's response to the recommendations.
- Conducting examination-in-chief or cross examination of the assessor in the event of litigation.

For the mental health professions, the following is provided:

- Procedures for receiving the referral, including necessary information

to obtain in order to decide on accepting or refusing the referral and to ensure payment.
- Initiating, conducting, and concluding the assessment, including step by step discussion of each component.
- Preparing the report and recommendations.
- Post-report discussions with the parties and lawyers.
- Preparing for and coping with being a witness on the witness stand in subsequent litigation.

Precedents for forms, orders and letters appear at the conclusion of some chapters. They were evolved in the respective practices of the authors and are offered as a starting point from which others may develop their own precedents reflecting local statute and custom.

This book is based upon the statutes and practices of Ontario. To assist in adapting the legal material in a book for other jurisdictions we have included in Appendix I the various statute sections from across Canada governing custody/access assessments. To assist assessors in framing their reports to take into consideration the criteria that courts consider relevant in determining custody and access, we have set forth those sections from across Canada in Appendix II. As of July 1989 some provinces lacked specific legislation in one or both areas.

Appendix III is a bibliography of selected resources grouped by general subject categories, relevant both to lawyers and assessors.

Throughout we have attempted to present the rationales underlying our suggestions for what to include and what to avoid. Ethical considerations for both professions are given specific attention. We have presented an integrated approach to the subject, in an effort to model the very cooperation we advocate: a similarity of philosophy within a context of compatible differences in tasks and responsibilities.

Although each of us has carried primary responsibility for the content of the chapters addressed to our own profession, the content of every chapter reflects cooperation and some contribution by us both.

Others may, and surely will, have differences of approach or in point of view. We welcome dialogue. Ultimately we all share the same goal, to participate with the separated parents who have turned to us in arriving at constructive plans for their children's futures.

Barbara A. Chisholm — Toronto, Ontario

H. Christina MacNaughton — St. Catharines, Ontario

September 1, 1989

Note: For ease of reading, we have throughout the text referred to members of the legal system as "he" and to the assessors as "she". No inference is to be drawn from this arrangement except that of convenience for clarity of presentation.

B.A.C.
H.C.M.

Acknowledgments

We would like to express our sincere thanks to the following people for their constructive comments, particularly to those among them who read portions of the manuscript as it was developed: Renata Block (Social Worker), Nancy Elgie (Psychologist), Gail M. Hilyer (Educator), The Honourable Francis J. Kovacs (District Court Judge), Samuel R. Luker (Psychologist), Marion Mann (Social Worker), Eileen Martin (Lawyer), and Audrey Rosenthal (Lawyer-Legal Accounts Officer, Ontario Legal Aid Plan).

We thank the Carswell Company, especially Marie E. Ferguson, Senior Legal Editor, for her continuing assistance.

We appreciate the swift and obliging assistance of Kelly Hildebrand and Myra Christiansen of the Lincoln County Law Library.

We are grateful to our friend, Margaret Weiers, who read the entire manuscript and challenged us always to grammatical precision.

Our friends and colleagues have been generous with their support, encouragement, and practical assistance. We thank them all, and in particular: Anne and Michael Barstow, Franklin Corner, Helen Davidson, Kate Davey, Cecil Fennell, Stephen Ireland and Mary Frances Richardson.

We owe a great deal to our respective business partners, Carisse M. Gafni (Chisholm & Gafni, Child and Family Consultants, Toronto) & Patricia Boyko (MacNaughton & Boyko, Barristers and Solicitors, St. Catharines). They were always available over the year of writing this book to listen, to read portions of the manuscript, and encourage our best efforts. They have generously tolerated our increasing absorption in the book and consequent occasional absences of mind and body from our respective practices.

We owe a particular debt of gratitude to Leona McKay for her tireless conversion of draft upon re-draft of longhand into immaculate manuscript and computer discs. She rose to every unreasonable demand upon her time and energy with enthusiasm and good humour. We cannot imagine having been able to do this book without her.

B.A.C.
H.C.M.

1

Assessment: Why and When

1. CHOOSING BETWEEN ASSESSMENT AND MEDIATION

When families separate or divorce the situation is fraught with disappointment, fear, and anger. The trust that marital partners, or former partners, feel in themselves and in each other is stressed and eroded.

Although agreements may be hard to reach when mutual trust is minimal, many separating couples do manage to make joint decisions about how to continue parenting their children through negotiation between themselves, with or without a mediator, and with or without the assistance of lawyers.

Some couples are unable to reach a negotiated agreement, however, and in that minority of cases the structure of child custody and access must be submitted to the court for decision. When dealing with matters quantifiable, the law is an adequate tool, but in matters qualitative, it is, at best, clumsy. Increasingly, lawyers and courts turn to mental health professionals for assistance through independent custody/access assessments.

(a) What is Assessment?

An assessment is a process in a custody/access dispute in which a qualified mental health professional undertakes to:

1. Reach an understanding of the family situation and of the individuals in the family.
2. Evaluate how the family situation affects the children of that family.
3. Recommend how the custody and access arrangement might be most beneficially structured for the children, given the capacities of the parents and the needs of the children.
4. Prepare a report containing recommendations about custody and access, including the data upon which the recommendations are based.

In custody/access assessments the skills of mental health professionals are applied in the service of the legal system. The two systems, mental health and the law, approach custody/access matters differently. With good will and some understanding of each other's professional approaches, the interaction of law and mental health becomes more comfortable for both professions, and therefore beneficial for those children whose futures depend in part upon the outcome of the cooperative venture.

Assessment is future oriented and predictive — it looks for what will work, not who will win. Increasingly, family law lawyers are learning that in matters of child custody and access their role should more often include helping their clients seek solutions that will work for the children, instead of trying to win at all costs. There is a difference between the best possible result and the best reasonable result. When the issues relate to children, the best reasonable result becomes, for them, the best possible result.

Having defined what an assessment is, let us be very clear about what an assessment is not. An assessment is not mediation. An assessment is not therapy. Many of the skills employed by a clinician in therapy and in mediation may be utilized in doing assessments, but they are three different processes. The client is different; the purpose is different; the clinician's task is different.

(b) Tasks of the Lawyer and Assessor: Whose Client Is It?

The task of an assessor is to understand and to recommend. The lawyer's task is then to use the recommendations to negotiate, and if that fails to resolve the issues, then to use the report and recommendations as part of the evidence in court. For the assessor to enter the arena to undertake those negotiations herself is to pre-empt the function of the lawyers and the legal system. In assessment, the court is the assessor's primary client, where the matter is already being litigated, with the children as secondary clients on behalf of whose interests the assessor will be making specific recommendations. The parties to the action (usually the parents) remain the clients of the lawyers, even though they are the assessor's main source of information, and, of course, have a major investment in the outcome of the assessment. The assessment process is vertical — that is, the assessor directs and manages the process and is responsible for the outcome.

(c) What is Mediation?

Mediation occurs when a third party facilitates the effort of the individuals (here usually parents) to negotiate a compromise resolution of the matters in dispute, which may be custody, access, or other claims arising out of separation or divorce. The mediator's clients are the disputants. The purpose of mediation is to reduce quarrelling, and to arrive at agreement. If litigation is already underway, it may reduce the number of issues to be submitted to the court for adjudication. The mediation process is horizontal — that is, the mediator shares and facilitates the process *with* the clients, who ultimately define their own agreement, terms, and outcome. The mediator does not make recommendations.

Confusion often occurs because assessment and mediation have similarities as well as differences.

(d) Similarities Between Assessment and Mediation[1]

ASSESSMENT:	MEDIATION:
1. Parties identify the problems.	1. Parties identify the problems.
2. The parties are the main source of information.	2. The parties are the main source of information.
3. Children must always be seen, and interviewed if practical.	3. Children may be seen or included in the process, if pertinent.
4. The aim is not therapeutic, although that may be a by-product of the process.	4. The aim is not therapeutic, although that may be a by-product of the process.
5. The focus is the best interests of the children.	5. Where the children are an issue in the mediation, the focus is their best interests.
6. Interviews are the main device.	6. Interviews are the main device.

1 The material comparing and contrasting mediation and assessment is adapted from material originally published in "Preparing Your Client for Assessment or Mediation", by B.A. Chisholm (1987) 1 C.F.L.Q. 385.

(e) Differences Between Assessment and Mediation

ASSESSMENT	MEDIATION
1. The process is for the court's assistance, where the matter is being litigated.	1. The process is for the parties' assistance.
2. The assessor uses her professional judgment to form opinion and make recommendations.	2. The mediator acts as a facilitator and neither expresses an opinion, nor makes recommendations.
3. The assessor seeks to understand as completely as possible the history of the marriage, early/later relationships, parenting skills, coping patterns.	3. The mediator seeks only enough information to establish the nature and context of the current conflict.
4. The assessor (with consent) contacts collaterals, both within and outside the family, to assist in full understanding.	4. The mediator does not go beyond the immediate family context (including new relationships).
5. No option exists for anything other than full disclosure in the assessment report of all verified information relevant to the best interests of the children.	5. (In Ontario) the option exists for open mediation with full disclosure to the court, or with very limited disclosure.
6. The assessor may be called as a witness at any subsequent hearing to explain or elaborate on the report.	6. (In Ontario) depending upon whether the parties agreed that the mediation would be open ("with full report") or closed ("with limited report") anything said to the mediator may be, respectively, compellable or privileged.
7. The assessor determines the structure of the process.	7. The mediator facilitates, but the parties determine, the structure.
8. The assessment report, with its recommendations, is a final document.	8. A temporary working agreement may be tried, subject to review in a specified period of time, and subject to alteration then.
9. The assessor prepares the report and its recommendations entirely by himself. The assessor is responsible for both form and for content.	9. The agreement reached by the mediating parties is prepared by them with the mediator's assistance in drafting. The mediator provides form, and the parties determine the substance.

10. The report is not vetted by anyone prior to completion.	10. The agreement must be cleared through each party's counsel prior to completion and signing.
11. The recommendations in the assessment report are just that, recommendations. They may or may not be ordered by the court.	11. So long as no one's rights are infringed, and the agreement is fair and is seen to be fair, its terms will likely be confirmed by the court, if the matter is being litigated, or incorporated into a Separation Agreement.
12. Assessment is undertaken to help the court make its decision, if the matter is being litigated, and to encourage decisions by the parties, if it is not.	12. Mediation is undertaken so that the parties may make decisions.

2. WHEN TO OBTAIN AN ASSESSMENT

Whenever the parenting of children is in dispute, courts and lawyers should be prepared to consider the utility of an independent custody/access assessment. With instructions from their clients, counsel may consent to the assessment and to the clinician to be retained for the service. If counsel disagree on either point, then the court can be asked to order the assessment. In many cases the court will do so even if one of the parties objects. An assessment report and its recommendations may increase the likelihood of settlement in cases in which the parties trust the assessor and are prepared to make their own decisions for their children in light of the assessor's independent professional opinion. In cases where the parties cannot come to consensus in light of the report, then the assessment may assist the lawyers in terms of the advice they give to their clients, and can materially assist the court in arriving at a decision.

(a) Assessor as Potential Expert Witness

The assessor's recommendations do not replace the court's decision. The court may concur with all, some, or none of the recommendations. All relevant evidence, not just the assessment, will be considered at trial in arriving at a determination of what custody and access arrangements will be in the best interests of the children. How the report and/or the *viva voce* testimony of the assessor will be weighed in evidence is a function of the care, expertise, and professionalism exercised by the clinician in the assessment process.

In complex technical matters courts often receive the evidence of experts. Family property distribution cases, for instance, may involve evidence from business valuators, accountants, real estate appraisers and actuaries, to name but a few. An individual, whether a party to the action or the judge in the case, might readily admit, for example, that the technicalities of valuing a business corporation are unfamiliar to him. He would readily seek the responsible professional to help him understand the principles involved before making a decision. The problem with child custody/access matters, however, is that many people, both lay and professional, who are also parents, or who vividly recall their own childhood, tend to believe that there is no particular expertise required to determine what is best for children. It can be a delicate task to help parents and triers of fact alike to understand that there are instances in which something other than societal norms (young children belong with their mothers), or economic factors (father is better off financially, therefore he can give the children a better life), or popular biases should be considered in determining the parenting arrangements that will best suit a particular child's needs.

The Nova Scotia Supreme Court stated in *Cashin v. Cashin*[2] that the use of technical experts and professionals to inquire into the matters at issue and submit reports to the court is for the benefit of the court in arriving at a proper determination of the issues between the parties. As Perras D.C.J. said in *Boody v. Boody*:

> The primary purpose of an assessment is to gather evidence for the court at a hearing or on a motion and, as well, to provide a professional opinion on the issues in dispute.[3]

Delineating the role of the independent assessor, Perras D.C.J. stated:

> The role of the assessor is not to make the final judgment in the case, but to provide expert assistance to the court in making its determination of where the child's best interests lie in a custody dispute.
>
> The following are general guidelines for the assessor:
>
> (1) He must assist the child and the court by ensuring that in his report the important facts affecting the best interests of the child are set out.
>
> (2) He must ensure that any recommendation that he sets forth in his report to the court has been presented to the parents, the children, and their counsel and has some chance of acceptance, especially if it involves some more than usual activity or co-operation by them.
>
> (3) The report must give to the court an insight into the needs of the children and the ability of each parent to best satisfy those needs.[4]

No matter how useful the assessment report or the assessor's evidence,

2 (1985), 48 R.F.L. (2d) 104 (N.S.T.D.).

3 (1983), 32 R.F.L. (2d) 396, at 398-99 (Ont. Dist. Ct.).

4 *Ibid.*, at 399.

they augment and inform, but do not replace, the court's sole responsibility to determine the issues of custody and access in accordance with the statutes, common law and facts relevant to the dispute. The New Brunswick Court of Appeal held in *McLean v. McLean*[5] that the trial judge erred when he made an award of custody based entirely on a social worker's report without considering the best interests of the children as defined in New Brunswick's Family Services Act.

Case law is unanimous that no matter how expert the assessor or thorough the report, the responsibility to determine custody and access lies with the court.[6]

(b) When an Assessment is Useful

(i) *Allegations of Abuse*

While custody/access assessments can be useful in any case in which parenting arrangements are a contested issue, there are several circumstances in which they are of particular assistance. When the parties accuse each other of physically, emotionally, or sexually abusive conduct toward the children, an assessment is critically important, even though the investigation of child abuse as such is the mandate of child protection authorities. In addition to evaluating the family relationships and functions the assessor has to form a professional opinion on the credibility of such allegations, weigh the risk of recurrence of abusive behaviour, and make recommendations that will reduce or eliminate such risk for the children in future. This is so even if the validation of abuse complaints is not the primary focus of the assessment, and whether or not the allegations appear to have validity. Allegations of sexual abuse are becoming more frequent in cases of separation and divorce. Great care must be taken to determine whether such allegations are true or false. Their presence in the dispute, whether proven or not, is an indication of the extent of the family dysfunction.

The specific methods used in the validation of physical or sexual abuse allegations are beyond the scope of this book. The bibliography contains references which will assist clinicians whose particular task it is to form a professional opinion as to whether abuse has occurred. A particularly useful text in the area of child sexual abuse is Suzanne Sgroi's *Handbook*

---

5 (1985), 49 R.F.L. (2d) 235 (N.B. C.A.).

6 *Garro v. Garro* (1982), 16 Man. R. (2d) 15 (Q.B.); *Gauci v. Gauci* (1972), 9 R.F.L. 189 (Ont. H.C.); *Jones v. Jones,* [1986] W.D.F.L. 389 (Ont. H.C.); *M. v. D.* (1982), 29 R.F.L. (2d) 288, at 293 (Ont. H.C.); *More v. Primeau*; *Primeau v. More* (1978), 2 R.F.L. (2d) 254 (Ont. C.A.); *Nanji v. Nanji* (1987), 8 R.F.L. (3d) 221 (Ont. H.C.); *Singh v. Singh* (1982), 26 R.F.L. (2d) 75 (Alta. C.A.); *Tapley v. Tapley,* [1983] W.D.F.L. 763 (Ont. H.C.).

of Clinical Intervention in Child Sexual Abuse.[7] Lawyers as well as clinicians will find it germane.

When an abuse validation assessment is sought, the choice of assessor will be influenced by the type of abuse alleged. Not every clinician is skilled in and comfortable with determining whether sexual abuse has or has not occurred. Consultation with other lawyers, mental health professionals, or the local child protection agency may be necessary to obtain referrals and recommendations.

(ii) *Parental Deficits*

Assessment is also beneficial in situations where one (or both) of the parties is alleged to have mental, emotional, intellectual, or behavioural deficits, or when family violence has been a feature of the relationship. Any of these may create marked differences between the parties in how they approach child rearing issues in areas such as education, religion, discipline, and the roles of men and women, to name a few. An assessor can determine the existence and extent of such problems, clarify the effects of such approaches and attitudes, and evaluate the impact they have on the parenting capacities of the parties.

(iii) *Special Needs Children*

If one or more of the children has special needs due to physical, mental, or emotional handicaps, or learning disabilities, an assessment can assist the court to match the child's needs with the capacities that each of the parents has to contribute to the child's care.

(iv) *Apparently Equal Potential Parental Placements*

Assessments can be a great help when either party would appear to be an acceptable custodial parent for the children, but the parties are still too embroiled in dispute between themselves to cooperate sufficiently for a joint custody order to be realistic. These "coin-toss" cases are common ones. The assessor may be able to delineate valid points of comparison and contrast between the parents that could not be demonstrated so readily or succinctly in the testimony of other witnesses in the court room, within the confines of the rules of evidence. Particularly sensitive attention will be paid in such cases to ascertaining the wishes of the children and the basis for those wishes, if the assessor can reliably obtain them. Those wishes

---

7 S. Sgroi, *Handbook of Clinical Intervention in Child Sexual Abuse* (Toronto: Lexington Books/Heath, 1984).

may carry more weight than in cases where there are more overt grounds upon which the court can pick and choose between the parties. Assessors must be alert to detect parental attempts to sway the child's wishes in such assessment situations.

Assessment ought to be considered as an instrument to assist the court in any custody/access case in which the parties have been unable to agree, with or without the assistance of a mediator, or through inter-lawyer negotiations. If the parties' positions on the custody/access issues have hardened and a court appearance seems likely, an assessment may break the deadlock, and focus the issues.

3. HOW TO OBTAIN AN ASSESSMENT

(a) Statutory Authority

(i) *Inherent Jurisdiction*

While the Divorce Act, 1985,[8] contains no provisions expressly permitting orders for an assessment, the courts in Ontario and other jurisdictions have made assessment orders by relying upon the inherent jurisdiction of the superior courts,[9] and the rules of the court.[10]

(ii) *Ontario Children's Law Reform Act*

In Ontario, an independent assessment is authorized by section 30 of the Children's Law Reform Act[11] in cases in which custody of, or access to, children is at issue.

> 30. — (1) The court before which an application is brought in respect

---

8 S.C. 1986, c. 4.

9 *Cillis v. Cillis* (1980), 20 R.F.L. (2d) 208 (Ont. H.C.). Affirmed (1981), 23 R.F.L. (2d) 76 (Ont. Div. Ct.); *El-sohemy v. El-sohemy* (1980), 17 R.F.L. (2d) 1 (Ont. H.C.); *Roschuk v. Roschuk* (1980), 15 R.F.L. (2d) 196 (Man. C.A.); *Ross v. Ross,* [1987] W.D.F.L. 1349 (B.C. S.C.), in which although section 15 of the Family Relations Act of British Columbia (R.S.B.C. 1979, c. 121) provides for assessment reports, the court held it had inherent jurisdiction in any event under the Divorce Act 1985, S.C. 1986, c. 4.

10 *Cashin v. Cashin* (1985), 48 R.F.L. (2d) 104 (N.S. T.D.); *Jones v. Jones,* [1986] W.D.F.L. 389 (Ont. H.C.) which applied Rule 70.01(1) (Ontario Consolidated Rules of Practice), which in turn invokes Rule 52.03 authorizing one or more independent experts to be appointed in a divorce action; *McIntosh (Burke) v. Burke* (1986), 1 R.F.L. (3d) 370 (N.S. C.A.), affirming [1986] W.D.F.L. 706 (N.S. T.D.) in which the trial judge, acting as a referee on application to vary the custody provisions of a *decree nisi,* had jurisdiction to order an assessment; *Norton (Korpeshko) v. Korpeshko* (December 22, 1980) (Man. Q.B.) which relied upon James McLeod's annotation to *Cillis v. Cillis* (1980), 20 R.F.L. (2d) 208-209.

11 R.S.O. 1980 c. 68 [as amended by S.O. 1982, c. 20].

of custody of or access to a child, by order, may appoint a person who has technical or professional skill to assess and report to the court on the needs of the child and the ability and willingness of the parties or any of them to satisfy the needs of the child.

(2) An order may be made under subsection (1) on or before the hearing of the application in respect of custody of or access to the child and with or without a request by a party to the application.

(3) The court shall, if possible, appoint a person agreed upon by the parties, but if the parties do not agree the court shall choose and appoint the person.

. . . .

The section is not mandatory and the court may refuse to order an assessment. The court may act on its own motion and may also postpone the hearing of a custody or access matter to obtain an assessment.

The Act does not define a person with "technical or professional skill". Psychologists, social workers, and psychiatrists with training and experience in child and family matters, adept at both assessment and the writing of reports are logical choices, although persons from other professions might, on the basis of particular skill and experience, also be considered. In some provinces the enabling legislation specifically names "family counsellor" (B.C. and Newfoundland); "family investigator (Manitoba); "probation officer" (B.C. and Newfoundland); "social worker" (B.C., Manitoba, New Brunswick and Newfoundland) in addition to any "other person approved by the court" (all provinces with legislation).

It is important that the person designated as the assessor be capable of being qualified in court as an expert witness able to give opinion evidence. If counsel for the parties agree on which person should be appointed, the court will make the order accordingly, although the wording of the subsection does not entirely preclude the court from substituting an assessor of the court's choosing for the person agreed upon by counsel.

(iii) *Relation Between Children's Law Reform Act and Divorce Act*

In Ontario, section 30 of the Children's Law Reform Act may be invoked even once divorce proceedings have been commenced, notwithstanding that section 27 of the Act stays all proceedings under that Act upon filing a Divorce Petition. In *Booth v. Booth,*[12] the court granted the wife's application for an assessment under section 30 of the Children's Law Reform Act in divorce proceedings stating that section 27 was not an absolute bar to taking further proceedings under that Act. The court was of the

12 (1983), 33 R.F.L. (2d) 330 (Ont. H.C.).

opinion that section 10(*b*) of the Divorce Act, 1970,[13] was wide enough to vest the court with the jurisdiction to make an order for assessment because it was corollary to an order for custody and was for the benefit of the children, the parties, and the court. Section 16(6) of the Divorce Act, 1985 is equivalent to section 10(*b*) of the 1970 Act. The *parens patriae* jurisdiction is wide enough to allow such an order.

(b) When the Court Will Order An Assessment

Section 30(2) of the Children's Law Reform Act is permissive. The court will not order an assessment on its own motion, or over the objections of counsel for one party in every custody/access case, although if parties consent it would be unusual for the court to refuse the order.

Professor James McLeod's annotation to *Chapman v. Chapman* suggests concerning the permissive rather than mandatory approach of subsection 30(2):

> It would seem to flow on general principles that the person requesting the assessment must show a reason the special remedy of an assessment is required in the particular case. The alternative is to say that in all custody disputes an assessment will be ordered, if requested, in order to provide impartial expert evidence, unless the resisting party can show a reason to the contrary. . . . . The onus should be on the moving party to show at least some reason for the assessment. There should be some reason to expect that the assessment will add to the evidence if, as our law provides, the parties and the child have a right to have the decision of custody or access made by a judge, not an assessor. . . . . There must be some evidence that the dispute is so intense as to prevent all the relevant factors coming out, or that there appears to be a parent-child problem that requires expert analysis and/or explanation, or finally that the assessment is necessary to allow the parties to understand the needs of the child and the need for cooperation.[14]

In *Cillis v. Cillis*,[15] the Ontario Divisional Court affirmed the ruling of the High Court in which Montgomery J. held that while he did not have the power to order assessment in the circumstances, he did have the power to stay the ex-wife's application to vary the access provisions of a *decree nisi* under section 18(6) of the Judicature Act[16] until an independent assessment was completed, stating that:

> . . . the High Court does have an inherent or ancillary jurisdiction to make such orders as are necessary for the purpose of promoting a fair and satisfactory

13 R.S.C. 1970, D-8.

14 (1985), 49 R.F.L. (2d) 47, at 48.

15 (1980), 20 R.F.L. (2d) 208 (Ont. H.C.). Affirmed (1981), 23 R.F.L. (2d) 76 (Ont. Div. Ct.).

16 R.S.O. 1970, c. 228, s. 18(6).

> trial. Where the access to infants is the issue the court has jurisdiction to order a family clinic assessment of the parties, where that assessment appears reasonably necessary to arrive at a just and proper decision in the best interest and welfare of the children.[17]

The court in *Clasen v. Clasen*[18] ordered an independent assessment over the objections of the mother who claimed that the husband was on a "fishing expedition" in the hopes that the assessment would turn up evidence to support his position. The court said that the father had legitimate concerns about the care of the children, but even if the court had agreed with the mother that the father was "fishing", the assessment might still have been ordered to satisfy the court which stated:

> The fates of the children, who are not parties to the proceedings, should not rest entirely on the evidence the parties choose to tender or challenge.[19]

A review of recent cases reveals situations in which courts have been ordering independent assessments over the objection of one of the parties, or on the court's own motion: hostility or intractable dispute between the parties on the custody/access issues;[20] equally apparently adequate parents;[21] allegations of abuse;[22] allegations of deficits in parenting skills and capacities;[23] where one parent's values or lifestyle is at odds with those of the other parent;[24] where a party seeks to change an existing custodial arrangement;[25] and where one parent seeks to alienate a child from the other parent, or has already done so.[26]

The court has also favoured a second assessment in the face of a pre-existing assessment where the court determined that the earlier

---

17 *Supra*, note 15 (Ont. Div. Ct.), at 76.

18 (1984), 42 R.F.L. (2d) 376 (Man. Q.B.).

19 *Ibid.*, at 379.

20 *Ross v. Ross, supra*, note 9; *Booth v. Booth* (1983), 33 R.F.L. (2d) 330 (Ont. H.C.); *Cashin v. Cashin* (1985), 48 R.F.L. (2d) 104 (N.S. T.D.); *Chapman v. Chapman* (1985), 49 R.F.L. (2d) 47 (Ont. Dist. Ct.)

21 *Bailey v. Bailey* (1987), 5 R.F.L. (3d) 354 (Ont. Dist. Ct.).

22 *M. (S.P.) v. M. (W.B.)* (1988), 15 R.F.L. (3d) 301 (Ont. H.C.); *R. (J.S.); Waterloo Family & Children's Services v. R (S.),* [1988] W.D.F.L. 1417 (Ont. Prov. Ct. (Family Div.)); *W. (S.) v. W. (M.L.),* [1987] W.D.F.L. 1410 (Ont. H.C.); *Cameron v. MacDonald* (1989), 20 R.F.L. (3d) 119 (N.S. Co. Ct.).

23 *Sturn v. Pardell,* [1988] W.D.F.L. 1163 (B.C.S.C.); *Clasen v. Clasen, supra,* note 18; *Hampel v. Hampel* (1983), 31 R.F.L. (2d) 462 (Ont. Dist. Ct.); *McKechnie v. McKechnie,* [1987] W.D.F.L. 1976 (Ont. H.C.); *Faulkner v. Faulkner* (1985), 47 R.F.L. (2d) 26 (Ont. H.C.); *Waddell v. Waddell,* [1989] W.D.F.L. 1185 (Ont. Dist. Ct.).

24 *Sutherland v. Sutherland,* [1987] W.D.F.L. 439 (Ont. Dist. Ct.).

25 *Asquith v. Marsh,* 10 A.C.W.S. (3d) 329 (Ont. Dist. Ct.).

26 *Ptashnik v. Ptashnik* (1988), 12 R.F.L. (3d) 377 (Man. Q.B.); *Heaton v. Heaton* (1988), L.W. 820-007 (Ont. Dist. Ct.).

assessment was deficient and incomplete.[27] In another case the court arranged for an independent assessment prior to appeal when the only mental health evidence at trial was from an on-side consultation, and there had been no on-side expert for the other party, or independent overview for the court.[28]

(c) When the Court Will Refuse to Order an Assessment

Courts have refused orders for independent custody/access assessments in such instances as: cases in which expert evidence has been filed for both parties or there have been previous independent assessments by several experts;[29] where there are no overt indicators of a child's maladjustment to an existing custody situation;[30] where a party seeks to continue or re-open a completed assessment that did not result in a recommendation that the party liked;[31] or where the court holds that there is enough evidence to come to a reasoned decision on factors relevant to the applicable legislation without an assessment.[32]

The timing of an assessment may be a factor in whether a court will order it. For instance, the court refused to order a psychological report too long ahead of the trial in the case of *Gilfix v. Gilfix*[33] Orders can be made, however, to update assessments to ensure current relevance for trial.

An order denying an assessment does not preclude the court from ordering an assessment later in the proceeding.[34]

4. CONCLUSION

The chief advantage of an independent custody/access assessment is that it provides the court with a view of the children and their needs and tolerances, and of the parties and their capacities and limitations, more subtle and complex than that which is otherwise available to the court under the strictures of the rules of evidence. Master Cork said in *Velanoff*

---

27 *M. (S.P.) v. M. (W.B.), supra*, note 22.

28 *Whey v. Brenton* (1984), 41 R.F.L. (2d) 30 (Nfld. C.A.).

29 *Nadeau v. Campbell* (1983), 21 A.C.W.S. (2d) 409 (B.C. S.C.); *Zaborsky v. Zaborsky*, [1986] W.D.F.L. 502 (B.C. S.C.); *Metzner v. Metzner* (1987), 10 A.C.W.S. (3d) 383 (B.C. S.C.).

30 *Nathani v. Nathani* (1983), 48 N.B.R. (2d) 410, 126 A.P.R. 410 (Q.B.).

31 *Naumetz v. Naumetz*, [1988] W.D.F.L. 1633 (Ont. H.C.). *McClinchey v. McClinchey*, [1989] W.D.F.L. 185 (Ont. Dist. Ct.).

32 *Ruiter v. Ruiter*, [1987] W.D.F.L. 289 (Sask. Q.B.).

33 [1979] 2 W.W.R. 190 (Man. C.A.).

34 *McIntosh (Burke) v. Burke* (1986), 1 R.F.L. (3d) 370 (N.S.C.A.) indicates that the issue of denying an order for assessment should not be viewed as *res judicata*.

v. Velanoff[35] that if the parties themselves could be made aware through an assessment of the potential effects of their demands upon the children, then by such foreknowledge they might be able to avoid or reduce the likelihood of harm to the children. He indicated further that any court would welcome an assessment done by a qualified assessor because it would assist the court to determine what would be in the best interests of the children. His view was like that of Master McBride in *Faulkner v. Faulkner* who, ordering an independent assessment on his own motion where the parties put each other's parenting abilities in issue, stated that "Such assistance as the court can get in aid of resolution is something to be desired."[36]

35 (1985), 7 F.L.R.R. 125 (Ont. H.C.).
36 (1985), 47 R.F.L. (2d) 26, at 28 (Ont. H.C.).

2

Choosing the Assessor: Notes for the Lawyers

1. THE SOCIAL WORKER
2. THE PSYCHIATRIST
3. THE PSYCHOLOGIST
4. AREAS UNIQUE TO EACH PROFESSION
5. OVERALL POINTS TO LOOK FOR
6. CONCLUSION

Once it has been determined that an independent custody/access assessment would be useful in a case, the next decision is who should be approached to undertake the task. It is not easy, unless you have your own favorite resource persons, to know who to recommend or agree to, when assessment is being considered. Word of mouth impressions may suggest professionals who have been used by other lawyers and found to be useful, reliable, and effective. On the other hand, such a list may not be readily accessible, or you are not comfortable considering the persons named therein. Does the particular case call for a social worker, a psychiatrist or a psychologist with specific skills to appraise the situation, or will any one of the mental health professions serve as well as any other?

There are not always clear lines defining the areas of competence and expertise among social workers, psychiatrists, and psychologists. There are important though less tangible qualities of skill, viewpoint, and professionalism, which may significantly influence the selection. While the three main mental health professions who engage in custody/access assessment work have clinical interviewing skills in common, each also has unique qualifications.

The following guidelines may be useful in choosing an assessor.

1. THE SOCIAL WORKER

A professional social worker[1] has a degree, either at the undergraduate (B.S.W.) or graduate (M.S.W.) level, or both, from a faculty or school of social work affiliated with a university. Training in social work involves both theory taught in the classroom, and supervised field practice placements. In Ontario, the designation C.S.W. signifies that the professional social worker is an accredited member of the Ontario College of Certified Social Workers.[2] In the United States, the designation A.C.S.W. signifies that the social worker is also a member of the Academy of Certified Social Workers, a national designation. In Ontario, it is useful to ascertain whether the social worker is a member in good standing of the Ontario Association of Professional Social Workers. Unlike all other Canadian provinces, there is as yet no licencing legislation for social workers in Ontario, such as

---

1 Many non-social workers are not clear about what a social worker or the practice of social work is. The following may clarify the extent and boundaries of social work as a professional discipline.

The Prince Edward Island Social Work Act, S.P.E.I. 1988, c. 62 (in force as of December 3, 1988) defines "social work" in section 1(f) as meaning:

> . . . service that is performed, for remuneration or in a continual way and without immediate supervision, to aid clients to understand and resolve personal, family, or social problems, in ways which, in the judgment of the [Prince Edward Island Social Work Registration] Board as supported by common opinion among social-work educators, authorities and practitioners, require expert and comprehensive knowledge, skills, judgment and ethical conduct of a distinctly professional nature as provided for in education at a university school of social work . . . .

The New Brunswick Association of Social Workers Act, 1988, S.N.B. 1988, c. 78 (in force January 1, 1989) states in section 2:

> "Practice of social work" includes the assessment, mediation and prevention of social problems, and the enhancement of social functioning of individuals, families, groups and communities by means of
>
> (*a*) the provision of direct counselling services within an established relationship between a social worker and client;
>
> (*b*) the development, promotion and delivery of human service programs, including that done in collaboration with other professionals;
>
> (*c*) the development and promotion of social policies aimed at improving social conditions and promoting social equality; and
>
> (*d*) any other activities consistent with the objects of the [New Brunswick] Association [of Social Workers].

The Ontario College of Certified Social Workers defines the practice of social work in Bylaw 2 (establishing the O.C.C.S.W.), clause 1(j) as:

> the application of knowledge and skills to improve the social functioning of individuals, groups, organizations, and communities.

2 Most other provinces have equivalent designations for accredited members of the social work profession.

there is for physicians (psychiatrists) and psychologists.[3] Some employees of public service agencies are called "social workers" when in fact they do not have a degree in social work and are therefore ineligible to be accredited as professional social workers. The background experience of a social worker who undertakes custody/access assessments will likely include clinical social work practice[4] with a focus on families and children, and the dynamics of separation and divorce.

Consider using a professional social worker if there is concern about understanding the interaction of family members; the reasons for the family breakdown; the relationships between the adults, and between the adults and the children; the patterns of parenting that have gone on in the past; the parenting that is going on now; and a sense of what environment will be provided by each parent now and prospectively into the future, to meet the needs of the children.

2. THE PSYCHIATRIST

A psychiatrist is a physician who, after obtaining an initial university degree in medicine, and completion of internship, has successfully completed a residency in, and essentially confines professional practice to, the

---

3 At the time of writing there is before the Government of Ontario an Application by the O.A.P.S.W. (Ontario Association of Professional Social Workers) for the enactment of a Social Work Act for Ontario.

4 "Clinical social work practice" is defined by the National Association of Social Workers' *Model State Licensing Statute for Social Workers*, Clause 103(d) as:

> the application of social work methods and values to the diagnosis and treatment of mental and emotional conditions and in providing psychotherapy.

The skills base required for social workers in Ontario to be able to be accredited as professionally competent and qualified for membership in the Ontario College of Certified Social Workers is defined in the *Guidelines for the Accreditation of Professional Competence in Social Work* which are prescribed for the College in By-Law Two. Of particular relevance in custody/access assessments are Guidelines 9 and 10 which are reprinted here:

> **Guideline 9**
> **Problem Identification and Assessment**
>
> The professional social worker is expected to be able to describe problems in terms of:
>
> 1. the individuals and/or groups involved in the problems;
> 2. the domain of the problem situation, that is, where it does and does not occur;
> 3. the frequency of the problem, that is, when it does and does not occur;
> 4. the essential characteristics of the presenting problem; and
> 5. whether other professions, organizations or persons should be involved or assume responsibility.
>
> In describing social problems, the practitioner must be able to gather data that is pertinent to assessing problems. This includes:

diagnosis and treatment of disorders affecting the mind.[5] In Ontario, a psychiatrist is accredited through the College of Physicians and Surgeons of Ontario, and will likely belong as well to the Ontario Medical Association.

Consider using a psychiatrist if the concern is to receive a diagnosis about the mental condition of one or both of the parents, or any or all of the children; or an indication of the emotional condition in either parent, or in one or any of the children that may require psychiatric attention. If a party to the action has already been diagnosed as suffering from a mental disorder, a psychiatrist will be able to comment on the probable outcomes of various treatment methods, as well as the implications that mental disorders and their treatment have for the lives of the children and others involved. There are many subspecialties in psychiatry, and those engaged in custody/access assessment work should be experienced and specialize in dealing with children or families.

---

1. collecting all of the information required for an adequate assessment;
2. obtaining multiple perspectives upon the same problem situation whenever possible;
3. encouraging specificity when seeking information so that the data can be readily mobilized for purposes of analysis.

The practitioner must be able to analyze the data collected in terms of the parameters of the problem and knowledge of resources which can be mobilized for reducing, solving or preventing the problem. With this background, the professional social worker is expected to be able to:

1. identify discrepancies among the perceptions and interests of the various parties to the problem situation;
2. distinguish, when appropriate, between the objective of the seeker and the target of the change effort;
3. relate relevant historical information and psychosocial theory to the current problem situation;
4. assess the impact of existing social policy upon his or her understanding of the problem under investigation.

Guideline 10
Identification of Alternative Courses of Action.

Objectives are defined in specific, meaningful and comprehensive terminology in order for them to be readily reviewed by the client or other decision maker. Thus the professional social worker should be able to interpret the original problem in the light of new knowledge and social science theory. This involves:

1. specifying the advantages of the chosen plan over other possible alternatives;
2. suggesting how the chosen plan will maximize the probability of achieving the objective of the change effort;
3. demonstrating the feasibility of the chosen strategy for conducting the intervention given the particulars of the problem situation;
4. support the choice with relevant theory.

5 The *Diagnostic and Statistical Manual of Mental Disorders* (known as the DSM-III-R) says a "mental disorder" is:

3. THE PSYCHOLOGIST

A psychologist has an undergraduate degree in psychology, following which he or she has usually obtained a Ph.D.[6] in psychology. In Ontario, the Psychologists Registration Act,[7] provides in subsection 11(1) that "No person shall represent himself to be a psychologist unless he holds a certificate of registration." Psychologists in Ontario are accredited through the Ontario Board of Examiners in Psychology. Membership in the Ontario Psychological Association is voluntary. The designation "C.Psych." indicates that the psychologist is certified by the Ontario Board of Examiners in Psychology. There are several areas of specialty in psychology.[8] Clinical psychologists engage in therapeutic practice, and it is usually clinical psychologists specializing in family and child related issues who engage in custody/access work.

Consider using a clinical psychologist if there is concern about the intellectual levels of the parents or one or all of the children; if there is

---

> . . .conceptualized as a clinically significant behavioral or psychological syndrome or pattern that occurs in a person and that is associated with present distress (a painful symptom) or disability (impairment in one or more important areas of functioning) or with a significantly increased risk of suffering death, pain, disability, or an important loss of freedom. In addition, this syndrome or pattern must not be merely an expectable response to a particular event, e.g., the death of a loved one. Whatever its original cause, it must currently be considered a manifestation of a behavioural, psychological, or biological dysfunction in the person. Neither deviant behaviour, e.g., political, religious, or sexual, nor conflicts that are primarily between the individual and society are mental disorders unless the deviance or conflict is a symptom of a dysfunction in the person, as described above.

Diagnostic and Statistical Manual of Mental Disorders, 3d ed. Revised (Washington, D.C: American Psychiatric Association, 1987), p. xxii.

6 In psychology, as in social work, legislative regulation of the profession followed the establishment of the profession by many years. Senior members of the profession who had degrees at the masters level and experiential equivalence to more formal training were granted registration or certification in appropriate cases on a "grandfathering" basis before 1964.

7 R.S.O. 1980, c. 404.

8 The definition of the scope of practice in psychology developed by the Ontario Board of Examiners in Psychology in consultation with the Ontario Psychological Association in 1987 was printed in the October 1987 issue of *The Bulletin*, Vol. 10, No. 3, as follows:

> The practice of psychology is the assessment, diagnosis and treatment of behaviour and mental processes, research and other professional services usually performed by a psychologist in Ontario for the purpose of assessing and understanding behaviour and mental processes, ameliorating maladaptive or undesired behaviour, and maintaining or enhancing the physical, intellectual, emotional, social and interpersonal functioning of individuals and groups.

As "licenced acts" permitted in the profession of psychology the Board suggested the following:

a wish for the information to be gained by various recognized tests concerning the developmental normalcy, or otherwise, of the children in areas of intellectual functioning and learning; or if there is a wish to compare the personality structure and coping styles of any of the family members to norms in a measured way through projective tests and personality tests.

4. AREAS UNIQUE TO EACH PROFESSION

Despite areas of broadly overlapping knowledge and skills, there are fields of expertise and endeavour in which each of the three major mental health professions has exclusive domain.

Only social workers are mandated by provincial legislation to investigate, intervene, apprehend children, and engage in case work with parents to protect children. Also unique to social work is training and experience in the practical adaptation of individuals to physical environment, and vice versa, and in the matching of the needs of individuals to specific community resources such as public welfare programmes, public housing authorities, etc.

Psychiatrists are the only mental health professionals licensed to prescribe medication or to admit persons to hospital. Although clinical social workers and clinical psychologists may be trained and experienced to recognize mental disorders when they are encountered, only a psychiatrist may make a formal diagnosis of psychopathology.

Only a psychologist may interpret standardized personality tests and projective tests, although such tests may be administered and scored by a psychometrist.

5. OVERALL POINTS TO LOOK FOR

(a) A Note of Caution

These guidelines are very general. Well-trained, experienced members of each of these disciplines may be of great value as assessors. All would be able to comment upon the observed relationships between parents and children, and to express professional opinions about the children's needs

---

(a) Making recommendations for treatment, placement or other interventions affecting the lives of individuals or groups based upon the results of standardized tests designated to assess intelligence, psychopathology, personality, neuropsychological functioning or perceptual disorders;

(b) Performing psychotherapy, behaviour therapy, hypnosis or biofeedback.

The Ontario Board of Examiners in Psychology. *The Bulletin*. October 1987, Vol. 10, No. 3, p. 3.

and the parties' capacities to meet them. All would be able to consult with members of the other mental health professions for input concerning areas outside their immediate specialty. The guidelines above serve only to illustrate broadly the main areas of expertise which may be relied upon.

Beyond the formal professional qualifications, there are other considerations in choosing which clinician to invite to act as assessor. Time taken to weigh them may ensure that the assessment is of acceptable quality and will be reliable.

(b) Credentials

The person should have a well-presented *curriculum vitae*, readily available, to share with the lawyers, the parties, and the court. The clinician should be prepared to discuss any aspect of her professional background.

(c) Experience

Is the person's professional experience pertinent to child custody/access assessments? If that is not readily apparent from the *curriculum vitae*, the person should be prepared to clarify what aspects of that background do contribute to skill in assessments, or to point out what additional steps she has taken to acquire the necessary skills.

(d) Point of View

Does this person have a particular point of view on such matters as separation, divorce, joint custody, sole custody, possible restrictions on access, the roles of men and women as fathers and mothers, lifestyle, *etc.*? Do these positions appear rigid, or is there flexibility of approach, and absence of prejudgment before even beginning to work, yet sufficient professional self-confidence that ensures emotional independence and a philosophical starting point? Is the person prepared to discuss these points openly and non-defensively?

(e) Definite Sense of Procedure

Is this person able to present a clear picture of how she undertakes assessment, including how to begin, what payment arrangements are to be made, how the first interviews are arranged, whether they consult collateral informants, what the assessment process itself will include? In other words, does the person appear in control of the process, but not so rigidly that accommodation is not possible to any unusual circumstances of the client's situation. Does the assessor have reasons for the assessment approach used? Does it make sense?

(f) Willingness to Do Home Visits

Some professionals resist seeing the children in the homes of the mother and the father (if both are possible), and base reports on office contacts only. Some assessors do not see the children and parties interacting. This point of view should be greeted with considerable caution: home visits may clarify much about the party's lifestyle, the care of the child, the stress or advantage a party is living under, etc. Absence of this perspective may affect the recommendations significantly.

(g) Acknowledgement of the Lawyer's Role and Responsibility

Does the clinician have some understanding, at least, of the role of the lawyer and the responsibilities that go with it? Does she seek clarification of the boundaries of the relationship between lawyer and assessor as they "share" the client; will she persist in such discussion until clarification is achieved and misunderstanding avoided?

(h) Thoroughness

Does this person have a reputation for being thorough in her work, or for being too quick and rather shallow, including the ability to write a professional report, setting out her findings and recommendations clearly and so as to assist the court?

(i) Willingness to Appear in Court

Is this person prepared, or not, to be asked to appear in court to support the recommendations of an assessment report, or to be cross-examined on them? Can the person explain how she arrived at those recommendations?

6. CONCLUSION

If the lawyer has not worked before with the suggested mental health professional, the lawyer should feel perfectly free to clarify every point before making a final decision on the choice of clinician. If resistance or defensiveness are encountered about any or all points, caution should be exercised on the client's behalf, and, ultimately, on the children's behalf.

Consideration of the intangibles of reputation, methodology, and reliability, is an essential element of the "expert" status of the assessor. For the assessment to be useful to the lawyer, the parties, and the court (and therefore to the children), the assessor must be one in whom all interested parties can have confidence. A careful, thorough assessment which both is, and appears to be, balanced and fair may be of more ready use in negotiated settlement of the case. If the case proceeds to trial, such an assessor is not only more likely to be accepted by the court as a person qualified to give opinion evidence, but the evidence will be accorded more weight.

In the long run it is more important to use a competent mental health professional with skill and credibility than to have a clinician of a particular profession merely for the sake of using *that* profession. In other words, it is sometimes necessary to compromise on the choice of the assessor's profession, but one ought never to compromise on the quality of the professional who is asked to perform the assessment.

3

The Referral Process

1. MAKING THE REFERRAL: THE LAWYER'S PERSPECTIVE
2. RECEIVING THE REFERRAL: THE ASSESSOR'S PERSPECTIVE
3. EXHIBITS

1. MAKING THE REFERRAL: THE LAWYER'S PERSPECTIVE

(a) Preliminary Contact with the Assessor

Before formal appointment of the assessor, either by court order or mutual agreement between the parties, the assessor's consent to act must be obtained. In some cases, as in Ontario, the assessor's consent to act is required by statute.[1] In every case it is required by common sense.

If the assessor is a person with whom either party's solicitor has worked before, that consent may be obtained initially with a quick phone call. Although it is not universal practice to obtain a written consent of the assessor to the appointment, the use of such a consent form may augment or even replace an affidavit in support of a motion requesting an assessor. FAX machines can be useful in the rapid transmission of consent forms where required in urgent situations. An alternative with assessors one often engages is to obtain in advance a series of consent forms signed in blank. An example of such a form follows at the end of this section as Exhibit (3.1). With a supply of such forms and a master copy of the assessor's up-to-date *curriculum vitae* in an assessment resource file, the brief telephone call to obtain the assessor's consent is all that is required before

1 Ontario: Children's Law Reform Act, R.S.O. 1980, c. 68 [as amended by S.O. 1982 c. 20], s. 30(4); Yukon: Children's Act, R.S.Y 1986, c. 22 [as amended], s. 43(2); Newfoundland: Children's Law Act, S.N. 1988, c. 61, s. 36(4).

filling in the appropriate blanks. Form (3.1) reflects the requirements of section 30 of the Ontario Children's Law Reform Act and can be augmented or amended to reflect statute or practice in other jurisdictions.[2] It provides a useful outline for the points to be covered in an order.

Every assessor has his or her own preferred method of procedure for the assessment process. As this is a growth industry, however, it is possible from time to time to encounter mental health professionals who are inexperienced in custody/access assessment work. Particular care should be taken in such instances to ascertain that the potential assessor not only possesses the requisite skills and experience, but will also use a thorough protocol for the assessment process. Just as there have been few, if any, courses in law schools on how to use assessments, there has been little, if anything, available to mental health professionals to help them adapt their skills to the demands made by the legal process in child related matters. In fact, the very word "assessment" can mean different things to lawyers (who think of it forensically) and to mental health professionals (who think of it clinically).

(b) What to Tell the Assessor

Explain to the clinician that a custody/access assessment is sought that will involve an investigation of the family and children and the preparation of a report embodying the assessor's recommendations as to custody and access. Indicate whether the report will be filed with the court for use in evidence in the event that post-assessment negotiations do not achieve settlement.

Not every clinician wishes to become involved in custody/access work. If the prospective assessor is not prepared to testify in court to expand upon and defend the report, it is a disservice to counsel and client alike to persuade the clinician, no matter how able as a therapist or diagnostician, to become involved as an assessor. Do not do it even if both parties to the litigation have indicated that they will both agree with whatever that clinician recommends. In custody litigation parties sometimes make such statements in advance of assessment expecting a favourable recommendation, and afterwards deny having made any such representation. To put either the client or the clinician in such a position is unreasonable and unfair to both of them.

Upon ascertaining that the clinician is qualified to undertake such an assessment, understands the nature of the task, and is willing to perform it and able to commence and complete it within an acceptable time frame,

2 For the texts of the statutory provisions mandating assessments, evaluations and investigations in child custody/access matters see Appendix I at the end of the book.

then work out the procedural details. Be prepared in the initial contact to give a general background of the facts to the clinician so that he or she may determine the likely scope of the process and the time required to complete it and to prepare the report.

The following should be clarified at the outset in the preliminary contact with the clinician:

- Will the clinician expect a financial retainer?
- Will the clinician invoice the lawyer(s) or the party?
- Will the invoice have to be paid before the release of the report?
- Will the clinician expect counsel's personal undertaking with respect to the payment of the fees?
- Does the clinician accept third party or legal aid billings?
- What is the clinician's hourly fee for private paying parties or third party (Ontario Legal Aid or insurance) billing?
- What is the clinician's preliminary estimate of the approximate number of hours expected to be required to complete the process?
- When can the clinician begin the assessment?
- Is it the clinician's practice to contact the parties for the initial appointment or to have each party responsible to set up first appointments on his or her own initiative?
- To the best of the clinician's knowledge is there any conflict of interest that would negate the clinician as the assessor of choice?
- Does the assessor read the affidavits and pleadings before seeing the parties? After the assessment but before writing the report? Or does the assessor not read the pleadings at all?
- Is there any bias on the part of the clinician that would make him or her less than the ideal assessor for the case at hand?

(c) Preliminary Three-Way Meeting

The assessor may wish to have a face to face meeting with both lawyers to discuss the clients' positions and the assessor's procedures before beginning the assessment, or indeed taking on the case at all. This is useful where a lawyer and assessor have not worked together before. Such a meeting could occur in the assessor's office, not only to demonstrate the neutrality of the assessor, but as a matter of professional courtesy. After all, it is the lawyers who seek to retain the services of the assessor. This stage-setting meeting is not a forum to argue the merits of the case, but an opportunity to clarify the process. The assessor may even suggest someone else as better qualified to perform the particular assessment as a result of information learned at this meeting.

Other clinicians, however, will not consider such a threeway meeting necessary. This is especially so when the assessor and one, or both, of the lawyers have worked together before. If an issue requires some discussion, a conference call among the lawyers and the assessor might serve to clear up the matter, and save time and travel expense.

Responsibility for the cost of such a preliminary meeting should be clarified at the time it is arranged, and might be incorporated in the subsequent account from the assessor, on whatever basis that statement will be drawn up.

(d) Vetting the Referral for Bias

Bias may be hard to ascertain at the preliminary contact stage, as counsel may not yet be aware of any circumstance in the case which might spark a biased reaction on the part of the clinician.

A brief discussion of the facts of the dispute with the potential assessor will serve to clarify the appropriateness of the referral for the clinician as well as allowing the clinician to make an intelligent judgment as to the time required for the assessment. For example, a particular clinician may not feel comfortable in situations in which allegations of child sexual abuse have been made; or where one parent's sexual orientation is other than the societal norm, or in which certain religious doctrines are a major factor in the dispute. The preliminary contact allows a clinician who knows her biases to decline the appointment. Otherwise the strength of the assessment recommendations might be weakened when a bias comes to light after the assessment has been completed. A responsible clinician will not undertake an assessment in which she recognizes either that her objectivity may be impaired or that it involves an area where she feels less than competent.

(e) Discuss the Choice of Assessor With the Client

The information gathered in the preliminary contact with the clinician, from her *curriculum vitae*, and from previous experience with that clinician, should be shared with the client. Determine whether the client would have any difficulty cooperating with an assessment performed by this particular person before proceeding to obtain an order or agreement to appoint the assessor. Remember, the cooperation of the client with the assessment does not mean that he or she is agreeing in advance to abide by the eventual recommendations of the assessor. Clients often need a lot of reassurance on this point.

(f) Anxiety About First-Contact Influence

Anxiety about first-contact influence sometimes occurs when the following circumstances exist:

- Lawyer "A" has worked with clinician "X" before and lawyer "B" has not.

OR

- Lawyer "A" has already had preliminary contact with clinician "X", obtained the clinician's consent to act as an assessor, and now asks lawyer "B" to concur in the appointment.

Lawyer "B" or lawyer "B" 's client may react to these circumstances with an anxiety that clinician "X" is already "onside" with lawyer "A" and/or will approach the assessment predisposed to the point of view of lawyer "A' "s client. On this concern of both lawyer "B" and lawyer "B" 's client, bear in mind that *someone* has to contact the clinician and reveal enough about the nature of the case so that the clinician can decide whether she is prepared to undertake the assessment.

The concern of prior relationship between lawyer "A" and clinician "X" is a common one. Lawyer "B" may enquire from lawyer "A" about why lawyer "A" feels secure in recommending clinician "X" for this particular situation. Discussion may indicate that lawyer "A" was impressed with the clinician's thoroughness or fairness in a previous report, whether or not his client's position had been favoured in the recommendation.

The lawyer who is already acquainted with the clinician might keep first contact minimal and encourage the other lawyer to speak at length with the clinician in order to ascertain whether he would be comfortable with that assessment referral. Lawyer "B" would wish to explore the clinician's credentials, procedures and general point of view. A three-way meeting between the lawyers and proposed assessor can be helpful in such instances. Other lawyers can be consulted for information as to the clinician's reputation.

An experienced assessor will be quite comfortable in suggesting the names of other lawyers as references, including ones whose client's positions have not been supported by the recommendations in past assessments. Such discussions should reassure lawyer "B" that this professional is not only competent, but arrives independently at her own evaluation of what is, or appears to be, in the best interests of the children concerned.

The concern as to a prior working relationship or even social relationship between lawyer "A" and clinician "X" speaks to a misperception of the assessor's role. The assessor is an independent consultant to the court, and in no way an on-side advocate for either parent, even in a situation in which the report wholeheartedly recommends a result that is in support of one party's position. Neither parent, who is each lawyer's client, is the client of the assessor. Unlike the lawyer, the assessor carries no responsibility to advance either parent's position, and, may indeed, support neither. As indicated earlier, the assessor's accountability is to the court on behalf of the children. Reputation in the professional community as to professionalism, responsibility, thoroughness, and fairness, is the acid test. Counsel should not refuse the requested assessor out of hand simply because the other side suggests her. To do so may in fact compromise the quality of the service counsel is able to provide to the client. Just because a lawyer has no prior relationship or experience with a clinician does not mean that the clinician will not be a good choice, or indeed that lawyer's own choice for this or for subsequent cases.

(g) Assessment Consents and Motions

It may be that all parties are in agreement on the need for an assessment, and on the issue of how it is to be paid for. If so, the parties may enter into a written agreement as set forth at Exhibit (3.2), or they may execute a consent to a court order for the assessment, as set forth at Exhibit (3.3).

If one party objects to the assessment, or to paying for all or part of its cost, then recourse to the court is necessary. A Notice of Motion requesting that the court order an assessment should set out the following elements pursuant to Ontario's Children's Law Reform Act (which is one of the most comprehensive codifications of custody/access assessment requirements in Canada at the moment of writing):

- Why the assessment is necessary.
- Who is proposed as the assessor.
- That the proposed assessor has consented to provide the service.
- Why the proposed assessor is the appropriate professional to complete the assessment.
- The proposal for responsibility for payment.
- Reasons for one's client's position vis-a-vis payment.
- Which parties should be required to participate in the assessment.
- The authority under which the court may make such an order.

An example of such a Notice of Motion appears as Exhibit (3.4). Motions brought under the rules of the court or other statutes ought to contain these or similar elements in order to be comprehensive. Ideally, the Notice of Motion should be served on every person for whom an order to participate in the assessment is sought.[3]

The supporting documentation for the motion will contain the following:

- The written consent of the assessor (Form (3.1)).
- The *curriculum vitae* of the assessor (if not already part of the consent form).
- Affidavit of the party setting forth:

  (a) reasons why the assessment is necessary in this particular case;
  (b) why the proposed assessor is the appropriate professional to complete the assessment;
  (c) financial information relevant to that party's ability to pay for the assessment;
  (d) financial information relevant to the other party's ability to pay for the assessment.

An example of a party's affidavit in support of a motion for assessment appears as Exhibit (3.5) at the end of this chapter.

(h) The Form of the Order

Whether or not the assessment is on consent, a formal order ought to be taken out to define the scope of the process and to protect all the parties. Section 30 of the Ontario Children's Law Reform Act[4] provides a thorough outline for the points to be covered in an assessment order made pursuant to the Act, and which it would be prudent to include in any assessment order.

Subsection 30(1) defines who is a person who may be appointed and

---

3 The Ontario Children's Law Reform Act, *supra*, note 1, provides in section 30(5):

> In an order under subsection (1), the court may require the parties, the child and any other person who has been given notice of the proposed order, or any of them, to attend for assessment by the person appointed by the order.

See also the Children's Law Act, S.N. 1988, c. 61, s. 36(5).

Subsections 3(2) of the Ontario statute and 36(2) of the Newfoundland statute state that an order appointing an assessor may be made "with or without a request by a party to the application", allowing the court to act on its own motion, but apart from subsection 30(5) (Ontario) and 36(5) (Newfoundland) the Acts are silent as to notice requirements.

Ex parte applications for assessment are specifically allowed by section 15(1) of the British Columbia Family Relations Act, R.S.B.C. 1979, c. 121 [as amended]; and the Newfoundland Unified Family Court Act, S.N. 1977, c. 88 [as amended], s. 16(1).

4 *Supra*, note 1. See also the Newfoundland Children's Law Act, S.N. 1988, c. 61, which is virtually identical to the Ontario legislation.

defines the scope of the assessment task:[5]

> .... a person who has technical or professional skill to assess and report to the court on the needs of the child and the ability and willingness of the parties or any of them to satisfy the needs of the child.

Subsection 30(4) indicates that the person so appointed must have consented to the appointment and be able to complete the assigned task within any time restrictions imposed by the court. Subsection 30(5) allows the court to mandate the cooperation not only of the parties and the child,

---

5 The person who may be appointed to perform an assessment is defined in other provinces as follows:

> ... person who
> (a) has had no previous connection with the parties to the proceeding or to whom each party consents; and
> (b) is a family counsellor, social worker, probation officer or other person approved by the court for the purpose.
>
> Family Relations Act, R.S.B.C. 1979, c. 121 [as amended], s. 15 (1).

> ... a person who
> (a) has had no previous connection with the parties to the proceeding or to whom each party consents; and
> (b) is a family investigator, social worker or other person approved by the court for the purpose.
>
> Family Maintenance Act, R.S.M. 1987, c. F-20 [as amended], s. 3(1).

> ... a psychiatric, psychological, social, physical,or any other examination or evaluation specified by the court ....
>
> Family Services Act, S.N.B. 1980, c.F.-2.2 [as amended], s. 8.

> ... a person who
> (a) has had no previous connection with the parties to the proceeding, and
> (b) is a family counsellor; social worker, probation officer or other person approved by the court for the purpose....
>
> Unified Family Court Act, S.N. 1977, c. 88 [as amended], s. 16 (1).

> ... a person who has technical or professional skill to investigate, assess, and report to the court on the needs of the child and the ability and willingness of the parties to satisfy the needs of the child.
>
> Children's Law Act, S. N. 1988, c. 61, s. 36(1).

> ... the director of family and children's services appointed under section 108 ....
>
> Children's Act, R.S.Y. 1986, c. 22 [as amended], s. 43(1).

> .... the Director of Child Welfare....
>
> Custody Jurisdiction and Enforcement Act, S.P.E.I. 1984, c. 17, s. 4(2).

but also of ". . . . any other person who has been given notice of the proposed order."

Requiring named individuals to attend for assessment in the order allows non-cooperation by a party to be used as evidence on the custody/access issue for actions brought pursuant to the Act. Subsection 30(6) states:

> Where a person ordered under this section to attend for assessment refuses to attend or to undergo the assessment, the court may draw such inferences in respect of the ability and willingness of any person to satisfy the needs of the child as the court considers appropriate.[6]

The responsibility for the payment of the assessor's fees and expenses shall, in the words of the Act, be specified in the order. Subsections 30(12) and (13)[7] provide respectively:

> (12) The court shall require the parties to pay the fees and expenses of the person appointed under subsection (1).
>
> (13) The court shall specify in the order the proportions or amounts of the fees and expenses that the court requires each party to pay.

For actions brought pursuant to the Act, subsection 30(14) makes it clear that the court can, for reasons of financial hardship, relieve a party from the obligation to pay for the assessment.

An assessment order ought to provide clearly on its face for the following:

- Who is to do the assessment?
- What is the scope and focus of the assessment?
- Which persons are being assessed?
- Who must attend for assessment?
- Who is paying for the assessment and in what proportion?
- The date, if any, by which the assessment must be completed, delivered to the parties, and filed with the court.

Exhibit (3.6) is a precedent for such an order based upon section 30 of the Children's Law Reform Act.

Sometimes counsel obtain orders that are very general in their wording. For example:

> An assessment will be performed at the expense of X by an assessor to be agreed upon by the parties.

---

6 Similar provisions are found in the Manitoba Family Maintenance Act, R.S.M. 1987, c. F 20 [as amended], s. 3(3); the New Brunswick Family Services Act, S.N.B. 1980, c. F-2.2 [as amended], s. 8; the Newfoundland Children's Law Act, S.N. 1988, c. 61, s. 36(6).

7 See also S.N. 1988, c. 61, s. 36(12)-(14).

Difficulties arise in such instances. Weeks can be spent arguing with counsel about which professional will receive the referral. A further court appearance may well be necessary to determine that issue. It is far preferable to do your homework about who would be the appropriate professional before, rather than after, the motion. Consider whether "significant others" such as new partners or spouses of the parties should be required to attend for the assessment pursuant to section 30(5). Consider requiring the participation of auxiliary caregivers such as babysitter or grandparents who are, or are proposed to be, involved with the child(ren) on a day to day basis.

(i) The Referral Letter to the Assessor

Whether the assessment is on consent, or is court ordered, the lawyer for each party should contact the assessor. A telephone call to confirm the appointment of the assessor may be an opportunity for some discussion of the process, but of more importance is a referral letter to clarify the task before the assessor as to scope and focus. A joint referral letter countersigned by each lawyer may, like an agreed upon statement of facts, save time for the assessor and money for the clients. Of course, each lawyer may prefer to write such a referral letter outlining the case from his or her own client's point of view for the assessor. Failure to provide a joint or individual referral letter deprives the assessor of a preliminary orientation to the issues from one's client's perspective.

A copy of the referral letter should be shared with opposing counsel so that all parties are clear as to the assessor's terms of reference. Indicate what documents are being shared with the assessor.

Once the assessor has been appointed all contact with the assessor concerning the case must be kept above board. If either party's lawyer does communicate concerning the assessment, copies of such letters should be furnished to opposing counsel.

The referral letter should achieve the objectives outlined below as (i) to (viii). (A sample referral letter appears as Exhibit (3.7) at the end of this Chapter.)

(i) *Confirm the Appointment*

If the assessment is court ordered, provide a copy of the order of appointment with the referral letter.

(ii) *Clarify the Method of Payment*

If your client has been ordered, or has agreed, to pay all or some portion of the assessment, specify whether the assessor is to bill the client directly for his/her share of the costs. Confirm whether the assessor should invoice the lawyer, and whether the lawyer or the client will furnish a retainer to the assessor. If third party payment by a legal aid plan is involved, provide the assessor with a copy of the authorizing letter from the plan.[8] There will be limitations as to cost, time to be spent, and stipulations as to what proportion of the total bill for the assessment the plan will be prepared to pay. The assessor will need to know the extent of such limits and whether and how they may be increased.

(iii) *Identify the Action and the Parties*

Provide the style of cause of the action in full, together with the court file reference number. State which party you represent, and give the client's full name, address and telephone numbers. State the names and dates of birth of each child and indicate with which party each child has his principal address. Provide as well the name and address of the firm representing the other side and the name of the lawyer in charge of the file. The assessor will need that information in order to ensure contact with the other party if that party, or his lawyer, does not contact the assessor or send a referral letter.

(iv) *Give a Brief Synopsis of the Facts*

Give a very brief synopsis of the facts. Is this a divorce action or not? When is the trial date, if it has been set already? Is this a custody dispute or is the issue one of access only? What is each party's position? Does the dispute involve all of the children or only some of them? Which ones? What are the major issues in contention concerning the children?

---

8 Providing a copy of the legal aid authorization to the assessor is also a matter of self-protection for the lawyer. The Ontario Legal Aid Plan's *Legal Aid Tariff Manual*, (Toronto: 1988), provides, in item 4010-43:

> The responsibility for choosing and paying the expert is the solicitor's.

If the lawyer does not put the assessor on notice of the legal aid authorized terms of payment, and secure the assessor's agreement, evidenced in writing, to bill in accordance with those terms, the lawyer risks personal liability to the assessor for his proper fees and expenses, and the Ontario Legal Aid Plan will not assume responsibility. This position is subject to items 4010-41:

> Unreasonable or improper bills need not be paid by solicitors and will not be paid by Legal Aid.

and 4010-42:

> Solicitors have a responsibility to ensure that all disbursements are reasonable and proper and that public funds are not wasted.

Are there allegations of abuse, either physical, emotional, or sexual? Who is alleged to have abused the children?

(v) *Provide Copies of Documents*

The assessor needs the pleadings, existing orders, and affidavit material filed by each party in the proceeding to date in order to have a sense not only of where the parties are legally, but by what route they arrived there. Affidavits reveal sore spots, issues, and the degree of anger or cooperation between the parties.

If counsel received an affidavit to which a reply has not yet been prepared, or if there is concern about potentially prejudicial content of an affidavit produced by the other side, be sure nevertheless that this is sent to the assessor. Counsel might comment, disagreeing with that material, but counsel should be able to rely on the assessor's capacity to approach such information with healthy skepticism. Some assessors indicate that they read affidavits less to learn the facts than to gauge the heat of the conflict. The other side will probably include the material in its package to the assessor in any event, and an up-front spirit of cooperation not only assists the assessor, it reflects well on your client.

Some assessors prefer not to receive the documents at all, or read them only at the conclusion of the assessment. Clarify this point early on.

(vi) *Indicate Existence of Other Reports*

If there are reports by other mental health professionals, ask the assessor if she wishes to have those as well. Psychological tests or medical reports by physicians or psychiatrists may be of use to the assessor to form part of the overall data in the assessment. If there is a previous assessment on the same issue upon which this assessor has been asked to recommend, the assessor may prefer not to see it lest she be influenced by it. Make sure nonetheless that she is aware of its existence and is given the name, address, and phone number of the person who prepared the report. The option is then open to the present assessor to call the previous assessor to consult, to clarify information, or to ascertain whether the terms of reference of the earlier assessment were the same as the present one.[9]

---

9 In some cases, a court may choose to restrict the assessor's access to material prepared by other professionals concerning the family. In *MacIver v. MacIver*, [1989] W.D.F.L. 180 (Man. Q.B.), Helper J. ordered that none of the material filed regarding the family

(vii) *Indicate Where the Report is to be Delivered*

Is the report to be provided to the court? To the parties and the court? To the parties only? Who is responsible for filing it with the court, the assessor, or the parties? Provide the mailing address for the court office and the correct designation of the court to which the report will be directed, if that is the case.

(viii) *Indicate Statutory Considerations*

Give the assessor a copy of the relevant statute sections that define the custody/access criteria with which the court will be concerned in the event that a hearing becomes necessary. Appendix II at the end of the book contains the legislative criteria for custody in those Canadian jurisdictions in which it is defined. Ask the assessor to bear those criteria in mind while formulating the report. Do not expect, however, that assessors should confine themselves solely to the criteria outlined in the statute.

(j) Payment Arrangements: Protecting the Assessor

The financial responsibility for the assessment will fall on one or all of the parties to the action. Their proportional allocation may be determined by agreement or by court order. The assessor's interests ought to be safeguarded by a memorandum of agreement between the assessor and the parties,[10] and also by the wording of the court order, if any, evidencing the allocation of financial responsibility. The proportionate share of one or more parties may be paid by a third party such as a legal aid plan. In that instance prior authorization must usually be sought from the plan.[11]

---

should be shown to the assessor, save only the separation agreement. The child had already been exposed to numerous psychologists and other professionals, and 14 affidavits concerning the child's emotional well-being had been filed with the court in the two months preceding the court appearance in which the independent assessment was ordered.

10 See a precedent for such memorandum as Exhibit (10.2) at the conclusion of Chapter 10.

11 The Ontario Legal Aid Plan stipulates in the *Legal Aid Tariff Manual* (Toronto, 1988) that no authorization is required for assessments in custody cases, or in access cases where child abuse is alleged if certain conditions are met:

4050-61 No other assessment has been performed in the last year; and

4050-62 The total duration of the assessment and report does not exceed 10 hours; and

4050-63 All parties have agreed that the report will be admitted into evidence; and

4050-64 The parties have agreed to divide the cost equally.

(i) *Seeking Legal Aid Authorization*

When seeking authorization from the Ontario Legal Aid Plan, be specific concerning the following:

- Whether the assessment is regarding custody only, both custody and access, or access only. The Plan will not usually fund assessment, the only focus of which is an access dispute.
- The name of the assessor of choice, and his or her professional designation.
- Whether there is a court order for the assessment (and, if so, enclose a copy of the order with the letter requesting authorization).
- Why the assessment is needed in this case.
- How many other parties are sharing the cost and in what proportions.
- Whether a child protection agency is involved and willing to assume all or part of the cost of the assessment.[12]
- Whether there have been previous assessments and, if so, by whom, when they were performed, how they were funded, and whether they were directed to the issue of the current case.
- Whether other parties to the dispute are covered by legal aid certificates and, if so, the reference number of the certificate(s) (if known) and the full names and addresses of such parties, together with the names of their respective solicitors.
- The likelihood of cost recoveries from other parties.
- Whether travel by the assessor will be necessary for home visits and,

---

If the situation differs from the guidelines, or more than 10 hours is needed, authorization is required.

The guidelines specify that the client's proportionate share to a maximum of one-half of the total cost of the assessment (4050-65) will be allowed.

Authorization must be sought for the payment of more than the client's proportional share of the fees, or where the assessor's fee structure falls outside the payment scale, or the profession of the assessor is not one of the three specified.

Granting authorizations is further subject to the following three caveats:

4060-12 Assessments will seldom be authorized when access is the main or only issue;

4060-13 Assessments may not be authorized where a family court clinic is available;

4060-14 Assessments will not be allowed in addition to mediation without prior specific authorization.

12 At the time of writing (summer 1989) there is, in Ontario, an agreement between the Ministry of Community and Social Services and the Ontario Legal Aid Plan whereby the Ministry will cover the cost of an assessment in legal aid funded cases in which an application is brought by such an agency under the Child and Family Services Act, (S.O. 1984, c. 55). Legal Aid will fund their cost attributable to a legal aid funded client in those cases under the Divorce Act, 1985 (S.C. 1986, c. 4) and the Children's Law Reform Act (*supra*, note 1).

if so, for how many trips.

- Whether overnight accommodation will be necessary for the assessor.
- Any special circumstances known at the outset that may affect the amount of time required to perform the assessment.

An example of a letter seeking Ontario Legal Aid Plan authorization appears as Exhibit (3.9) at the end of the chapter.

(ii) *Conditions and Restrictions of Legal Aid Authorization*

The authorization from the Ontario Legal Aid Plan will contain restrictions and conditions as indicated in the points (A) to (D) below.

(A) *Restrictions as to time.* The authorization will be for a stated maximum number of hours for which charges for the assessment may be submitted to the Plan. The time allocated will cover both the investigation and the writing of the report. Travel time for the assessor will not normally be addressed in such an authorization unless counsel requests a consideration of travel time at the time of requesting authorization, and then a common restriction would be two trips, one to visit the children in each party's home. The Ontario Legal Aid Plan expects the parties to travel at their own expense to the assessor's office for their own interviews. If it is known in advance that travel will be required, request coverage for it, and state the reasons for its necessity in the request for authorization. Estimate the travel both as to time and distance. Often the two parents will live in different communities from the assessor, and may be in different communities from each other. Travel may be necessary not only for home visits, but also for meetings with collaterals such as teachers, physicians, and the friends and relatives of the parties. If so, request specific authorization providing details of the circumstances necessitating travel to see collaterals. The assessor can usually arrange appointments so that a trip for a home visit can also encompass appointments with other collaterals.

If overnight accommodation is necessary for the assessor for such home visits and interviews with collaterals, make sure to request that, estimating the costs in the request for authorization. A motel or hotel will be necessary if the assessor cannot readily make the round trip in one day.

In some cases, the need for travel time, or accommodation, or indeed the scope of the investigation time, may well not be known at the time the original request for authorization is made. Open communication and cooperation on procedural matters between the lawyers and the assessor are vital so that the assessor can indicate the need for such further authorizations at the first opportunity, and a supplementary request for authorization can be made. An example of a letter from an assessor to a lawyer asking for further time authorization appears as Exhibit (3.9).

A letter which the lawyer might send to the Ontario Legal Aid Plan requesting expanded time authorization based on the request from the assessor appears as Exhibit (3.10). The lawyer's letter may have to be quite detailed, or may merely enclose the letter from the assessor if it contains enough detail.

A telephone call may do in some instances for contact with a collateral source, or where a co-professional is being called to verify facts. Face to face meetings are important, however, and the lawyer should not hesitate to urge that funding be available so that the quality of the assessment is not compromised.

(B) *Restrictions as to fees payable.* The Ontario Legal Aid Plan usually authorizes payment of the assessor on a profession-specific fee tariff that is, like the fees paid to lawyers under the plan, often considerably lower than the assessor's usual hourly rate. At the time of writing in the summer of 1989, the usual fees paid to clinicians for assessments under the Ontario Legal Aid Plan were as follows:

Psychiatrists: (in accordance with the prevailing O.H.I.P. rate) $98.40 per hour.
Psychologists: (registered with the Province of Ontario) up to $80.00 per hour.
Social Workers: (holding an M.S.W. or equivalent qualification at the masters level) up to $68.00 per hour.
All other clinicians: $50.00 per hour.

These rates are reviewed periodically. Verify the applicable rate before communicating it to a potential assessor. The Ontario Legal Aid Plan appreciates being provided the name and address, and profession designation of the proposed assessor. When asking a clinician to undertake an assessment where one or both of the parties is funded by a legal aid plan, do the clinician the courtesy of informing her that legal aid is involved before obtaining the consent to act as the assessor. Just as there are lawyers who do not accept legal aid certificates, so too there are assessors who do not accept legal aid work.

(C) *Restrictions as to proportion of costs borne by legal aid.* Usually the Ontario Legal Aid Plan will make its authorization contingent upon the costs being borne by the parties in equal shares. The wording of such authorizations may seem to suggest equal responsibility dollar for dollar. This works if both parties are funded by Legal Aid. If one party is, however, capable of paying the assessor's usual hourly rate, then it is fairer to the assessor to bill the cost for one-half the time of the process to the private pay party at regular rates, and other half of the time at legal aid rates to the other party.

If there are more parties to the action than just the mother and the father, then each party's proportionate share of responsibility for costs is usually reduced.

It is possible that a case may involve other parties such as child protection agencies or government departments. The participation of such agencies in the payment for an assessment should be clarified in advance of engaging the assessor. The existence of such other parties should be made known to Legal Aid at the time the authorization is requested.

(D) *Conditions as to the use of the report.* The Ontario Legal Aid Plan authorization will stipulate that all parties must consent to enter the report in evidence. This is usually satisfied by filing the report with the court. Such a condition does not preclude one party or the other from requiring the presence of the assessor to testify at any hearing or trial. Separate arrangements must, however, be made with Legal Aid for the payment of the assessor's fee for a court appearance. Usually the party who requires the attendance of the assessor at court will pay the fees, which may, at the conclusion of trial, form part of a claim for costs.

(iii) *Retainers and Solicitor's Guarantees*

If the client is paying directly for all or part of the cost of the assessment, clarify with the assessor how the fees will be established, account rendered, and whether any security of payment will be required. Some assessors require a retainer by cash, certified cheque or lawyer's trust cheque. Some assessors will only release the report once their final account has been satisfied. Others will require the lawyer to guarantee personally that portion of the account attributable to that lawyer's client.

Clarify all such arrangements and requirements in advance, preferably in writing.

2. RECEIVING THE REFERRAL: THE ASSESSOR'S PERSPECTIVE

(a) Preliminary Contact With the Lawyers

If a clinician is to undertake an assessment, someone has to make the request. This will be a lawyer for one of the parties (or occasionally, the lawyer's secretary). The purpose of the phone call will be to ascertain the clinician's interest in and availability to undertake an assessment, when the process might begin, how much it will cost, and how long it will take. Sometimes these calls are made just prior to going into court: the lawyer wants to be able to recommend a particular assessor, if assessment is to be proposed in the matter. Even though that may put pressure on you to give a quick "yes" or "no" answer, certain basic information must be obtained before answering.

(i) *The Nature of the Assessment*

Is it a custody/access dispute, just access, or just custody? Who is the lawyer on the other side? The assessor needs to clarify this latter item in case there is any reason or impediment that would preclude the assessor from being able to work with that particular lawyer, such as previous unhappy experience in cooperative work which has led to a decision not to work again with that lawyer.

(ii) *The Marital Situation at the Moment*

Are the parents already separated and/or divorced, or are they still resident in the matrimonial home with each refusing to leave (usually on the advice of counsel) until the matter of the children is resolved?

(iii) *How Many Children are Involved and Their Ages*

Are all the children in the family involved in the dispute? If not, which ones are involved?

(iv) *Are There Any Other Parties?*

Are there any other parties to the action who would be participants in the assessment? This could be grandparents or other relatives who are seeking access to the children or their custody.

(v) *Are There Any Special Circumstances?*

Are there any special circumstances in the situation, such as allegations of abuse; religious, racial, or cultural matters; or personal lifestyle issues on the part of one or both of the parties that cause or complicate the dispute? This information is important from the start because one may wish not to accept the referral if one or more of these factors are present. Assessors must be professional, which includes an awareness of self. If the presence of a special factor such as religious persuasion or sexual orientation would, or might, impinge on professional objectivity in the assessment, you have a duty to refuse the referral. Establishing that in the very beginning is a courtesy to the lawyers and the court, and considerate of the parents and children concerned. As well, an honest self-appraisal is in your own professional best interest. It is preferable, certainly, to refuse some work than to have a report attacked in court, perhaps successfully, as showing (regrettable) bias. One can always plead "too busy" to accept it.

(vi) *What the Payment Arrangements Will Be*

What will the payment arrangements be, if this is known at this stage? Many assessments are paid for through a legal aid plan. That may involve accepting a pay rate lower than the regular fee to privately-paying parents. The lawyer retained by a client with a legal aid certificate needs to know right away if payment at the going legal aid rate is acceptable. If not, then the lawyer will start looking for another assessor, and not use up valuable time presenting your name and qualifications to the other side and to the court.

(vii) *Suggested Time Frame*

What is the suggested time frame for completion of the assessment? If a court date has already been set, can an assessment reasonably be completed in the interval, and if not, what can be done about that (*e.g.*, requesting an adjournment)?

(viii) *How the Lawyers Will Obtain Copies of Your Signed Consent*

Most of this information can be exchanged over the phone. If prepared to undertake the assignment, indicate so verbally, and wait for the lawyer to make contact again to formalize the referral.

(b) Clarifying the Nature of the Service

During the initial conversation another important matter needs to be explored, unless you are dealing with a lawyer with whom you have worked before and each of you is clear about the matter. That involves making absolutely sure that both clinician and lawyer know what is being requested and what is agreed to be undertaken. There is, as indicated earlier, both confusion and difference of opinion about assessments, mediation, and/or counselling, or therapy. Sometimes referral inquiries request assessment when mediation is, in fact, being sought; or mediation is the service requested when, in fact, as the conversation progresses, it becomes clear that recommendations are being sought indicating assessment. From time to time a lawyer may ask a clinician to counsel the couple about their pending separation and then, if they choose to go forward with it, to conduct mediation about the children or other matters, and if that fails, to undertake an assessment. One-stop-shopping may be very appealing at first glance but is to be avoided. The ethical dilemmas should be obvious.

Occasionally, the lawyer may only be exploring possibilities, and wants to think out loud about the various options that might be considered in trying to achieve resolution. This may lead to a tentative query about the same clinician undertaking all three activities. The lawyer is responsible for determining which service is to be requested.

The lawyer who raises such a query is not being intentionally manipulative: he is genuinely seeking a way out for the client in what is becoming daily a more stressful and difficult situation. One must have a clearly thoughtout policy and ethical position about the interfaces between and among assessment, mediation, and counselling. It is, as stated, preferable to lose the occasional referral because of not subscribing to the one-stop-shopping theory, than to perpetuate the myth that a mental health professional can be all things in any given situation, regardless of the subsequent impact on the parents and the children. As the clinician is so clear, then (potential) referring lawyers become more and more clear with their clients. They present the pros and cons of each process more effectively, and assist their client in choosing the route that appears most appropriate to the situation. Well- prepared parties, who understand clearly what it is they have consented to, approach the service they have chosen, not anxiety-free, but calmer, with a sense of having retained or gained a modicum of self-control over their lives.

(c) Clarifying Credentials

One or both lawyers and the assessor may be unfamiliar with each other. The assessor's name may have been suggested by a colleague or the judge, and the positive recommendation has moved them at least to call. Or the assessor may be a compromise appointment, their earlier suggested clinician having been rejected for one reason or another. Assessors should be prepared for requests for information about themselves, their professional training, experience, background, other assessments, even particular religious affiliation. Offer to send copies of your *curriculum vitae*, and to provide the names of other lawyers with whom you have worked.

The lawyer who feels comfortable with the choice of assessor will convey that to the client, and will be less likely to "ride herd" on the assessment through asking for on-going reports on its process and progress. Such behaviour can increase rather than alleviate the client's anxiety about the process. Good working relationships built on mutual respect and understanding lead to additional referrals. Those relationships begin at the referral stage.

Ask the lawyer to confirm your appointment as assessor in writing as soon as it is made, or to inform you if you are not appointed, so that you may accept other referrals.

(d) Referral Letter and Litigation Documents

Once the appointment to undertake the assessment is confirmed, specific details about first and next steps need to be clarified. Many of these points may have been discussed at the time of the referral phone call. In any event, they should be covered as soon as the appointment as assessor is confirmed, especially if assessor and lawyer(s) are unfamiliar with one another and have not worked together before. Other assessors may work differently, and unless procedures and requests are made explicit, the lawyer(s) may be forgiven for assuming that all assessors use the same policies and procedures that they have encountered so far.

Request clearly, the following:

- A copy of the assessment order, if any.
- A letter from each lawyer setting out briefly:

  (a) The identifying information — family names(s), and address(es); children's full names, birth dates, and present residence address; and which party is the lawyer's client.
  (b) An indication of the nature of the present dispute and what specifically the assessor is being asked to address within that dispute. For example, there may be matters other than custody/access being disputed but the assessor is being requested only to consider and make recommendations on the custody/access issues).
  (c) The name and full address of counsel for the other side.
  (d) A clear statement of how the assessment is to be paid for. In the case of private payment by the client request enclosure of the retainer cheque; in the alternative a copy of the legal aid payment authorization.
  (e) An indication of their client's ability and willingness to attend at the assessor's office for (at least) the initial interview.

- Copies of pertinent materials, such as notice(s) of motion, affidavits, replies, previous court orders, statements of claim, divorce petitions, previous assessment reports if such have been done, relevant letters or reports from other professionals who have worked with the family or the parents or any one of them. Some assessors indicate that they wish not to receive such material in advance, preferring, they say, not to be influenced, but to form their own opinions and gain their own impressions. While, of course, every assessor must do precisely that (form their own opinions and gain their own impressions), it is very helpful to be familiar with some of the history of the situation in advance, if only to be able to listen intelligently as each parent's version of the situation is presented. One does not have to accept or believe everything stated in the materials, but they are reflective of the quarrel. Affidavits often reflect less the actuality of events than the reality of the temperature of the situation. Being aware of that temperature allows the assessor to be both focussed and tactful in the early stages of the assessment, when each parent is still very uneasy.

If the file is a very large one because the dispute has gone on for some time, it may not be useful to see every scrap of paper. Trust the lawyer's discretion in sending selected items, and perhaps arrange to read other materials at the lawyer's office later, if that seems indicated. Acknowledge receipt of the materials in writing or by telephone.

As a labour-saving device, one lawyer may prepare the referral letter, setting out the above details and enclosing relevant materials, and the other lawyer may be content to add a post script indicating concurrence with the information contained therein, and signing his name at the bottom of the letter. Such a device not only advances the referral process, but it may spare the assessor receiving too many duplicate copies of the relevant materials. Knowing what materials have been sent by the first lawyer, the second one may then need to send only copies of materials or reports specifically related to his client.

(e) Preliminary Three-Way Meeting

With the materials, letters, and court order in hand the assessor may be prepared to begin the assessment, or a further step may be undertaken first by way of a pre-assessment meeting with the lawyers.

Such a meeting may be useful if there are unusual or potentially awkward aspects to the dispute (religion, sexual orientation, allegations of inappropriate behaviour with one or more of the children, a previous criminal record, etc.), and the lawyers are unsure of the assessor's (potential) objectivity about the matter. Perhaps one side has been inflamed by a recent affidavit, and not knowing the assessor, needs to be reassured about the impact the allegations in the affidavit appear to have had. Whatever the reason, if one or both lawyers suggest a meeting, by all means agree to it. The assessor's office provides a neutral location. Or if one lawyer seems distressed on his client's behalf by the action of the other side, and is concerned about whether the assessment has been compromised even before it has begun, the assessor can suggest such a meeting. It will help to clear the air, facilitate expression of concern or irritation, and allow the assessor to demonstrate professional neutrality. At the conclusion of the meeting you may clarify whether the cost of the meeting is to be incorporated into the statement at the conclusion of the assessment, in accordance with whatever the payment arrangements are.

Pre-assessment meetings are not indicated in every case. Where lawyers and assessor know and trust each other, and the dispute is a straightforward one, they are an unnecessary, additional expenditure of time and money. But if there is uneasiness which could affect the lawyer's confidence in the assessor's ability and professionalism, they are most worthwhile. A reassured counsel will prepare his client much more positively. Then, at the conclusion of the assessment, if the recommendations do not support that parent's position, the subsequent consultation between lawyer and client will be less subject to suggestions that the assessor was biased right from the beginning. The implications of this for the children, for the future of parental cooperation, and not the least of it, the assessor's reputation, arc obvious.

Now, the assessor is ready for the assessment to begin.

3. EXHIBITS

(3.1) Consent to Act as Assessor
(3.2) Agreement to Submit to Assessment
(3.3) Consent to Order for Assessment
(3.4) Notice of Motion Requesting Assessment
(3.5) Affidavit in Support of Motion for Assessment
(3.6) Assessment Order Under Section 30 of the Children's Law Reform Act
(3.7) Referral Letter to Assessor
(3.8) Letter Seeking Legal Aid Authorization
(3.9) Letter to Lawyer from Assessor Seeking Authorization for Additional Time
(3.10) Letter to Legal Aid from Lawyer Requesting Authorization for Additional Time for Assessor

EXHIBIT (**3.1**)

Consent to Act as Assessor

IN THE MATTER OF the Children's Law Reform Act, R.S.O. 1980, c. 68, as amended,

AND IN THE MATTER OF:______________________________

____

____

____

1. I, ______________________, a ______________________ practicing in the City of ________ in the Province of ________, state that I am a person who has technical or professional skill to assess and report to the court on the needs of children and the ability and willingness of parties to satisfy the needs of such children pursuant to Section 30(1) of the Act. Annexed hereto as Schedule "A" is a copy of my *curriculum vitae.*

2. I hereby consent to perform an independent custody/access assessment and to make a report to the court concerning the needs of the child(ren):

   ______________________________ d.o.b. ______________

   ______________________________ d.o.b. ______________

   ______________________________ d.o.b. ______________

   and the ability of the following parties to meet those needs:

   ____ (father)

   ____ (mother)

   ____ (   )

   ____ (   )

3. The extent of my previous contact with the children and the parties is as follows:
   None: [ ]
   Other (specify) [ ] ______________________________

   ____

   ____

4. I agree to deliver a copy of the completed report to the Registrar of the ____________________ Court at

____

and at the same time to furnish a copy of the report to each of the adult parties and their respective counsel.

DATED at ____________ this ___________ day of ___________ 19___.

____

Name: _________________________
Address: _______________________
____
____
Phone: (___) ___________

EXHIBIT (**3.2**)
Agreement to Submit to Assessment

THIS AGREEMENT made this _____ day of ____, 19__

BETWEEN:

____

referred to as "wife"

— and —

____

referred to as "husband"

THE PARTIES ACKNOWLEDGE THAT:

(a) The husband and wife are living separate and apart/intend to separate;
(b) They are the parents of the following:

Name: ______________________ d.o.b. ______________________

Name: ______________________ d.o.b. ______________________

Name: ______________________ d.o.b. ______________________

(c) Both the husband the wife wish to have the custody of the children;
(d) The husband and wife cannot agree on arrangements for access to the children;
(e) The parties wish to have the matter evaluated by a mental health professional to determine the needs of the children and the abilities of the husband and the wife to meet their needs;
(f) Each party acknowledges that the nature of assessment has been explained to each of them and that an assessment report is a recommendation which may form the basis for settlement but is not binding on the parties.

NOW THEREFORE in consideration of the mutual covenants herein the husband and wife agree as follows:

1. ______________________ will be retained to perform an assessment and make recommendations concerning the custody of and access arrangements for the children:

______________________________ d.o.b. ______________

______________________________ d.o.b. ______________

______________________________ d.o.b. ______________

2. The husband and the wife shall each pay one-half of the fees and disbursements for the assessment.
3. The husband shall pay the wife's half of the cost in the first instance and shall be reimbursed from the wife's share of the net proceeds realized on the sale of the matrimonial home.
4. The husband, wife, and the children will submit to the assessment together with any other members of their extended family as the assessor deems advisable.
5. It is agreed that either party may submit the report prepared by the assessor, ______________________, to a court of competent jurisdiction as evidence in the event that the husband and wife are unable to resolve the custody and access dispute, having had the benefit of ______________________'s assessment and recommendations. The assessor will be subject to subpoena and nothing said in the assessment is confidential.

IN WITNESS WHEREOF WE set our hands and seals at the City of ______________________ this ____ day of ____, 19__.

______________________	____________
Witness as to the signature of	Husband
______________________	____________
Witness as to the signature of	Wife

EXHIBIT (**3.3**)
Consent to Order for Assessment

__________ COURT OF __________

(Action commenced at __________________)

BETWEEN:

____

Plaintiff

— and —

____

Defendant

CONSENT

SUBJECT TO THE APPROVAL of this Honourable Court, the parties hereto Consent to an Interim Order as follows:

1. ________________________________ shall be appointed by this Honourable Court pursuant to subsection 30(1) of the Children's Law Reform Act to perform an assessment and make recommendation to the Court concerning custody of and access to __________________ ______________________________, born the ____ day of _____, 19__; ____________________________, born the ____ day of _____, 19__ and __________________________________, born the ____ day of _____, 19__;
2. The Plaintiff and Defendant shall attend interviews as requested by the assessor together with such further examination by a psychologist, physician, or psychiatrist, as the assessor may require;
3. The Plaintiff and the Defendant shall sign such authorizations to release information directed to doctors, schools, and other parties or institutions, as the assessor may from to time request;
4. The Plaintiff and Defendant shall each pay one-half of the fees and expenses of the assessment upon such terms as the assessor may request from time to time;
5. The assessor's report shall be filed in evidence;
6. Either party may require the attendance of the assessor as a witness; and both parties are at liberty to cross-examine the assessor at trial;
7. Neither party shall, except with leave of the court, commence or continue any motions, discoveries, or other proceedings, pending completion of the assessment;
8. Each party will make the children available to be observed during

any home visits requested by the assessor in the home of the other party;

9. There shall be no order for costs of this motion.

DATED at the City of ____________ this ____ day of _____, 19__.

____________________________ ________________

Witness as to the signature of Plaintiff

DATED at the City of ____________ this ____ day of _____, 19__.

____________________________ ________________

Witness as to the signature of Defendant

EXHIBIT (**3.4**)

Notice of Motion Requesting Assessment

__________ COURT OF __________

(Action commenced at ____________________)

BETWEEN:

____

Plaintiff

— and —

____

Defendant

NOTICE OF MOTION

TAKE NOTICE THAT a motion shall be made to a Judge on ______ day, the ____ day of _____, 19___ at 9:30 o'clock in the forenoon, or as soon after that time as the motion can be heard at the Court House ________________ Street, ________________, Ontario.

THE MOTION IS FOR an order pursuant to section 30 of the Children's Law Reform Act, R.S.O. 1980 c. 68, as amended by S.O. 1982, c. 20, as follows:

1. Appointing ______________________________ as a person who has technical or professional skill to assess and report to the court on the needs of the children ________________________, born the ____ day of _____, 19__; __________________________, born the ____ day of _____, 19__; and ____________________, born the ____ day of ____, 19__, and the ability and willingness of the parties or any of them to satisfy the needs of the children pursuant to subsection 30(1);
2. Requiring the mother ____________________________, the father ________________________________, [the mother's common-law partner, ______________________________, the father's wife ______________________________, and ______________________ (name any other relevant parties)] and the children to attend for assessment by ______________________________ pursuant to subsection 30(5);
3. Relieving the [Plaintiff/Defendant], ________________, from responsibility for payment of the fees and expenses of the assessor by reason of financial hardship pursuant to subsection 30(14);
4. Requesting that the [Defendant/Plaintiff],____________, pay all of the

fees and expenses of the assessor pursuant to subsection 30(12) and (13) of the Act;

5. Allowing both parties herein to cross-examine the assessor at the trial of the action, pursuant to subsection 30 (11) of the Act;
6. Allowing the [Plaintiff's/Defendant's] costs of this Motion fixed in the amount of $________;
7. Such further order as this Honourable Court may deem just.

THE GROUNDS FOR THE MOTION ARE:

1. Custody of and access to the children is at issue between the parties;
2. The family situation is such that an assessment will be of assistance to the court, and includes the following circumstances: ____________
____
____
3. An assessment is authorized pursuant to subsection 30 (1) of the Children's Law Reform Act, R.S.O. 1980 c. 68 as amended by S.O. 1982, c. 20;
4. ______________________________ has consented to act as assessor pursuant to subsection 30(4) of the Act;
5. The moving party cannot afford to contribute to the cost of an assessment, whereas the responding party can.

THE FOLLOWING DOCUMENTARY EVIDENCE will be used at the Hearing of the Motion:

1. The affidavit of ______________________, sworn the ____ day of ________, 19__;
2. The consent of ______________________ to be appointed as assessor, dated the ____ day of _____, 19__;
3. The *curriculum vitae* of ______________________, the proposed assessor;
4. The financial statement of the moving party, sworn the ____ of ____, 19__;
5. The financial statement of the responding party, sworn the ____ day of ____, 19__;
6. Such further and other material as counsel may advise and this Honourable Court may permit.

Date: Name, address and telephone number of moving party's solicitor or moving party.

To: Name & Address of Responding Party's Solicitor or Responding Party.

EXHIBIT (**3.5**)

Affidavit in Support of Motion for Assessment

_________ COURT OF _________

(Action commenced at ________________)

BETWEEN:

____

Plaintiff

— and —

____

Defendant

AFFIDAVIT

1. I, ________________, am the [Plaintiff/Defendant] herein and as such have knowledge of the matters hereinafter deposed to.
2. I am the father/mother of the children ____________, born the — ____ day of ____, 19__; ____________________, born the ____ day of _____, 19__; and ____________________, born the ____ day of _______, 19__. ____________________ is their mother/father. Both the [Plaintiff/Defendant] and I claim sole custody of the children.
3. The responding party and I separated on or about the ____ day of ________________, 19___. The children are currently living with ________________. I have experienced the following difficulties with their custodial and access arrangements: ______________

    ____

    ____

4. The following facts concerning myself, the responding party, and the situation of the children, both before and after separation, indicate that an assessment will be of assistance to the court in determining the custody and access structure for the children:

    ____

    ____

    ____

5. I propose that ______________________ be appointed to perform an assessment as to the needs of the children and the respective ability and willingness of ______________________ and myself to satisfy those needs.
6. Annexed hereto and marked as Exhibit "A" to this my affidavit is a consent to appointment as assessor executed by ______________ ______________________________.
7. Annexed hereto and marked as Exhibit "B" to this my affidavit is a copy of ______________________'s current *curriculum vitae* illustrating his/her qualification as a person who has the requisite technical or professional skill to perform the assessment.
8. I propose that the responding party, ______________ be ordered to pay ____% of the assessor's fees and disbursements.
9. The responding party can afford to pay ___% of the assessor's fees and expenses because ______________________________.
10. I cannot afford to pay more than ___% of the assessor's fees and expenses because ______________________________, and annexed hereto and marked as Exhibit "C" to this my affidavit is my statement of financial information verifying that my income and expenses, assets and debts, preclude my making any greater contribution.
11. ______________________________ lives with the responding party and therefore will have constant contact with the children if they are required to live in that household. His/her participation in the assessment will assist the court in making a determination as to custody of and access to the children.
12. I make this affidavit in support of the motion for the appointment of an assessor and for no improper purpose.

SWORN before me at the City)
of ______________ in the)
______________________________)
of ______________ this) ______________________
______ day of ______, 19__)

A commissioner, etc.

EXHIBIT (**3.6**)

Assessment Order under Section 30 Children's Law Reform Act

__________ COURT OF __________

(Action commenced at __________________)

THE HONOURABLE JUDGE) _____ day, the ____ day of __________, 19__

BETWEEN:

____

Plaintiff

— and —

____

Defendant

INTERIM ORDER

THIS MOTION made by ____________ for the appointment of an assessor was heard this day at ________________.

UPON READING the motion record of the Plaintiff and the Defendant, filed, and the consent to act as assessor and *curriculum vitae* of ______________________, filed; and upon hearing the submissions of counsel for both parties;

1. **THIS COURT ORDERS THAT** ____________________ be and is hereby appointed to perform an assessment pursuant to subsection 30(1) of the Children's Law Reform Act;
2. **THIS COURT ORDERS THAT** the parties and their children ____________________, born the ____ day of _____, 19__, and ____________________, born the ____ day of _____, 19__, will attend interviews as requested by the assessor, together with such further examination by a psychologist, physician, or psychiatrist as the assessor may require;
3. **THIS COURT ORDERS THAT** each party shall sign a medical authorization to the children's physician and a consent to authorize the release of information by the school, and other such releases that the assessor may from time to time request;

4. **THIS COURT ORDERS THAT** each party will co-operate in making full disclosure and ensuring the co-operation of the children;
5. **THIS COURT ORDERS THAT** the assessor's report will contain recommendations as to custodial arrangement and access arrangements, together with reasons, to assist the court in making its determination of what is in the best interests of the children pursuant to section 24 of the Children's Law Reform Act R.S.O. 1980, c. 68 as amended;
6. **THIS COURT ORDERS THAT** the assessor's report shall be filed with the court as soon as possible;
7. **THIS COURT ORDERS THAT** the assessor's fees and expenses shall be paid by the parties in equal shares on such terms as the assessor may request;
8. **THIS COURT ORDERS THAT** in the event that a trial of this action becomes necessary the assessor may be called as a witness and each party shall be entitled to cross-examine the assessor;
9. **THIS COURT ORDERS THAT** there shall be no order as to costs.

____

EXHIBIT (**3.7**)

Referral Letter to Assessor

Dear ________________________:

Re: ______________ **v.** ________________

I am pleased to confirm our telephone conversation of this morning and that you have been appointed under subsection 30 (1) of the Children's Law Reform Act to perform a custody/access assessment in the __________________ case.

Enclosed are the following documents:

(a) the court order appointing you dated the ____ day of _____, 19__;
(b) the Statement of Claim of my client;
(c) the Notice of Motion returnable on the ____ day of ____, 19__ for interim custody;
(d) the affidavit of my client in support of the above-noted motion;
(e) the affidavit of my client's mother, also in support of the above noted motion;
(f) the interim custody order of ______, 19__.

You will note that the order of _________, 19__, provides that the parties are each obliged to pay one-half of your fees and disbursements. I have instructed my client, as you requested, to bring a certified cheque for $1,000.00 for her share of the retainer. I confirm that you will be invoicing the parties directly for your account and that the report will be released following receipt of payment of your final account. This has been explained to my client who will contact you to arrange an intake appointment.[*]

Our firm represents the wife, ___________________, in a ____________ Court action, court file number __________, commenced at ______________. She seeks sole custody of the children of the marriage, namely, ________________________ born the ____ day of _____, 19__ and ____________________, born the ____ day of _____, 19__. She lives at ____________________ in ______________________; telephone: (res) _____________ and (work 9:00 - 4:30 _____________).

The husband is _________________________ who resides at __________________________ in _______________. He is represented by ________________________ of the firm of _______, _______________________. He seeks sole custody.

Both children live with their mother under the interim order of ___________, 19__. The parties were married _________, 19__, and have been apart since ________________. No divorce has been commenced yet. The children were with their father for the first month of separation. The couple tried a shared custody arrangement beginning around Christmas ________, but that broke down when the mother and her husband had difficulty sharing the necessary decisions when the mother realized that he had begun dating a woman the mother does not like.

The husband's lawyer will be sending you copies of his pleadings and affidavits.

There have been no prior assessments, but the older child has had some learning difficulties in the past and there was a psychological report prepared concerning her about three years ago by the school board staff psychologist. If you wish to see it please tell me and we will obtain a copy for you.

Please submit your report to the Registrar of the ______________ Court at ____________. I understand it is your practice to send a copy to each of the lawyers and our respective clients separately.

This action is under the Children's Law Reform Act. I enclose a photocopy of the relevant sections of that Statute outlining the elements to be considered by the court in determining custody. Please address those concerns as part of your assessment and recommendations.

Thank you for consenting to be appointed. If I can do anything to facilitate the process, please do not hesitate to call.

Yours sincerely,

____

* *Alternative wording if the client is funded by legal aid*:

I confirm that my client is funded by the Ontario Legal Aid Plan. Enclosed is a copy of the authorization letter from the Plan indicating approval of a total of 16 hours of time for the assessment and report writing at an hourly rate of $____. The Plan will pay reasonable long distance telephone charges and for travel time and mileage for one home visit with the child(ren) in each party's home. Mileage is chargeable at _____ cents per km. In the event that 16 hours will not be sufficient, please let me know immediately and provide full particulars on how you have calculated requisite time for this assessment. Authorization for such additional time will be requested from the Plan. I would caution you that the Legal Aid Plan will not pay for unauthorized time, and I am not in a position to pay for any services not funded by the Plan. Neither myself, nor my client will accept responsibility to pay for services unauthorized by the Plan.

EXHIBIT (**3.8**)

Letter Seeking Legal Aid Authorization

Date: ____________________

The Ontario Legal Aid Plan
Legal Accounts Officer
Suite 200 - 481 University Avenue
Toronto, Ontario
M5G 2G1

Attention: ______________________

Re: Client's Name: __________________
Certificate Number: _____________

Dear ______________:

I represent ____________________________ in an action for ________________ in which custody of and access to the children [of the marriage] is a contested issue.

Would you please authorize an expenditure for a custody/access assessment pursuant to subsection 30(1) of the Children's Law Reform Act [or as the case may be]. [Name and address of the assessor] who is a [social worker, psychiatrist, psychologist, or as may be] has been appointed by the court to perform the assessment pursuant to an order dated the ____ day of _______, 19__, a copy of which is enclosed.

The court has ordered my client to pay for one-half of the cost of the assessment, and the assessor has consented to accept payment at the legal aid rate for a [social worker, psychiatrist, psychologist, or as may be] in the amount of $_______ per hour for half of the time involved.

There are ______ children, the two parties to the action; their respective current partner(s), the paternal grandfather, the maternal grand parents, the children's teachers, babysitter, and several other collaterals to be consulted. The assessor, upon a preliminary review of the pleadings and affidavits, has estimated that _____ hours will be required, including _____ hours to write the report. The assessor anticipates that [one] visit out of town to the [mother's] home will be necessary to see the children in that environment. Because that home is located in ________________ ____________________, overnight accommodation will be necessary for one night, at an estimated cost of $______, as well as the travel time from ____________ to ________________ and back again and an estimated mileage charge at $0.29 per km of $________. Long distance phone calls will likely be necessary costing not more than $________.

The client, ______________________, has certificate number ____________ pursuant to a lien agreement for $_______. Interim bills in the amount of $________ have already been submitted on this file. We estimate that, including the cost for the assessment, the total fees in this action will be approximately $__________ if settlement is effected as a result of the assessment recommendations, and $_________ in the event that the matter proceeds to trial. We estimate disbursements of $__________. The lien will need to be increased by a further $__________ in the event of a trial.

Costs recovery is [un]likely given the nature of the case.

I look forward to your response.

Yours sincerely,

____

Solicitor number: ________

EXHIBIT (**3.9**)
Letter to Lawyer from Assessor Seeking Authorization for Additional Time

Dear ____________:

Re: ____________ v. ____________
Custody/Access Assessment

Thank you for your referral letter of ____________ and its enclosures. I note that the Ontario Legal Aid Plan has authorized payment for my fees to a maximum of 16 hours. Having now had an opportunity to read the materials filed by both sides, and having conducted intake interviews with each party, it is apparent that authorization for more time is needed.

There are three children in this case, each of an age to require a fairly lengthy individual interview. Your client was very upset at the first interview and I believe I will need at least two more sessions with your client to obtain her point of view and history. Each party has asked me to speak with their own parents, and there are several other potential collateral sources. Two school visits will be needed because the children are in different schools.

I estimate that about 22 hours, inclusive of report writing, will be needed. Please advise as soon as possible whether the additional time will be authorized. I will proceed only with the bare essentials of the assessment until you are able to advise whether the additional time has been authorized.

If you need further information concerning my procedures, please call.

Yours sincerely,

____

EXHIBIT **(3.10)**

Letter to Legal Aid from Lawyer Requesting Authorization for Additional Time for Assessor

Date: ____________________

The Ontario Legal Aid Plan
Legal Accounts Officer
Suite 200–481 University Avenue
Toronto, Ontario
M5G 2G1

Attention: __________________
Re: Client name: ____________________
Certificate number: ____________

Dear __________________.

Your letter of ________________, 19__, authorized a total of sixteen (16) hours for ____________________________ to perform a custody/access assessment in the client's case. You have my initial letter of __________ 19__ requesting authorization on file.

Please find enclosed a copy of a letter dated _______, 19__, from the assessor setting out the reasons twenty-two hours is the estimated time to complete the assessment.

I can verify the information contained in the assessor's letter concerning my own client's state of anxiety, and that interviewing these children and their teachers will require substantial time.

Would you kindly consider an authorization of twenty-two hours total for the assessment? Less time would compromise the quality of the assessment and impair its potential utility in negotiations and at trial.

Your early response would be appreciated.

Yours sincerely,

____

cc: Assessor*
Opposing counsel

* A copy is sent to the assessor to confirm that the request for time has been made. The request breaches no solicitor-client privilege; it is a matter of courtesy to let opposing counsel know of the request as it may affect his own client's obligations.

4

Preparing the Client: Notes for Lawyers

1. CLIENT APPREHENSION
2. STRATEGIES TO REDUCE CLIENT ANXIETY
3. BRIEFING THE CLIENT
4. SOME CAUTIONS

Even though the lawyer will already have had some discussions with the client about the nature and function of the assessment before the order for the assessment was obtained, a thorough briefing on what to expect should take place before the client meets the assessor for the first time.

1. CLIENT APPREHENSION

To the client, the assessor is a person of great potential power, and is therefore no inconsiderable threat. There is a myth that parenting is a skill that comes as automatically as breathing, and we all believe that myth in whole or in part. The assessor will have to make a recommendation favouring one particular type of custody (joint or sole); and one party's proposal for custody of the children over another. This can result in a recommendation that thereby implicitly "rejects" the other party as parent. Clients are already at a low ebb in their self esteem when the marriage breaks down, and then they will have to share the painful secrets of their married lives with strangers. The assessment is an experience that will call for sharing the pain with yet another stranger, this time one who will express opinions about them that may appear to say, "You are not capable of parenting your own child." No responsible assessor would phrase the message that way, but for the "loser" of the assessment that is how the message may sound.

A thorough preparation with the client can help to minimize fear about the process itself, and to put the potential assessment recommendations into perspective.

2. STRATEGIES TO REDUCE CLIENT ANXIETY

The lawyer should reinforce the message that the assessment is helpful precisely because choosing between the parties can be so difficult; that the neutral assessor will be trying to determine the needs of the children, and to match the capacities of the parties to those needs. The recommendation of the assessor is therefore neither a wholesale endorsement, nor a wanton rejection, of the lawyer's client as either person or parent.

Underscore that the assessor's recommendation is just that, a recommendation, albeit a professional one. The assessor does not decide the case. The parties remain free to negotiate a settlement that embodies all, some, or none of the assessment recommendations. If settlement is not possible, then the ultimate decision still rests with the court which can accept or reject the assessment recommendations in whole or in part.

Remind the client that assessment is neither mediation, nor therapy. The clinician doing the assessment cannot become the client's own social worker, psychiatrist, psychologist, or counsellor. Likewise, it is not the role of the assessor to negotiate settlement of the case, nor to help either side "win" or "beat" the other party. The goal of assessment is to assist the court with its responsibility to decide the direction of the children's future. Encourage clients to be honest and open with the assessor (even about their own flaws). Such information will usually be mentioned to the assessor by the other party. Negatives are less harmful if mentioned first by the client. Likewise, suggest that the client not devote all his or her energy in the assessment to slinging as many stones as possible at the other party. Such name-calling can reflect badly on the client.

Often there is a wait of several weeks from the time that the assessment order is made until the assessor can begin the process. The assessment itself will take several weeks to complete in many instances. Let the client know that while waiting is hard, and causes increased stress, it is better for the assessor to be given the time that is required for a thorough service, than for the assessment to be rushed and incomplete. If the lawyer has confidence in the approach and integrity of the assessor, and such confidence is communicated to the client, the waiting to begin and to complete the process will be easier.

Make sure to share the assessor's *curriculum vitae* with the client. It gives the client some sense of who the assessor is, which can serve to increase the client's confidence. In some cases, seeing the *curriculum vitae* may allow the client to indicate a possible conflict of interest that might not be apparent either to the lawyer or the assessor this early in the process. The client may, for example, have been involved in the same community organization as the assessor, or have some other such close connection.

3. BRIEFING THE CLIENT

By the time the lawyer knows who the assessor will be and has spoken with the assessor, forwarded documents, and provided a written referral, the lawyer is in a position to brief the client on what to expect from this particular assessor in terms of the way things will be approached. If the lawyer's preparation of the client has been inadequate, then when the assessor begins to ask the parent questions in the first interview the following may result:

Assessor: "Do you know why you are here?"
Parent: "My lawyer said I had to come to see you."
Assessor: "Do you know what for?"
Parent: "No." or, "You'll tell me what I have to do with the children."

In order to take full advantage of the opportunity the assessment affords each party to be understood in his claim for custody or access, the party needs to understand what an assessment is, what the role of the assessor is, and how the assessment fits into the context of the dispute resolution/legal action as a whole.

Make sure the client knows what the payment responsibilities are for the assessment; whether to take a retainer cheque to the first meeting with the assessor; what materials the assessor will have access to; and how to arrange the initial interview.

If the assessment has been ordered over the client's protest, it is crucial to advise that client of the legal implications of failure to cooperate with the assessment. Clients and lawyers catch each other's attitudes. It is important, if the lawyer objects to assessments on general principles, for the lawyer to reveal that bias to the client. The client then has an opportunity to consider whether a second opinion about assessments in general, and this assessment in particular, is in order. The lawyer's client needs an ongoing sense of the lawyer's support and accessibility, and at the same time needs also to be freed by the lawyer and encouraged to participate as openly and securely as possible in the assessment.

Ask the client to think of other people the assessor might be able to talk to in order to gain a broader understanding of the case from the client's perspective. Most assessors will want to speak to the children's teachers, each parent's current partner, and significant others in contact with the family, both friends and relatives. If the assessor does not ask for such a list of "collaterals" then suggest that the party offer it.

4. SOME CAUTIONS

Making use of other professions to undertake a role in the lawyer's case and with the lawyer's client may be difficult. Such interprofessional cooperation is a relatively recent development in custody/access work, and both the legal and mental health professionals are still gaining experience about how to do it effectively and efficiently. Both professions need to know a great deal more about each other in order to develop protocols that will effectively guide their interaction in the resolution of custody/access disputes. The previous material has been directed toward establishing some needed "do's" for lawyers. There are also some "don't's", or at least some areas to try to avoid if possible.

The lawyer should avoid consenting to a process that he does not really agree with. It is not then possible to really support the client in the process. As well, the lawyer should not use an assessment needlessly as a tactic to delay the action and continue a status quo.

Avoid undercutting the process. The effective use of an assessment relies in part on a base of good faith among lawyer, client and mental health professional. "Second-guessing" the assessor by coaching the client may make it impossible for an open, fair and reliable assessment to be conducted.

This in no way suggests that the lawyer should not maintain some contact with the client, deal with other matters as they arise, and express interest in the client's well being. The lawyer should, in fact, ask for some feedback from the client during the assessment. Concerns about issues such as the amount of time the assessor is spending in interviews with the client; the way contact with the child(ren) is being structured; or whether or not the assessor is interviewing the client's chosen collateral informants, are legitimate issues for the lawyer to raise with the assessor. Be sure always to let the other side know if such matters are being queried with the assessor. If, however, the feedback from the client indicates that the assessment is proceeding as expected, then stay in the background and do not interfere from the sidelines.

During the ongoing assessment, avoid, if at all possible, such steps as examination for discovery, cross-examinations, motions, or fresh moves in the litigation. Such actions anger the other side, alter the reality with which the assessor is trying to work, and may lead to "acting-out" behaviour that will mislead the assessor. If such litigation steps are unavoidable during the assessment, let the assessor know what is happening, why it is being done, and provide copies of any relevant affidavits or further pleadings.

Avoid making requests of the assessor that would impugn her neutrality or impartiality. Do not, for instance, ask the assessor to try to arrange holiday access for the family while the assessment is ongoing. Like justice needing to be *seen* to be done, as well as *being* done, the assessor must be seen as professionally fair, neutral, and ethical.

Avoid inexact language. If a lawyer wishes to retain the services of a mental health professional to assist in a better understanding of the client, or the client's situation, or the children in the care or custody of the client, but not with reference to the other side or even in discussion with them, then this relationship and function cannot be called an assessment. It may be referred to as a "consultation". This is a legitimate use of the expertise of the mental health professional, but must, of course, be subject to the mental health professional's ethics and standards of practice for her own profession. Any communication resulting from such an on-side consultation cannot be considered or referred to as an "assessment report".[1]

Avoid guaranteeing an outcome for the client at the beginning of the assessment. Building unrealistic expectations is unfair to the client, and will severely limit the lawyer's ability to make use of the assessment report if it is unfavorable to the client's expressed position. Until there has been an opportunity to read the complete report following the assessment it is impossible to know whether the advice to the client will be to consider agreement with the recommendations made, negotiate a variation upon them, or proceed to court and challenge the assessment recommendations.

1 In *Whey v. Brenton* (1984), 41 R.F.L. (2d) 30 (Nfld. C.A.) the court ordered an independent custody/access assessment in a situation in which, at trial, the custodial party had the benefit of expert evidence from an on-side consultation, and the non-custodial parties, with limited access, had been unable to have such an on-side consultation to balance the effect of such evidence for the custodial parties.

5

The Assessment Process

1. INTRODUCTION

The purpose of an assessment, as indicated earlier, is to assist in the process of deciding the custody of and access to the children of separated or divorced parents, or those in the process of becoming separated and/or divorced. Such decision should not only resolve (or at least conclude) the present dispute, but it should as well go a long way toward providing for the children's long range constructive upbringing, to the extent that can be foreseen. The recommendations contained in the assessment report, supported by the information that precedes them, should enhance the lawyers' and the court's understanding of the dispute, its antecedents, the children's needs, and in particular what it is of themselves that the parties[1] would bring to the task of ongoing child care.

High on the list of factors to be understood by the assessor is that of each parent's motivation in seeking the children's custody, or enhanced access to them. Experience has taught that not all claims for custody are rooted in genuine parental concern for children. Some actions reflect more

1 The terms "parties" and "parents" are used interchangeably in this chapter.

ongoing spousal provocation or retaliation behaviour, masked as parental longing.

Participating in an assessment is not easy. The stakes are high. Not only does it deal with children's lives and futures (the decisions that are made at the conclusion of the case stream children's lives in certain directions for the foreseeable future), it shapes the parents' view of themselves. The timing of most assessments makes that inevitable. Each parent is usually still smarting or hurting from the end of the marriage, and is feeling in some sense a failure as a husband or wife (at least in that relationship). Now in the unresolved dispute about the children, the assessment looms, carrying with it the potential for a second identified failure, as a parent, if the recommendations are not favourable. Even though each parent has consented to the assessment, and may have actively sought it, there is a sense of risk. Anxiety is inevitable. Getting the assessment off on the right foot therefore is not only important, it is a crucial aspect of learning about and fairly evaluating each parent's motivation. Although it may appear at first glance not so important an issue, who phones whom to arrange the first intake interview is, indeed, just that: important.

2. ORGANIZATIONAL MATTERS

(a) Who Makes the First Call

In the initial discussions with the referring lawyers the assessor should make it clear that the parties should phone to arrange the first appointment. This is not just a matter of caste and class, nor of too-formal and too-rigid professionalism. There are reasons. Sometimes that request is missed or forgotten, and in the lawyer's confirming letters of referral the assessor is requested to phone the client to get the assessment started. If that is the case, phone the lawyer or the lawyer's secretary, and explain the policy again and the reasons behind it. Repeat the request that the client arrange the appointment. Here is why.

Asking the parent to call places the responsibility right where it should belong — with the parent. As with the content of affidavits, first-call behaviour will indicate something (or raise questions) about each parent's attitudes. Some parents will phone almost the moment they conclude the conversation with their lawyer, indicating their concern about getting the assessment under way as soon as possible. They may sound worried or harried or angry. They may be tense and irritable at first, but they have called, and are ready to start.

Other parents will delay calling. The reason may be unclear because based on the referral information concerning the background and nature of the dispute, an early contact might have been expected. The silence becomes noticeable, raising questions in the assessor's mind. Is this avoidance and resistance in spite of consent and demanding affidavits; is it fear; is it anger; is it innocent, and is the parent unaware of your request? A phone call to the parent's lawyer is in order. Sometimes under the pressure of work there has been a communication problem and the client has not been told to arrange the appointment. In these instances, the parent's phone call to you follows hard on the heels of yours to the lawyer, and the matter is soon cleared up.

But if dealing at a distance with resistance, it is essential to learn of it, and something of its extent. If the assessor phones the parent she may not gain evidence of that serious resistance. The momentum has changed, particularly if you connect on the first call and the parent masks his or her real feelings and makes an appointment. While it is of course true that a competent professional will tap into the parent's attitudes during the course of the assessment, nevertheless the assessor may not gain a full understanding of the extent of parental resistance. Waiting for the parent to call provides an unavoidable insight into motivation.

Sometimes a parent requires two or three reminders from his or her lawyer before phoning. Very occasionally a parent will not phone at all. That parent's lawyer is entitled to be kept aware of the situation. Most lawyers keep a hands-off, arms-length relationship to the assessment and if no other matters are pressing in the case, may not be in touch with their client. Thus, the lawyer will be quite unaware of the no-call situation unless kept informed by the assessor. After two or three requests have been passed on to the parent, with no result, the lawyer may begin to re-evaluate his position in the matter. In any event, it is probably fair to suggest that the parent who is clear about the request and who has not phoned after several reminders, is sending a message that raises a query about his or her committment to the children and their future. This procedural policy about first appointment calls places and keeps the responsibility for cooperation with an assessment in the proper place: with each parent, with the assistance of each lawyer. It is not the role or responsibility of the assessor to ensure, or to attempt to ensure, compliance. This is very different, of course, from the necessary and usual negotiations that take place in setting up appointments, which involve mutual awareness of matters of availability, location, other obligations and so forth.

In Ontario, the legislation allows the court to draw whatever conclusions it wishes from the non-compliant behaviour of a parent in an assessment. Section 30(6) of the Children's Law Reform Act[2] states as follows:

2 R.S.O. 1980, c. 68 [as amended by S.O. 1982, c. 20].

> Where a person ordered under this section to attend for assessment refuses to attend or to undergo the assessment, the court may draw such inferences in respect of the ability and willingness of any person to satisfy the needs of the child as the court considers appropriate.

(b) Setting up the First Appointment

When the parent calls for the first appointment, the assessor may demonstrate right from the beginning that she is flexible, fair, and non-threatening. Making the first appointment may take several minutes of give-and-take negotiation; in the course of the conversation, parent and assessor make their first impressions on each other. A friendly, pleasant, low-key, professional approach is indicated. Willingness to arrive at a mutually possible time and location demonstrates flexibility, and may reassure a very anxious parent that you do listen. Imposing a date, time, and location, suitable only to the assessor's convenience, conveys a message that (perhaps) the assessor does not listen very well. If this should be so, the parent's anxiety and/or resistance level will escalate, and the assessment may be in difficulty already.

(c) Location of the First Appointment

The first two (or even a third, if indicated) interviews should take place in an office, not in the parent's home. Although the assessor will, of course, visit each parent's home later, in the initial stages of the assessment certain boundaries need to be established. The assessor wants to establish that the relationship and the undertaking are professional, that she is a qualified professional, and that she is "on top" of the process that is beginning. Confidence in these capacities is important for the parent, not only during the assessment but at its conclusion, when that parent is responding or reacting to the recommendations.

Location is a function of who is in charge. If the first contacts, before any trust base has been built at all, are held in a parent's home, a subtle personalizing, socializing, de-professionalizing atmosphere will result. It is the parent's home; the assessor is the guest; the parent is in charge. The assessor's office, on the other hand, however warm, attractive, and comfortable to be in, is just that, the office, the place where the professional self functions, and where the assessor is in charge. It is professional turf; the parent's home is personal turf. If it is manageable, the early contacts with each parent should be held at the assessor's office. Quite apart from anything else, the location demonstrates neutrality and professionalism, while offering each parent some opportunity to get acquainted with the assessor. The office inevitably reflects the person, and while the assessor is busily trying to get to know the parent and his or her life, the parent picks up information about the professional from certificates, diplomas, pictures, and decorative touches. That is only fair — it helps to humanize the professional.

(d) Time of the Appointment

Daytime appointments may work a real hardship on some parents. They may face losing a day's pay, or the irritation or even anger of a supervisor or boss at a request for yet another day off on a personal matter. Remember that parents have already faced appointments with lawyers, for examinations for discovery, for court hearings, or for meetings of one kind or another with one professional or another. Most of these will have pre-dated the contact with the assessor; any one of them may have cost that parent not only time but money. Asking for more time off may bring on more stress. Indicate your awareness of this, and a wish not to be the cause of it; the assessment brings its own added stress, and that is enough. Recognition of this point is welcomed by the parent.

The parent may ask when they have to come to your office. Or they may anticipate an inconvenience, and already stressed and angry about the whole situation, attempt to establish some sense of control (of something!) by announcing angrily that they cannot come during the day. Whatever the opening remarks, enquire pleasantly whether they need an evening or a weekend appointment. Many parents seem surprised by the offer: is this a commentary on their experience to date with professionals? Affirm your willingness to make such an arrangement if they need it; after all, they have lives and obligations outside the assessment that may not fit into a daytime office schedule. Suggest that they provide one or two possible dates and times, to see if they can be accommodated. In almost every case this flexibility and consideration is met with echoing flexibility and good will. The offer may come quickly to manage things on their end to meet the demands of the assessor's schedule, and a date, time and location are in place. By empowering parents this way in the very first exchange, through demonstrating respect for them as persons, the stage is set for a first meeting with a parent who has begun to view the assessor as reasonable, sensitive, practical, fair, and democratic.

(e) Structure of the First Appointment

Each parent will want to know how long the appointment is likely to be; whether the child(ren) or the current spouse should come at the same time; what documents or files you want brought along; and where the office is. Take the time to answer these questions and explain the reasons behind the answers.

- The first interview usually lasts an hour and one-quarter (this helps plan the amount of time needed to keep the appointment, and to arrange for someone to pick up the children at school or daycare if they will not be back home in time).
- The parent will come alone this time, without the children or spouse (there is a lot of getting acquainted to do, and a process to set in place, and questions that may need to be considered; it will be easier to do all that if the parent is alone; the spouse and the children are very important and certainly will be seen in the course of the assessment).
- No, they don't have to bring any documents at this time, as you have some already from the lawyer, but if they wish to, that's fine, (this may later produce very useful materials, such as a personal diary of events, personal letters received from the other parent since the separation, and so forth).

If the matter of a retainer has been confirmed with their lawyer and it has not yet been received, it may be useful at this point to suggest that the parent bring that along with them at the time of the first appointment.

(f) Using the Lawyer's Office for Interviews

For some parents, especially those who live in another community, it will not be feasible to get to the assessor's office. Certain physical disabilities, lack of transportation, or other situations may make it obvious that this is the case. In that event, offer to meet them in their lawyer's office. Ask them to phone the lawyer's office and enquire about the availability and use of interviewing space; suggest a possible date and time and ask them to confirm the plan with you. All lawyers will be cooperative and helpful with that request. Indeed, the matter may have been discussed with the lawyer at the time of referral. Information about the parent's circumstances may have led to a query as to whether the parent could get to the assessor's office, and if not, whether space in the lawyer's office could be made available.

Every parent will already have been to their lawyer's office on several occasions. They know the way, and are familiar with its layout. A parent who might be overwhelmed at having to find the way to the assessor's office, knows that he or she can safely meet the assessor at the lawyer's office. This allows parents to retain some sense of control in the unfamiliar assessment situation, and maintains the context of "office" for the assessor. That way, everyone's needs are satisfied.

If indicated, all subsequent interviews with the parent, except during the home visit, may be conducted at the lawyer's office by, of course, arrangement with the lawyer's staff. As a side benefit, such cooperative activity between assessor and lawyer serves to increase their working-relationship comfort. It facilitates friendly chatting, allows the lawyer's secretary to meet the assessor, and contributes usually to an enhanced opportunity for understanding of each other's role. All grist for the future mill of repeat referrals.

If this solution is not possible, however, two other options are open: asking the lawyer's help in seeking the use of a colleagues's office, or in arranging the use of an interviewing room at the local court house. Either alternative is an acceptable compromise.

(g) The Intake Interview: Two-Parent or One-Parent?

Some assessors require the parents to meet together at the assessor's office at the beginning of the assessment process. During that meeting they are challenged to consider their responsibilities as parents to their children, the impact on the children of their ongoing dispute, and the potential value implicit in their arriving at a shared resolution of the dispute. The possibility of using the assessment to lead to a mediated or negotiated agreement is held out to the parents. The assessment is then begun.

While this approach has its rationale, of course, there is another point of view: by the time the assessment has been requested, much effort has already been expended on attempting resolution, unsuccessfully. Even if the parents are speaking to each other, there is considerable strain in the communications. Their positions have polarized, and even their lawyers have been unable to effect acceptable resolution. Being together is very stressful. At this stage they are not really amenable to listening to how they should cooperate; if there was reason to believe that they could manage that, mediation would have been the process of choice. Each parent needs to experience an opportunity to be heard on his or her own, and to connect with the (potentially so powerful) assessor from the beginning as an individual. The assessor can demonstrate neutrality by a careful presentation and respectful listening that does not suggest a pre-held opinion. Too early discussion about parents' obligations may give the impression that the assessor has already chosen sides and prejudged the issues. Better not to risk it: if mediation seems indicated at the conclusion of the assessment, it can always be included as one of the recommendations. Seeing the parents together in order to be convinced of their inability to agree about the children puts an unnecessary added stress upon them. It is not diagnostically necessary.

3. CONTENT OF THE FIRST INTERVIEW

There are a number of items to be covered in the first (intake) interview. A summary of these, in the general line of progression, is as follows:

- The parent's understanding from the lawyer of the purpose and conduct of an assessment.
- Clarification of the role of the assessor.
- The limitations on that role.
- Focus and purpose of the assessment.
- The process of the assessment.
- The assessor's approach to children.
- The general structure of the assessment report.
- The use of the assessment report.
- Payment arrangements.
- The beginning of recording the story.
- Recording the basic identifying information.
- Requesting a collateral names list.
- Answering the parent's questions.
- Setting the next appointment.

Sometimes all of the items will be covered, although not necessarily in the order indicated; in other cases, the parent will be so nervous or upset or single-minded about what they need to say, that only a portion of the issues will be touched on. Not to worry: there is always the next interview in which to catch up.

Some parents will be so nervous that you will have to carry the responsibility for getting things started and for keeping them rolling. Others, as indicated above, will be so single-minded about what they want to say, or so compulsive in their speech that the assessor's role becomes almost that of traffic manager. Compulsive parents will not want to hear a discussion about the assessment process, that will have to come later. It takes patience, clarity, flexibility, and quiet firmness to navigate around either extreme.

(a) Clarify What Assessment Is

It is useful very early on to ascertain parents' understanding of what an assessment is. Some will have been very well briefed by counsel; others will not. Some will have been given quite accurate information; others will have been incorrectly informed. Some will have listened carefully to counsel; others will have been so anxious that virtually all they heard was the assessor's name, address, and telephone number. Ask the parent to explain his or her understanding of the assessment, its purpose and process, as presented by the lawyer. Explain how important it is for parents to understand what they are participating in. They will each be the main source of information, and they will be able to assist you more thoroughly if they understand the process, and the reason for seeking certain information. Depending upon the description provided by the parent, you may support it, and suggest some elaboration, or indicate that the process goes beyond what they have described. Indicate awareness that the outcome of the situation is of great importance to them, and indeed to the children. As well, it is of equal importance that as parents they understand what the assessment is for, how it will be conducted, what the report will contain, how they will receive the report, and what may occur afterwards.

(b) When There Has Been a Prior Assessment

Some parents will have had an earlier assessment experience; you may represent a second opinion. This prior experience will have led them to expect the same process now. Indeed, their lawyer may have made the same assumption. Ask each parent how he or she found that first assessment; what the process was; and for any comments about it before starting the new one. Clarify any differences in your policies and procedures. If parties felt unfairly treated in a prior assessment, you need to be aware of this and what they perceived as unfair or inappropriate. Indicate a concern to be fair and ethical in this assessment: if the results still do not favour their position, they should nevertheless be able to feel heard and fairly treated. They are entitled to know and understand the process. It is the future of the children that is being shaped, and that responsibility is serious. So you seek their help in building an understanding of what this is all about.

(c) Explaining the Assessor's Role and Procedure

Take time to give parents details of the assessor's role and procedures. It is an investment in cooperation, in full disclosure, and in their response at the conclusion of the process when the recommendations are in. It may be necessary to present this in bits and pieces if the parent is very anxious or needs to tell his or her story without waiting for the context information. It is up to the assessor to ensure that all the introductory material is covered. An informed parent who understands what is being requested in the assessment will be a more effective participant, and a more equable recipient of the report at the end.

The points to be covered now are as indicated below under headings (i) to (vii).

(i) *The Assessor's Role*

Explain that an assessor is not there to help one parent win or defeat the other parent. The assessor is not a parent's advocate. Each parent has a lawyer, whose valid role it is to advance his or her position, clearly and forcefully, in negotiation or at trial. An assessor has two clients: the court, and the child(ren). Although parents are a main source of information (after all, they have been living the situation) the assessor's responsibility is as follows:

- First, to assist the judge by providing information and an understanding that he would not have had available before about the dispute and all the people involved in it.
- Second, to make recommendations which act as advice (only) to the judge. The assessor cannot make case decisions. That is the prerogative of the court alone.
- Third, to be a spokesman for the interests of the children, not as the children's lawyer, but speaking on their behalf through the recommendations.

Indicate that any recommendations are just that, recommendations. They are not binding upon the court which is independent and free to use them or not. Add, however, that for the assessment to be of value (else why spend money and time on it, and put up with the added stress?), it must be thorough.

(ii) *The Assessment Process*

Indicate a wish to get acquainted with each parent (and/or the other parties who may be involved). There is much to learn: what happened to the marriage or the relationship; how it started and why it has reached the state that it is in now; what went wrong (after all, none of us enters an important relationship expecting or wanting it to fail). You will want to meet and learn about the child(ren), how they are coping and what they need; to understand what each parent sees as the way they can and will care for the child(ren), and how they can arrange things when the child(ren) are ill and can't go to school or daycare. You will want to get acquainted with them as persons in their own right: learn something of their own childhood and their own parents' marriage. We are, all of us, turtles; we carry our childhoods with us wherever we go. Learning something about their perception of their parents' marriage helps to indicate what they learned as children of how men treat women, how women treat men, how their parents handled stress and anger, and how they each treated their children. Those examples form part of what we all bring with us to our own adult relationship expectations, especially the early ones. This information will help to put the present situation in a context that leads to understanding.

(iii) *Collaterals*

Another way of getting to know parents and their points of view in the situation is through contact with persons they may recommend to you. Ask the parent to prepare a list to bring to the second interview, with the names and phone numbers, and addresses if available, of people you may speak to, who know them in a way and over a period of time which you, of course, cannot hope to duplicate. There is no right number of such names, nor right kinds of persons.

Parents will want suggestions about choice of collateral names. Indicate that the purpose of the request is twofold: (1) to ensure that you have been thorough in your efforts to understand them and their position, by speaking to persons who have known them in a way that you cannot; and (2) to ensure that your reaction to their version and position is balanced and fair, by holding it up beside the opinions and information of others. The list might include their own parents (very useful always); siblings and their spouses; other relatives; close friends; work mates or supervisors; professionals whom they have seen, such as counsellors or therapists; physicians; and neighbours. The choice is theirs, and you will respect the list. On their behalf you will speak only with those persons authorized by them. Names may always be added, and indeed names originally given may be withdrawn subsequently if they change their mind.

Parents should not submit names without the individual's permission; those whose names are presented should be assured that the assessor will not quote them in the report (unless requested to do so); and that speaking to you does not automatically mean that they will have to be a witness if there is a trial. The decision to call witnesses, and the choice of witnesses, will be made by each parent and his or her lawyer; collaterals will not automatically be called upon to go to court because they spoke to the assessor.

Be sure parents know that not everyone on the list may be contacted, especially if the list is long. Sometimes people are missed, even after repeated calls. Sometimes if the information gained in previous collateral interviews has been consistent, further interviews may not be needed. While you do not undertake to speak to everyone on the list, you do undertake not to go outside the list without the parent's knowledge and consent.

If the children are of school age, you will want to consult their teachers. Ask the parent of current custody to inform the principal of the assessment and your anticipated request for a school visit, indicating consent to the release of information, and to then add the relevant names to the collateral list. If both parents are currently custodians, then ensure that each is aware of your wishes in this regard.

It is useful to pause at this point to allow for questions and to ensure that the parent is "with you". Misconceptions may have been cleared up, and there is notable relaxation of tension. Preparation of the collaterals list provides an assignment, something a parent can do, although the discussion may also raise new concerns: What will it mean to the assessment if both parents suggest the same collateral names? What good would it do to speak to relatives who are on their side? What good would it do to speak to relatives who are not on their side? What can they do if they don't have any really close friends to suggest? What if they haven't told anybody at work about the situation?

Such matters will stimulate remarks about the situation and the parent's feeling about it. Crying or strong anger may ensue, feelings of desperation about the children may be shared. These need to be listened to with patience and respect. The parent may even demand a "quick and easy" assessment, the conclusion of which is obvious to him or her and must be to you. Speaking to the anxiety behind the demands, combined with a clear intent to be thorough and fair, will help to calm the situation. Your respect for the issue of the children's future will require the assessment to take some time; you recognize that that adds to their already heavy stress. But a shallow report, incomplete and/or poorly thought out, may serve their children over the long run far less well than a more careful and thoughtful one, upon which the court can rely with confidence, or upon which the parents may agree.

(iv) *Speaking to the Children*

A common focus of concern is how an assessor will involve the children. Already they have been caught in the middle of the situation, their loyalty sought by each parent and possibly by grandparents as well. If a previous assessment was done, perhaps this was one focus of the parent's discontent: the previous assessor may have greatly upset the children by a direct, insensitive, ill-timed question as to which parent they wanted to live with. Make clear your belief that such a decision is the full responsibility of adults, and that children should not be placed in the position of having to express choices, much less make them. Indeed, you will want to meet the children in the home of each parent, and, if possible, speak to them. But not right now. Now there is need to get on with learning about the situation and the parent. When the times come to meet the children, you will ask the parents' help with introductions, so that the children will feel comfortable (or as comfortable as possible) with your being there.

(v) *The Report*

Once the assessment itself is completed (that includes all the interviews with parents, collaterals, and children, home visits, school visits, test applications if used) you will re-read everything, think about it, and arrive at a position as to how the children can best be raised and cared for from now until they have grown. Then you will prepare a report. That report will present a summary of your understanding of the situation, past and present; of the people concerned; of what happened to their marriage or relationship; who the children are and what their needs are; what, if any, wishes, opinions, or messages the children want conveyed; what each parent wants and offers; and, finally, the recommendations. The recommendations will describe the best possible arrangements *for the children* in the circumstances. They will be spelled out in some detail, and will reflect your professional judgment as to the working arrangement most likely to ensure that the children will be properly and effectively brought up until they can be on their own.

(vi) *Distribution of the Report*

The report will be sent to each parent (or party), each parent's (or party's) lawyer, and to the ordering judge, or master, or court registrar.[3] Upon reading the report — all of it, not just the recommendations — each parent should then consult with his or her lawyer about it. Any questions or concerns about the report may be raised with the assessor by the lawyers. Assure the parents that you will be quite prepared to meet with them and their lawyer to discuss the recommendations and their basis. A happy resolution occurs when each side is prepared to negotiate an agreement based on the recommendations (which may be modified or amended if everyone agrees). Such an outcome is to be encouraged; it reduces costs for everyone, financial and emotional, saves court time, and spares the children the added tensions associated with a trial. But settlement may not be reached. One parent is bound to feel disappointed, even perhaps initially angry, when the recommendations do not favour his or her position, and may choose not to settle.

Indicate to each parent that if that proves to be the case, you will be prepared to attend at court, where the disaffected parent's lawyer could challenge the report. Conversely, you will also be prepared to attend at court in order to expand on and clarify the reasons and reasoning that

3 As was noted earlier in this chapter under the heading "The Intake Interview: Two-Parent or One-Parent?" 2(g) some assessors present their recommendations to the parents in a joint interview. This approach is not favoured for the reasons indicated there.

led to the recommendations. Parents need to know and understand the assessor's thinking here: the report and its recommendations should be of genuine value to the court, as part of the evidence brought out if there is a trial; therefore, the assessor should be prepared to explain the basis of the recommendations, and the conduct of the assessment. No assessor should have it both ways: with the power to make recommendations that will or may effect the lives of children, but shielded from accountability as to the means employed to arrive at those conclusions. So if it becomes necessary to attend at court, you will, of course, comply.

(vii) *The Bill for the Assessment: Fees and Expenses*

This point in the interview may be a useful time to introduce the subject of the cost of the assessment and how it is to be paid. If the parent was asked to bring a retainer cheque, it is appropriate now to ask for it and issue a receipt if requested. Indicate to a parent who is paying for, or contributing to the cost of the assessment, that when the report is sent a complete statement will be enclosed showing the full cost and the portion that is theirs. You will ask for the retainer to be replenished along the way to cover remaining costs and items such as preparation and typing of the report, photocopying, and sending out the copies. This way the cost is spread over the time of the assessment, rather than being faced in total at the end. If there remains a small balance owing at the end, this will be reflected in the statement. If there is a balance in favour of the parent because not all of the retainer was needed, a cheque in the parent's favour will accompany the statement. If the parent is being supported by a Legal Aid Plan certificate in meeting the cost, then the detailed account will be sent directly to that parent's lawyer with the report.

(d) Who Discusses the Report with the Parents

There is a point of view that the conclusions and recommendations contained in an assessment report should be discussed directly with the parents and/or their counsel, either separately or together, before or after release of the report. The aim seems to be to facilitate each parent's understanding of the recommendations, to deal with the attendant feelings and reactions, and perhaps even to initiate some mediated joint approach to a cooperative implementation of the recommended structure for custody and access. While positions on this question vary, experience shows that such a process is not of consistent value. Each parent needs time to read and absorb the entire report, not only the recommendations. Seeing themselves in print is startling to some parents, and again they need time to react and recover from that. Discussion with their lawyer may serve to give balance to their reactions (sometimes just to a sentence or even to one word), and to direct attention to the question of how the report and its recommendations fit into their case. Following such a discussion, a meeting of the assessor with the parent and lawyer will be of much more value. Questions about content of the report, questions about the recommendations, questions about procedure, will have been identified and may be addressed more effectively at the subsequent meeting. At a meeting with the assessor alone at which a parent learns that his or her position has not been supported, anger and disappointment may be so high that useful discussion is obviated, then or later. It is preferable to remember that the parent is their lawyer's client, and to reinforce that recognition by directing the parent back to the lawyer to discuss the assessment results.

(e) Clarity of the Assessor's Role

There is another dimension of this last point that might well be raised here, although not discussed with the parent. That dimension refers to a current point of view among some assessors that, as a part of their assessment process, they may move into the case, either as possible mediator or as counsellor. For mental health professionals such an undertaking may seem not only logical but advisable. Their training as "helpers" leads them into that role, and they see the activity as a valid expression of that helping mode. The rationalization that by so doing they may hasten settlement of the disagreement or improvement of an emotional disturbance allows them, in effect, to depart from the assessment and their role as assessor.

As admirable as such intent may be, and however well motivated, the policy is faulted on two counts: the assessor's relationship to the lawyers, and the impact on the parents of such mid-stream attempts to change horses.

The assessor's individual decision to interrupt the assessment reflects an assumption that the parents are the assessor's clients, and that the case itself is the assessor's to resolve. Neither assumption is correct. As indicated earlier, the parents are not the assessor's clients: they were and have remained their lawyers' clients. The assessor's role is to understand, explicate, and recommend on behalf of the children; it is not to undertake to resolve — that belongs to the lawyers and the court. However benignly intended, moving away from the function of assessment (which the assessor has agreed to perform) into that of agent of resolution is an unwarranted incursion into the lawyer's role and the court's responsibility. The case was the lawyers' first and has remained theirs to serve. The assessor does not own the matter, and was not retained to be either counsellor or mediator. The assessor is a specialist, ordered by the court or retained by the parties on the recommendation of counsel, to prepare a report which will be but one item of evidence, albeit an important one, in the matter. Each lawyer is entitled to receive what he expected: a report of a completed assessment, which contains specific and focussed recommendations, and a thorough discussion of the reasons for them. If the assessor's professional opinion is that these parents are now prepared to cooperate and mediation or negotiation is indicated, or that one or both of the parents requires counselling, then such opinion should be directed to counsel as part of the assessment recommendations, for consideration by counsel with his client.

A change-of-direction decision taken by the person retained to do an assessment may have quite an effect on one or both parents. Each parent has already been through the process of considering and agreeing to the assessment. Much apprehension may still be in place, especially for persons whose capacity for trust has been damaged. Risking putting their child's potential future in the hands of a stranger has called for a real leap of faith, and genuine confidence in their lawyer's advice. They nevertheless agreed, with some understanding of the process in which they will be participating. They try to cooperate, and they share their fears and anxieties, their anger and frustration, their demands and wants, their history and hurts, with this person, the assessor, who needs to know in order to make recommendations for their children.

It comes as a confusing change to find themselves now meeting with an assessor who indicates that the parents need help, or that mediated resolution of the dispute is indicated, and that the assessment process will be altered to provide that service. This is so whether that change in direction comes before or after recommendations have been circulated. The change may be complied with on the surface, but underneath the parents may feel angry. If their behaviour is addressed, there may be a sense that they are being targeted as a problem, or even as "the" problem, even before the assessment is completed. The impression may thus be gained that the assessor has taken sides. Parents have little choice but to accommodate to the process or to try the new approach of mediation. Otherwise the assessor (what should she now be known as?) may report negatively about them as parents.

If counselling is suggested by the assessor, the outcome is questionable with a non-trusting parent. If the counselling attempt proves ineffective, the professional may decline to complete the interrupted assessment on the grounds that the (confused) parent is now not prepared to cooperate further. In fact what has happened is that the assessor has lost or vacated the neutral ground she originally occupied, and cannot retrieve it. Confidence has been weakened and little advancement made toward resolving the dispute about the children.[4] Initiating a second assessment following such an experience is difficult for everyone, a difficulty and stress avoidable through a careful husbanding of the role and boundaries of being an assessor. The temptation to become the mediator or the counsellor can be very real when the assessor is faced with a hurting, needful parent. The temptation has to be resisted. Getting caught in the trap will compromise the assessor's objectivity which, like justice, must not only be maintained, but must have been seen to have been maintained.[5]

An additional point is worthy of note. Some parents will be covered by a legal aid certificate to meet their portion of the cost of the assessment. The Ontario Legal Aid Plan's written policy concerning disbursements specifically indicates that "Mediation will not be allowed in addition to an assessment without prior authorization." If mediation is authorized, the time limit allowed is five hours, and any extension of time beyond that must be authorized by the Plan in advance as well. Thus, a change by the assessor from assessment to mediation in a case in which one or both parties is/are receiving legal aid may have specific financial implications for the assessor, and should therefore be approached with care. If the Legal Aid Plan declines to pay the bill, the lawyer for the legally-aided parent is liable for the account.[6] This may result in the lawyer not using that assessor again in future.

(f) Gathering Information

(i) *Getting the Story*

Depending upon how readily the first part of the intake interview has gone, setting the stage, outlining the process, and ensuring the parent's grasp of the steps, it is now time to begin to get the story. Check the clock, to gauge how much time is left. Occasionally a very upset parent has had a compulsive need to tell it all in one sitting, or has been crying heavily and needs recovery time. As a guideline, an hour and one-quarter to an hour and one-half should suffice. There is too much to learn; you

4 It is fair to acknowledge that some efforts to resolve the dispute may find willing respondents. Perhaps that result indicates that a service such as mediation should have been undertaken from the outset and that assessment as such was premature.

5 Once the assessment is completed, the report delivered, and the situation settled by agreement or court order, a parent may seek counselling or advice from the former assessor. So long as such counselling or advice in no way violates the right of the other parent, there is no reason to refuse the service. One area about which to be very careful is the matter of who has custody. Do not see a child without the knowledge and consent of the custodial parent, no matter how pressing a problem appears to be.

6 *The Ontario Legal Aid Plan*, "General Principles in Disbursements", ss. 4060-84 and 4060-83.

cannot do it all in one sitting. If you have indicated when first setting up the appointment that an hour and one-half at the most is what is needed, remind the parent of that, and even if there is only 15 or 20 minutes left, get started on the story. Beginning to really talk about it makes the interview feel more real to the parent, imparting a sense that the assessment has really begun.

(ii) *Taking Notes*

Take notes right from the beginning. Make notes on the whole process, to the extent that you can, especially trying to capture actual words or phrases used by the parent. Quite apart from wanting to be accurate and detailed, so that upon review preparatory to writing the report you are able to really recall the interview and its content, detailed note-taking may stand you in good stead at the post-report stage. An angry or disappointed parent may indicate to his or her lawyer that he or she nevér made such a statement, nor did he or she ever give you such information or impression. In order to cite the basis for the offending sentences in the report, and to support earlier statements that you tried to be fair and accurate, it is of obvious value to be able to indicate that the notes don't substantiate the parent's claim. Occasionally, showing the actual notes to the parent and the lawyer is useful. In the event that the matter proceeds to trial, and you are called upon to testify, notes which you have made at the time of the interviews and kept unaltered will be available to refer to on the witness stand to refresh your memory.

Most parents are quite comfortable with notes being taken during the interviews. They understand their value and will even pause to ensure that you have finished writing something down. Occasionally, however, one meets a parent whose anxiety and level of suspicion makes note-taking something of an issue. In such situations it is necessary to address the worry. Ask if the parent understands why you need to take notes — it is imperative when coming to write the report that each party's information and point of view be recalled accurately. Since more than one assessment is going on at the same time, it is essential that you rely not just on memory, and risk getting details mixed up or lost. Good note taking adds to the materials sent by the lawyer, and since this is such an important matter, enlarging on those materials through the conversations with the parent ensures accuracy in the report.

Such an approach usually calms the parent's anxiety about what is being written down. It is not useful to ask an anxious parent if he or she minds if you take notes while you talk. What do you do next if they say, "yes"? Rather, an approach that speaks to the parent's stake in the outcome usually suffices. If anxiety continues or re-builds as they are becoming upset in talking about the situation, offer to show the parent your notes right then; hand over the pad and let the parent read what you have written there. Even the more seriously suspicious parent will usually settle down after a second offer to read your notes, having seen there what you said was there: a record of what you are learning about the matter and their point of view about it.

Care should be taken to avoid personal or attitudinal comments in the notes, especially negative descriptions of a parent, their mode of dress, or their interview behaviour. Such observations could prove embarrassing later, and are best avoided. This is not the same as noting that the parent was very anxious, seemed angry and resistive at first, or cried off and on throughout the interview.

(iii) *History*

Except for the compulsive-flow-of-speech individuals who cannot stop talking, most parents want guidance as to where to start. There is no one "right" place. They may start anywhere — you will put the pieces together.

Some parents may begin with a linear approach from the beginning: "Well, I was born on the 5th of March, 1957, in Etobicoke, and I was the third of six, ..." and go on from there. Others will start with when they first met their former or separated spouse or partner. Still others will start with a clear statement of the present dispute and what the other side is and has been doing that is so wrong. It doesn't matter, because it will be up to you to put it all together eventually anyway. And where they start may give you some clue about them and their particular personality.

Let the telling go on for a bit, just as they want to present it, interrupting only to clarify. Do not challenge a position taken or an accusation made — simply note it. Once a more secure relationship is established and there has been another opportunity to talk to the parent, and to listen, you may then decide to seek support for an allegation or more information about a position articulated earlier.

Keep an eye on the clock, and on the parent's fatigue level (and your own). You need to allow at least 10 or 15 minutes for obtaining the basic identifying information. Not only do you need to have this, but waiting until the end of the interview to obtain it serves a dual purpose: time has been spent on beginning the working relationship, and has allowed the assessor to focus directly on the parent and how he or she appears to be feeling and handling the matter. As well, waiting until the end to obtain this information allows the parent to participate successfully in a straight forward, brief exercise, giving you the basic identifying data. This provides time for individuals to compose themselves emotionally, and if they have been talking about upsetting and volatile material, to return to the emotional safety of relating objective information. Even though much of the information may be available in affidavits or the lawyer's referral letter, asking for it directly from the parents acknowledges them as individuals. As well, having the details on one page makes them easier to refer to later when preparing the report. Ask for the following: full name; birth date and birth place; their number among how many siblings; if foreign-born, when they came to this country and their present citizenship status and date of change; how far they went in school; what post-secondary education, courses, or training they have had or are taking now; their present address and telephone number; their present employer, if working, and the nature of the work and their title if they have one; the employer's name, address, and telephone number (with an explanation that you would call them at work only if absolutely necessary); the date and place of the marriage or when they and their partner had begun to live together; the dates and places of the children's births; the date being used as the date of separation; the date of the divorce, if there has been one; the full name of a current partner or spouse; the date of beginning to live together or the re-marriage; the names and birth dates of children born to this relationship; the names and ages of any children of their new partner or spouse who are living with them; dates and nature of current custody and access orders if there are any; if religion is an issue in the situation, what denominations are involved; and, if there is a Separation Agreement touching on custody and access, when that agreement was signed. Most people are encyclopedias of the important dates and events in their lives, and upset parents feel pleased at being able to recall them all.

There remains now only the reminder about the collateral list for the next time, and the making of the next appointment. This should also be an office interview, following which you will be arranging to visit them. A comment such as that you were pleased to meet them and get things started usually evokes a positive response to the effect that they were pretty nervous coming in but they feel much better now, and relieved that things are finally underway.

4. THE SECOND INTERVIEW

The second interview with each parent is usually a much calmer and more relaxed affair. There is recognition of each other, driving and parking or using public transportation are easier through a now-familiar area, and the location of the interview (your office or the lawyer's office) also is no longer strange. Although there may still be some crying, it is less intense and of briefer duration. Indeed, in the second interview humour may arise naturally from time to time, further contributing to a noticeable relaxation on the parent's part. Three goals are present:

1. To obtain the collateral names list.
2. To obtain further information about the parent and the situation as he or she sees it.
3. To make tentative plans for the home visit.

Additional time may also be devoted to answering the parent's questions.

(a) The Collateral Names List

It is useful to open the interview by asking if the parent has brought the collateral names list. Focusing on the list provides a comfortable, direct way to get into the interview.

Collateral names lists come in many forms: typed, carefully written or printed on a separate piece of paper; scribbled on the back of a rumpled, former shopping list; contained in a tiny address book; or parents may indicate that they know who they have selected, but they haven't had time to write the names down. In the latter instance, it is useful to hand a note pad and pen to them and ask them to write the list out for you. In any event, go over the list carefully. Be sure that you understand the spelling and pronunciation of the names, their relationship to the parent or the situation, their location, and whether the telephone numbers are long distance numbers. If so, ensure that you have the correct area code.

Enquire if there are any potential problems the parent can foresee concerning contact, such as availability only in the evening, or plans to be away over a certain period. Note the presence or absence of the children's grandparents on the parent's side, and enquire about that. Grandparents are very often significant collaterals, and their (usually) strongly-held opinions about the children's future quite important. If a parent's own parents are alive, live near by, or relatively so, and they are in touch with each other, their absence from the collateral names list is to be noted, and discussed at some point. This omission may reflect uneasiness on the parent's part about what might be said to you, or a deteriorated relationship between the two generations.

If the parent has or shares custody (whether full or interim) of school-aged children, ensure that the list contains information about the school name and location. The names of the principal and of the relevant teachers are necessary, and the grades or subjects they teach. Remind the parent of two aspects mentioned at the first interview: you might not speak to everyone listed; and you will not speak on their behalf to anyone not listed.

(b) The Parent Who Declines to Provide a List of Collateral Names

Occasionally it occurs that a parent brings no list of collateral names.

Experience indicates that such behaviour suggests either a very isolated, alienated, loner, or a parent afraid that the information obtained would be universally critical or at least not supportive. Perhaps this parent is a very untrusting, insecure person, or one defensive about his or her part in the former marital situation. The submission of collateral names is not mandatory; it is entirely voluntary. In the case where no names are presented it is appropriate to acknowledge the parent's right to that choice. However, they may wish to reconsider: perhaps the other parent has already agreed to submit such a list or has even already done so, and the issue of balance and fairness is present. You want to ensure, insofar as one can, that each parent's perceptions and wishes in the matter have — and appear to have — been offered "equal time". If the refusal persists, note it for the file, and proceed. During a subsequent contact with that parent, check again. If the decision remains not to submit a list, note that again in the file.

Such notation is important: a parent who has declined to provide a list of collateral names and who is later upset if the recommendations go against his or her wishes, may suggest to counsel that the report is invalid because it is so unbalanced: there were no interviews with anyone on their account. It is essential to be able to produce your notes at that point, to indicate to enquiring counsel that the request was made to the parent on at least three occasions, on such-and-such dates, and declined each time. The client understood that you were proceeding without such assistance.

(c) Consent to Release of Information

Once the collateral names list is accepted, however, identified as either father's or mother's, and dated, the parent is then asked to sign the Consent to Release of Information Form (Exhibit (5.1)). Possession of the signed Consent may not be of import to friends and relatives of each parent, but it is essential for all professional contacts such as schools and counsellors or therapists. A separate Consent form should be requested of each parent, and should contain the following:

- A clear statement of consent to the release or sharing of information or records with the assessor (by name).
- On behalf of the named children.
- The full name and address of the parent (or guardian).
- That parent's (or guardian's) signature.
- The date.
- The relationship of the signer to the children (*i.e.*, mother, father, *etc.*).

(d) Picking Up the Story

Once the formalities are completed, the interview picks up the story begun in the first contact. Reviewing your notes of that first interview prior to this second contact will facilitate this process. You will refresh your memory about names, dates, and events already mentioned and can guide the parent now in completing more of the picture for you. During this second interview, with the parent more comfortable, important background information can effectively be solicited. The parent understands why you are seeking it, or, if still unsure, you may repeat the explanations and rationales set out at the first contact.

The tendency for most parents in this situation is to generalize at first that they had a good childhood, or a normal childhood, or that it was "all right, I have no complaints". Patient, low-key exploration will help here. Questions that help to clarify may focus as follows. How was discipline handled in their home? Who was the main disciplinarian? Was the discipline the same for all the children? How did they have fun in their family? Did the family members do things together on the whole or more likely individually? Which parent, looking back now, were they closer to? Which siblings were they closer to? How did the parents handle disagreements? What was it like at their house when there were disagreements? What were the good things about growing up in their family? Were there any not-so-good things about growing up in their family?

These items are not to be treated like a check list, of course. They may be introduced from time to time in the conversation to facilitate recall. Judiciously raised, they help the parent to address their experience, and to remember anecdotes and incidents until now forgotten, or not considered for a long time. Such details take them well beyond the generalization that "it was a good childhood, or at least not a bad one."

A logical sequence of that discussion then may be an enquiry about their parents' present point of view about the situation: the separation or divorce, the dispute about the children. Sometimes the current nature of the inter-generational relationship becomes clearer here: there may be strongly expressed reaction to their own parents' attitudes in the matter. Some grandparents are very supportive to their own adult child; some try to effect a reconciliation "for the sake of the children"; some actively support the other parent against their own child; and still others as actively avoid involvement at all. Some grandmothers are prepared to provide babysitting or sick day care, some are not. This information adds to the assessor's understanding of how each parent plans to care for the children, and the support resources available to them to meet the inevitable illnesses and the unexpected accidents.

In the course of this discussion parents may begin to share negative aspects of their childhood and/or their present relationship with one or both of their parents. They may express sadness, anger, or frustration. Some indication of the extent of the poor experience may help you to understand them better now, and to perceive more clearly why their marriage broke down. Ask concretely whether there was domestic violence in their family of origin, as between parent and parent, child and child, or parent(s) and children. (This information is rarely volunteered, but is frequently disclosed if the parent is asked directly.) Returning at this point to the positive experiences in their childhood will help to balance any discomfort or guilt aroused by having criticized their parents, and facilitate regaining any lost composure such recollection may have caused.

A shift now onto the relationship with their former spouse or partner is facilitated by asking simply how they met. This will lead into a discussion of what was good in the beginning and what, from their point of view, began to make it go wrong. At first, perhaps, there comes a description of what the other person did to upset things. Unchallenged acceptance of that may then lead into some acknowledgement of their own part in the situation, even if that is within a context of having been (as they see it) provoked or stressed too much or for too long, or reacting to a situation (the separation) they did not want.

Moving from the history to the present situation focuses on two issues:

1. What they want regarding the children.
2. How they would propose to structure the necessary arrangements.

Clarity is important here: is custody what is really being sought, or in fact is access the real issue? Sometimes what emerges is that a parent has sought custody (following a failed effort at joint custody), "because the other one did and that made me angry". Exploration of this statement may result in clarification that regular, guaranteed, flexible and cooperative access to the children is what that parent is really seeking, with an emphasis on "guaranteed".

If each parent *is* seeking custody, what form should that take? Can the parent see joint custody as a viable option, and why? If not, why not, and what does he or she seek instead? What visitation arrangements between the children and the other parent should be set up? Would the parent anticipate any changes in such an arrangement over time? What is the basis for resisting the other parent's requests now?

The answers to these questions provide more than just structural details. They give insight into attitudes as well. Is the parent resistive or open concerning sharing the children with the other parent? Is there recognition of the children's feelings about the other parent, whether these be loving, angry, hurt, or confused? Can this parent yet separate his or her own feelings about the other parent from the children's feelings and needs? Can they believe and accept that a child may continue to love someone they have ceased to love? And if there is real resistance to sharing the parenting or to frequent, relaxed access, what are the reasons being presented? Careful listening is indicated here: lip service to sharing and cooperation could mislead. If the parent has earlier repeatedly indicated their undiminished anger at the other parent, or even their contempt, how could they expect to handle the frequent interactions, talks, discussions, and decisions implicit in any shared parenting arrangement? Indeed, if they are still this angry, what are the implications for the children? Would this parent allow the children the psychological and emotional space needed to really continue to know and love the other parent? Is this even an appropriate goal for the children in light of past events? If not, how will this parent deal with the children's hurt, or anger, or bewilderment? How have they been handling these things until now? Is the parent clearly opposed to increased or relaxed access of the children to the other parent? For what reasons? Can these reasons be documented or supported?

Exploration such as this is just as important as learning how the parent plans to care for the children while at work, how to get them to and from school or day care, who will manage such errands as shopping, doctors and dentists appointments, and so forth.

Of course, not all parents are still so hurt and angry. Even though a dispute has arisen, and even though they required an assessment, the very process of considering and talking about it all may have led to a much more reasonable and cooperative attitude. In such instances equally thoughtful examination of options will provide direction for resolution. In any event, what is important is that you have understood their position and requests clearly, and that both parents understand that you will be considering these points carefully when approaching your recommendations.

(e) Special Problem Areas That May Require Attention

(i) *Dealing With Allegations Against Each Other*

In some custody/access disputes specific allegations may have been made by one parent against the other of some form of neglect or abuse of a child. Such allegations will have inflamed the situation and led to a state of denial/counter allegations/denial affidavits. The presence of such allegations needs to be directly but calmly faced with each parent. What is the basis of the allegations? What is the basis of the denials? Why, in one parent's opinion, is the other parent behaving as he or she is or appears to be?

Dealing with such allegations is like walking through a mine field on a foggy day. A misplaced-step can create quite a problem. Feelings will be very strong, and escalate quickly. Denials of any impropriety with the children may lead to a counteraccusation that the other parent is lying just to defeat their wish to see or have the children, a position that may be forcefully presented also by the upset parent's lawyer. The recent apparent increase in complaints of impropriety as part of custody/access disputes, has already led to a noticeable cynicism about their validity in some quarters. This has to be a matter of concern: too-ready dismissal of the allegation as only manipulative may obscure situations in which there is indeed reason for concern. Careful willingness to be thorough is indicated, in order to ensure the children's well-being, and to deal correctly with the matters of a parent's reputation and future role in the children's lives.

It is not the function of the assessor to be a protection worker for the state. Investigation, amassing of evidence, and the taking of necessary steps to protect children, within the context of pertinent child welfare legislation, is the responsibility of the mandated protection authorities. However, the assessor cannot side-step the issue: indeed, legislation in all jurisdictions places a particular onus upon a professional to report to a protection agency if that professional has reason to believe that a child is or has been at risk, and may be a child in need of protection.

In such difficult situations it is desirable that the professional retained to undertake the assessment is one familiar with, skilled in, and comfortable with the methods currently used to verify such allegations. Such an assessor will specifically request authorization to consult with any other previously involved professionals, through inclusion of such names on each parent's collateral names list. If a protection investigation has been concluded, or is currently taking place, the results will, of course, be of great import. Discussion with both lawyers may have been held prior to commencing the assessment. If allegations arise after the assessment is begun, then a mid-assessment meeting may be in order.

A professional dilemma has arisen about the timing of a protection investigation while a custody/access assessment is underway. Some protection agencies are reluctant to initiate an investigation if the allegations come within the context of a custody/access dispute, or if an assessment concerning the dispute is already in place. It is not within the purview of this discussion to examine that policy issue. Suffice it to say, again, that the assessor's responsibility is to formulate recommendations on behalf of the children.[7] When a difficult judgment call must be made in a confusing

7 The assessor has a responsibility, of course, under provincial child welfare legislation, to report to an appropriate authority if he or she believes a child has been or is in need of protection and no report has been previously made. Here, we are considering a matter in which that reporting requirement has already been met.

context, it must be acknowledged as such, with clarifying reasons, be professionally supportable, and reflect a focus on the child or children's best interests. Ultimately, of course, the court will determine the weight that will be given to such allegations and to the assessor's discussion of them in the report.

(ii) *Religion and Values Conflicts*

Considerable upset and aroused emotions can also be generated by religion. The conflict usually focusses on the religion of one parent who may have converted to that belief-system sometime after the marriage or cohabitation. Or, religious practice may emerge as an issue at the time of assessment. Significant difference in viewpoint, value systems, and child-rearing practices may have surfaced, leading to allegations and counter-allegations between angry parents. In such cases, tact and respect are called for, and a continuous focus on the needs of the children and the parenting capacity of each parent. The risk of later suggestions of bias or prejudice is always in front of the assessor, and arises not only in the conduct of the assessment itself, but as well in the framing of the report.

(f) Discussion of the Child(ren)

In assessments where allegations of abuse or conflicts about religion are absent, the second interview discussion may now have turned to a consideration of the children themselves.

As was the case in learning about the parents' childhoods, there are specific pieces of information about the children that will be useful to solicit. Again, these are not offered as a checklist, but as a guide. Were there any special circumstances (positive or negative) surrounding conception? Was the pregnancy welcomed or not? What was the pregnancy like? What was the impact on the marriage or relationship? Was the baby full term — how was the delivery? What kind of baby was he or she — passive, compliant, good natured, or fussy, a crier, with lots of food intolerances? What was it like having the baby at home? Who helped with the baby's care? Who provided most of the care? Was the child well or were there medical problems? What did the arrival of a child or children mean to the parents' relationship with each other? How did they rate their former spouse as a parent? What do they see as the strengths and the weaknesses of the children's relationship with the other parent? What do they believe the children might be wanting with respect to custody and access? Why?

Other important information, some of which will be obtained later, addresses the children's adjustment in school or daycare, their behavioral response to the separation and/or divorce, or other significant events in the family, and their special needs or problems, if any.

During this part of the assessment, the meaning of the children to each parent may emerge more clearly. Eventually, one needs to understand this. Of course children may fill important needs in their parents' lives, and do so in a way that encourages the parents to continue and deepen their commitment to caring for and raising the children, sometimes in the face of considerable difficulty. The rewards of being loved and being needed are significant and self-enhancing. But the blood-tie cannot be relied upon as an unfailing gauge of parental competence or emotional maturity.

From time to time, one meets a parent whose own emotional and dependency needs have taken precedence in the relationship with the child. In those situations, one often sees "role reversal": the child, in effect, takes care of the parent, instead of the other way around, and receives love and attention back in proportion to the acceptance of and performance of that role. In separation and divorce, such an emotionally needy parent may work hard on the child's sense of loyalty by repeated comments about how lonely it is when the child isn't there, or "isn't it too bad that the other parent won't let them visit more often, when he or she *knows* that the visits are really the only happy times in the week or month." Such parents may discourage the children from making new friends to play with in the neighbourhood: "But this is *our* time, don't you want to be with me, just us together?" Children may quickly learn not to report what a good time they had on the access visit because of the (sometimes quite emotional) reaction of the custodial parent, alleging that the enthusiasm means that they didn't miss him or her, that maybe they love the other parent more, and so forth.

The parent's description of interacting with the child, of handling coming and leaving from (or going and returning from) access visits may give important clues. Such emotional manipulation is not healthy for a child, and may impede later normal, healthy, social and inter-personal development.

On the other hand, the parent's discussion of the child may reflect a real recognition of the child as a separate person, an awareness of personality, and comfort with the requirements of parenting. Discipline is handled frankly and is related to the precipitating behaviour. The parent-child relationship is not at risk, even when the parent is annoyed or angry with the behaviour, and the child is encouraged to undertake new experiences and to make new friends. Access is seen as important, and there is no emotional blackmail associated with it.

(g) A New Relationship

In the course of the interview information about a new relationship may emerge, whether a second spouse, a live-in partner, or a new "other" who may develop into a significant person in the parent's life. Discussion will reveal the meaning of that new relationship, and that parent's perceptions of how it differs or compares to the former one with the other parent. Are there concerns about the new person's interaction with the children, and if so, in what areas? How is the situation being handled? If the interaction seems very positive, what is the parent's feeling about that? Is there any suggestion of competition or jealousy, if the children have really taken to this new person? How have the children reacted to the arrival of this person on the scene? What have they said about it, and how have they behaved? Has there been any change in the children's behaviours or attitude toward this person lately? Will this person be prepared to meet with you in the course of the assessment?

There may be another side to the coin: the *other* parent has made a new relationship. This can create real problems, when the first parent is threatened and defensive. Angry exchanges and/or problems with access arrangements may follow, especially if the child or children indicate happily that they really like so-and-so, or begin to call that person "Mommy" or "Daddy". Discussion will indicate how the parent is handling things, and whether or not feelings are so high that they dominate the parent's response. In such situations the children may be getting a very clear, very direct message that interacting with the new person, much less really liking them, spells trouble. What is the basis of the parent's resistance? Is it related to actual information or just strong feelings? Is a clash in value systems at the root of at least part of the upset? Is sharing the child or children with anyone else an apparent part of the situation? If so, what implications may there be for this parent's future capacity to allow the children to grow and to foster new loving or modeling relationships with other adults such as teachers, camp counsellors, coaches, or older relatives who take an interest? How does the parent anticipate dealing with this scenario in future, if it hasn't happened yet?

(h) Further Interviews

The amount of material to be covered in an assessment is considerable. Depending upon the complexity of the situation and the emotional status of one or both of the parents, two interviews of some hour and one-quarter, to an hour and three-quarters may suffice. But a third interview or even more may be necessary for complicated cases. An emotionally distressed parent may not be able to focus or concentrate well enough in an interview to facilitate early completion of that first phase. Some parents will try to keep the contact going because they want to try to influence the other party to reconcile. Some will be so fragile emotionally that they can only move a bit at a time. Some may be avoiding discussing important aspects of the assessment (*e.g.*, their recent employment history, and/or an emotional breakdown) by the device of bringing up problems with the child, the other parent, the school, the former in-laws, "which you must understand", and in relation to which they "wish your professional opinion and advice".

It is wiser to see these parents for more than two interviews, rather than attempt to cram everything in. A third interview and occasionally more, is indicated. Two valuable results ensue.

1. That parent at least will be able to see your effort to be thorough and fair, an important aspect in itself but of real value later if the recommendations favour the other side.
2. The more extensive interviewing will allow for a more definitive judgment on your part about that parent's emotional status and their potential capacity to parent.

(i) Closing This Phase

When the assessor reaches the point of believing that the parent's portion of the assessment information is understood, it is time to discuss a home visit. An appointment may be made then or a plan agreed upon for a visit further along. It is useful to obtain the driving directions at this point. Some time will also be spent outlining your approach in a home visit, and soliciting the parent's support and participation in preparing the children for your arrival. Questions can be answered at this time, but indicate as well that you will be talking with them again closer to the date of the visit, and will review this again then. Phase One of the assessment is now complete. Phase Two, reaching out to schools, the children, and the collaterals will now commence.

5. SCHOOL VISITS

School-aged children spend a significant amount of their waking time at school. Teachers and principals get to know their pupils well, at the same time forming clear impressions about their families through repeated contacts. Their information, opinions, and impressions are invaluable to the assessor, especially as a way of becoming acquainted with the child(ren) concerned, and of gaining further data about parental child-care patterns.

School principals and boards of education are anxious to avoid or at least reduce the possibility of unpleasant incidents at their school involving separated parents. This is quite understandable. Certain protocols are therefore in place, and ready cooperation with them will facilitate and ensure full access to the teachers and to the information you want.

The principal will have been contacted about the assessment by the parent of custody. Some principals may request the parent to sign a consent form prepared by their own Board of Education, over and above that signed for the assessor. No sharing of information about a pupil will be authorized by a principal unless proof of signed consent is made available.

Plan to visit the school yourself. While copies of report cards are useful, of course, and can be used if a visit proves impossible, a personal meeting with principal and teacher is much richer. As well as providing you with much more information, a successful school visit contributes to later good public relations. Some principals have to cope with what seems like a continuous flood of other professionals moving in and out of their buildings. Not all of these encounters may have been pleasant or constructive, and there may be some initial resistance to your coming. The successfully conducted visit, therefore, may help to mend some professional fences, and pave the way for subsequent, equally successful visits on other matters.

(a) Guidelines for the Structure of School Visits

- Phone the principal to request an appointment to meet the teacher. If the principal is unavailable, you might speak with the vice-principal, if that school has one. Some vice-principals feel comfortable about arranging appointments, others do not, and will refer you back to the principal.
- When speaking with the principal, as you introduce yourself and explain your reason for calling, add that you have a signed consent form from the parent(s), which you will bring to the appointment, so that he or she may photocopy it for the files. It is tactful, too, to indicate that you will be pleased to accommodate to the demands of their schedule. You may be asked to explain your role as an assessor. Most principals are aware to some degree of the stress at the child's home, but occasionally one has not been informed even of the separation, and has been taken by surprise by the parent's call.
- Agree with the principal as to how much time will be available to you on the day suggested; a thorough interview can take up to an hour, but a shorter time can also be very productive.
- If more than one teacher will be involved, a group meeting after school hours may be best.
- Confirm the date and time of the appointment and the names(s) of the teacher(s) with whom you will be meeting, and obtain instructions for finding the school.
- Always report to the principal's office first. Some principals will have

made time to talk to you, and want to do so, either alone or with the teacher(s) present. All principals want to know who is in their school. Some principals will want to see some identification: cooperate graciously. Present your professional card early, it helps to validate you. Offer the signed consent form right away also, before any formal conversation has started, so that a copy may be made. Make sure the original is returned to you, as you may need it again.

- At the beginning of the formal meeting, explain again why you are there, and the nature of your responsibility as the assessor. Answer questions of the principal or teacher(s) to the extent possible without breaching confidentiality; indicate what kind of help you are seeking. Take notes.

(b) Information to Obtain from the Teachers

The report from the teachers will touch upon the child's academic performance; the child's social performance; the child's behavioural performance; and the child/parent performance.

(i) *The Child's Academic Performance*

Is the child's academic performance up to, below, or in advance of grade level? What is the overall level or area(s) of special achievement or deficit? Have there been any changes in performance level, and, if so, when these occurred? (You, as assessor, may associate the change to a particular event in the family situation to which the child may have been reacting.) What are the expectations of promotion? What is the child's classroom attitude? Are there any special resource teachers or other personnel who have worked with the child? Are reports available of reading or speech or intelligence assessments undertaken by the school which could be shared with you?

(ii) *The Child's Social Performance*

Does the child have friends among the other children, a special friend or two or not? Find out about the child's capacity and readiness to share, take turns, cooperate. Does the child engage in fighting either in the classroom or on the playground? Is he or she a target for other children?

(iii) *The Child's Behavioural Performance*

Are there discipline problems in the classroom or on the playground? Does the child challenge authority or cooperate with it? Does the child cry easily? Is there good will toward other children or a hostile, bullying, or provocative attitude? Does the child talk of away-from-school behaviour that is potentially or actually delinquent? Is the child so quiet and/or withdrawn as to be almost invisible? Does the child talk about the family situation, about access visits, about either parent (or other caretakers, such as grandparents)? Does the child's usual behaviour change in the classroom or on the playground just before or after an access visit weekend? Is the child more aware of some adult behaviour than is appropriate to the child's age? Does the child seem reluctant to leave school each day?

(iv) *The Child/Parent Performance*

Is the child's custodial parent cooperative with the school? Does the other parent indicate an interest? Has the non-custodial parent requested reports and other information from the school, and has that information been forwarded?[8] Does the child appear to be well-rested, well-nourished, well-clothed for the climate? Does the parent come to the school for meetings with the teachers upon request? Is the child pleased to see that parent when he or she does come to the school? Is there positive or negative parental response to matters of poor school performance or the unacceptable behaviour of the child? Is the custodial parent's current, common-law partner or new spouse involved with parent-teacher meetings?

(c) The Child's Relationship to the School

For many children caught in the middle of a custody/access dispute the school is an emotional oasis, a haven, where they are accepted as they are, and where there are no loyalty struggles for them to navigate. Sometimes the child will turn to a teacher for reassurance and security, even to the extent, among young children, of becoming over-clinging and over-demanding. Such children may or may not verbalize to the teacher about the parental dispute situation, and the behaviour may not be initially understood as an expression of that situation. Your visit may thus be useful to the teacher to enhance his or her understanding of the child.

Some children use the school as an oasis so completely that they keep their mask on all the time that they are there. These children are usually quiet, even shy. They make no mention ever of the family situation, nor do they speak about what they do with either parent. They are socially

---

8 If the school has been unaware of the separation they may be unaware that the custodial parent has refused, for example, to forward such information to the other parent, whose no-show at the school events has thereby been interpreted by the teacher and principal as lack of interest.

somewhat withdrawn, but present no behavioural difficulties at all. A teacher may not even be aware that the child is under stress.

Other children, caught in the custody/access struggle and angered by it, act out at school. Discussion with the teachers and/or principal will indicate not only how the child is behaving, but how the teacher and principal respond. This in turn reflects the general atmosphere of the school and the particular environment which the child experiences each school day.

(d) Conclusion

Whatever the situation, and the child's school adjustment within it, a personal visit to the school provides vastly more information than can be elicited from a report card. The child's behaviour and academic/social performance may resemble that described to you by the parents or seen at home, or be in surprising contrast. Either way, you have learned more about the child and how he/she is coping. At the same time, you have had the benefit of others' opinions and experiences with the parent(s) as caretaker(s), in a context you could not have seen yourself. Placed against your own impressions, the picture begins to take on more colour and depth. If the child is troubled, the impression you gain about the school's response to him/her, and the resources they have brought, or could bring to bear to assist the child, may emerge later as a real factor in arriving at recommendations, especially if each parent seems about equal in what they will offer the child. Continued attendance at that school may be the factor that tips the scales in the direction of one parent in spite of some reservations, because the school is meeting the child's special needs.

If circumstances make a personal school visit impossible, a phone discussion with the teacher, arranged in advance through the principal, is an acceptable compromise.

It is possible that the family has moved after the separation or divorce, and the child is registered in a new school and not yet well known there. In that case, it is worthwhile to contact the child's former school, and conduct the same interview outlined above. Previous-year teachers may be helpful, also, if the school visit occurs in the first two months or so of the academic year.

If the child is younger and attends a daycare or nursery school, the same guidelines apply. Contact the Supervisor, make an appointment, and take good notes.

Sometimes during a school visit the teacher or principal asks if you wish to speak to the child. A general rule is to decline such an offer, to avoid the possibility of embarrassing the child.

6. HOME VISITS

(a) Making Home Visits

The impressions gained so far by the assessor about each parent, and the opinions beginning to form about the situation and its possible outcome, have been shaped largely so far through interviews with the parents. Those interviews have been mostly office-based. Each parent has usually come "dressed for the occasion" to some degree. Each parent has wanted to make a good impression, and initially at least, has tried to "fit in" to the atmosphere of the office setting. Behaviour, even when very upset, has been an expression of the commonly-held conventions associated with being in a professional office setting. But, even if the interviews have been very productive, they have not provided the full picture. To gain the missing dimension the assessor needs to see each parent in his or her own home, with the child(ren) if possible.[9]

Not all professionals who perform custody/access assessments agree that home visits are necessary. Some believe that the observations they can make in their office of each parent, and of the parent-child interactions, assisted perhaps by the use of various standardized and recognized tests, are enough to give them the information and impressions needed to arrive at reliable recommendations for the children. Such professionals routinely do not make home visits. If for no other reason, however, thoroughness suggests that home visits *are* indicated.

Each parent's home is his or her turf, even if it is considered temporary. Just as your office reflects you, parents' homes reflects them. They convey messages (that have little to do with affluence or lack of it), of priorities, attitudes, values and interests, which cannot be as effectively conveyed in office conversation. If the matrimonial home is still being lived in by one or both parents pending the outcome of the assessment, useful insights can be gained of the couple's lifestyle during their time together. References made by the parents during earlier interviews now take on a clearer meaning, as you can actually see what they were talking about — the

9 In some Assessments, observation of the relationship of the child(ren) with one parent may prove impossible to arrange or must be conducted under very controlled conditions. Such circumstances may exist when a Court Order is in existence forbidding any access between that parent and one or all of the children (because of established physical or sexual abuse, or an earlier civil kidnapping for example), or, ordering only supervised access between that parent and one or all of the children, to be conducted outside of that parent's home (for the same or similar reasons). The dilemma of distance may also make it impractical to seek to arrange a visit, particularly if there has been a long period of no contact between the parents or between the absent parent and the child(ren). In such situations the Assessment proceeds without this aspect, and the omission is noted and explained in the Report.

paneling in the basement he put in himself to make a rainy-day play area for the children; the hole in the bedroom wall where a fist went through; the proximity to a busy highway; the special attention obviously paid to the children's rooms, with wallpaper, curtains and bedspreads all matching, and a shelf for special treasures; the limited space of a one-bedroom apartment, with almost no place to keep toys, and a constant clutter that grates on the nerves; a small house or apartment that is clearly arranged with children in mind; the even larger house or apartment that is clearly arranged with adults in mind.

The parent's home is their turf and you are the guest, there on consent. The welcome will vary in enthusiasm, from pleasure that you are there to a barely concealed irritated tolerance of your presence. In some situations you may be invited for a meal or offered coffee or a cool drink; in others, the television set will continue to blare throughout and no offer of refreshment will be forthcoming. In some cases, friends or relatives will be there when you arrive, will not leave, nor be asked to. But in most instances the parent, the "significant other" (spouse or common-law partner), and the child(ren) will be the only ones at home. The children may or may not have been well prepared for your arrival. Each situation must be handled at the time, and each requires a judgment call: do you suggest that the television be turned down (hoping it will be turned off), or do you suggest sitting in the kitchen instead, if that is possible? You have to try to "read" the atmosphere, and go along with it as best you can. Sometimes it seems there is a kind of "test", to gauge your attitudes, and if you "pass", the television set is turned off voluntarily, with no suggestion from you. In such instances, an offer of coffee or tea usually follows. This would suggest that the parent may have been feeling defensive initially, and worried that you would convey a disapproving, or what is perhaps even worse, a patronizing attitude about what they have and how they live. Reassured by your pleasant adaptation to what is, their defensiveness subsides and their more cooperative self takes over.

It goes without saying that a home visit is arranged in advance, at times when the parent can be available and least likely to be disturbed by other obligations. For working parents, this may mean an early evening or after-supper, and before-bedtime, arrangement; for non-working parents, it may mean arranging times when the child(ren) are home from school or the baby is likely to be awake. Either situation may make an afternoon on the weekend more suitable and productive. The accommodation to the parent's convenience is an investment: a parent who feels free to participate in the visit is likely to be more relaxed, and to have conveyed to the child(ren) the idea that your visit is a helpful step in the situation.

(b) Guidelines for Home Visits

Although these may be considered basic and obvious, the following points outlined in (i) to (ix) provide some guidelines for a useful home visit.

(i) *Punctuality*

Be on time or as close to on-time as possible. If an unforeseen development significantly delays you, phone to inform the parent. If necessary, cancel and make an appointment for another day. The parent may have had to make changes in other arrangements in order to accommodate your visit; an untoward delay may really complicate things. The courtesy of a phone call at the first opportunity will help the parent to decide with you what to do. In most cases the response will be to urge you to keep coming.

(ii) *Where to Sit*

After the initial greetings and chit-chat about such items as the weather, the driving conditions, and so forth, wait for the parent to indicate which room they would suggest that you sit in, and go there. Some parents will ask you which room you prefer; it is useful to indicate that any place where they will be comfortable is fine for you. Occasionally, a parent will "just stand there". You can help to relieve the tension and paralysis by simply asking "where would you like me to sit?"

(iii) *Greeting the Children*

Greet the children by name, be friendly and pleasant, but make no specific effort to engage them in significant conversation at this stage. Respond, of course, if a youngster is wanting to tell you or show you something.

(iv) *Non-Assertive Approach*

When you know which room you will be in, sit and stay put. A low-key, pleasant, physically non-assertive approach will help an anxious parent feel less threatened, less intruded upon, and less "inspected".

(v) *Touring the Home*

Wait to be asked if you would like to see the rest of the house, or the child(ren)'s bedroom, *etc.* Somewhere in the course of the visit this will usually arise naturally. Sometimes a parent will suggest that the child(ren) show you their bedrooms or trophies or whatever; sometimes the parent will ask you directly if you would like to see around the house or the apartment. If the offer is not forthcoming, however, it is usually better not to make a specific request. Nor is it a useful device to announce that that will now be done. (In one instance, the assessor not only announced that it was now time to see the bedrooms, but crisply told the parent not to come along. Needless to say, such behaviour was viewed as very high-handed and intrusive, and alienated the parent significantly from the assessor.)

In most situations, if you wait patiently the conversation will come around to the parent's wishes or plans or ideas about the house or the apartment, if the outcome of the present dispute goes his or her way. Mention may then be made of the work already put into the place; or to the recognized inadequacy of the space if the children come, or as they grow and need separate rooms; or to the ideas that have already been considered for adding on one or two more rooms. Such comments pave the way for a response from the assessor, showing interest in what has been accomplished or what might yet be done. In many cases the parent, seeing the interest, will ask if you would like to see around.

But if no such offer is made, it is, in the long run, better to get along without the tour than to ask for it or to impose it. While the physical environment in which the children live when with this parent is, of course, of interest, of far greater value are the impressions and information gained about lifestyle, priorities, and relationships. Watching the interactions between children and the adult(s), between the adults themselves, and between and among the children, will help the assessor reinforce or alter earlier impressions or opinions. Lifestyle interests are often reflected in the decorative touches on the walls or shelves: reference to them or queries about an item may lead to discussion about hobbies or experiences that further acquaint you with the parent as a person. Reactions of new partners to the discussion may clarify their relationship to the parent, and their shared value system. This, in turn, adds to the enlarged picture of the context in which the children have been living or to which they would be exposed in future.

(vi) *Taking Notes*

Decide whether or not notes are to be taken during the visit. Some assessors are comfortable doing so and have no difficulty. In some situations, notes at the time will be in order. The parents may have specific information to impart which requires accurate recording on the spot, such as names, addresses, phone numbers, dates of events, or descriptions of incidents whose chronology the parent wants to convey in some detail. It is obviously responsible to record such data accurately at the time of telling, otherwise note-taking is more usefully left until after the home visit is completed. Even though parents observed the note-taking during the interviews, the context of being in their home changes its implications somehow. Having what they say or do in their own home written down while they are saying or doing it, is hardly conducive to spontaneity. Better, indeed, to sit quietly and participate/observe the visit in a friendly, relaxed manner, and to make notes afterwards, at the first available moment, while your impressions and recollections are fresh.

(vii) *Interviewing the New Partner*

If a new spouse or common-law partner has not already been interviewed, plan to do so as an adjunct to the home visit. As indicated earlier, most such persons are more than willing to be interviewed, some even eager to "have their say". In the context of visiting their home (or about-to-be-home), on familiar ground and with the cooperation of the parent, their comments and opinions can be easily elicited. A direct matter-of-fact request results in the privacy necessary for the (possible) sharing of concerns or reservations attached to the prospect of assuming or continuing a significant role in the situation. Having had the benefit of observing some interaction between the partner and the parent during the earlier part of the visit, (including non-verbal interaction such as eye contact or avoidance of eye contact, passivity or assertiveness with each other, warmth or apparent coolness with the child[ren] [his/hers/theirs]), their remarks and the feelings they express take on even more import.

Second partners, however loyal, have taken on history as well as a relationship. By the time they talk with the assessor, they have had some considerable experience with that history. Perhaps they had not expected the struggle over the child(ren) to develop or to have continued for so long, or to have taken such a prominent place in their lives. Perhaps they were unprepared for the darkening the shadow of the former relationship has cast on their current one. Perhaps they are worried about that, or their own future, or are just angry at what to them is an unjustified provocation by the former spouse, costing time and money and upsetting everyone. Whatever their viewpoint, as interested stakeholders, not quite in and not quite outside the quarrel, such persons bring most important insights to the assessment. It becomes a matter of real concern, then, if a second spouse or new partner declines to be interviewed or even present during the home visit.

(viii) *Confidentiality*

During the second home visit to the other parent, avoid discussion of topics mentioned or observations made during the first home visit. This can be done tactfully and avoids the possibility of unwittingly conveying information the first parent might prefer not to share with the former spouse, and maintains the appearance of discreet neutrality. Each home visit should stand on its own merits as a separate part of the assessment. In most cases the common bond is the presence of the children on each occasion.

(ix) *When Parents Are Still Under the Same Roof*

If both parents are still residing in the matrimonial home during the assessment (neither parent will leave until the custody matter is settled), individual visits with each parent with the child(ren) are still in order. Asking each parent to absent themselves for a period of time so an uninterrupted visit with the other parent and the child(ren) may be held is the simplest approach. The tension in such situations is usually quite high, but each visit is conducted as though the parents were living separate and apart. Care must be taken during the visits not to get caught in the parents' quarrel because of the speed of conveying messages one to the other following each visit; any suggestion of support for one side's position may (and probably will) be communicated at the earliest opportunity to the other, worsening the situation. While this caution applies generally of course, it is of particular concern in situations where neither parent has yet agreed to leave the marital home.

7. MAKING CONTACT WITH THE CHILDREN

Every assessment dealing with matters of custody and access is an assessment about one or more children. The decisions made at the conclusion of the dispute (court order or agreement by the parties), will stream each child's life in a certain direction; will shape each child's relationships, perceptions, and opportunities. A process of that importance must therefore ensure contact with each affected child, which includes meeting them, speaking with them, and observing them in their interactions with each of their parents, to the extent that that is possible (either in each parent's home or within the necessary restrictions as to arrangements referred to earlier). The dispute is, after all, about them: they are entitled to participate in the assessment to the extent that they can and in a way that is appropriate to their age and their status as children. Their opinions, wishes and wants, if they can be expressed, form an important part of the critical data being amassed by the assessor. How that information is sought, and the manner of the discussions with the child(ren) is a matter of particular concern. The skill involved should be rooted in a philosophy of respect and an understanding of the structure of adult/child relationships. Children whose parents (or caretakers) are quarreling over them are already undergoing considerable stress: the assessment process should not make it worse.

Fundamental aspects of contact with a child as part of an assessment are: the philosophical context; the matter of timing; and the technique(s) to be used.

(a) The Philosophical Context

Children are people. They have feelings, fears, and needs, and our approaches to them in the course of an assessment must reflect respect for all of that. While the contact may precipitate crying or upset or show of anger, those emotions should reflect their feelings about the parental situation, and *not* a response to an insensitive or ill-timed approach by an assessor. Careful thought ahead of time will facilitate a productive contact and ensure a critical goal: the assessor's contact must not be harmful. The guidelines outlined below will assist.

- Children involved in custody/access disputes must always be seen in the course of an assessment, and interviewed if possible.
- The reality of the family situation (parents are not going to remain together, or get back together), and of the dispute (they can't agree on where you are going to live or how you will be seeing them, for example) needs to be directly, truthfully, and supportively acknowledged.
- The responsibility and role of the assessor must be presented within a context of the limitations on those activities (I can't make your parents get together again, *etc.*).
- The decisions to be made in the situation are the responsibility of the adults to make, whether parents or a judge, and are *not* ever the responsibility of a child to make; those decisions may or may not concur with a child's stated preferences or wishes.
- One may assume that (regardless of any claims to the contrary) the child has been already subjected to a tug-of-love between the parents, and is potentially or actually caught in a loyalty/love/anger conflict that feels frightening and sometimes overwhelming, but also makes the child sad.
- Because of that, the child is wary of talking to the assessor, and anxious about how anything he/she might say will be used (the child, after all, is the one who would experience the repercussions if a parent is angered or upset by quoted statements of the child).

- At the same time, the child is anxious about who will continue or begin to take care of him or her, and hopes the assessor/adult will understand this.
- One *NEVER* asks a child directly which parent he or she wishes to live with. The question is unfair, and is a "Catch-22" for the child: if he or she answers, there is disloyalty felt to the other parent; if he or she does not answer, there is disloyalty felt to the parent of preference, if there is one, and so they lose either way. There are other, safer, ego-protecting ways to solicit information about wishes or preferences, and the reasons for them, without placing a child in such an invidious position. Such a question suggests to the child that he or she has the power, and perhaps the responsibility as well, to determine the outcome of the parental dispute. If the final resolution does not concur with their stated wish, the child may feel betrayed by the assessor or other adults. If the outcome concurs with his or her choice, the child may feel that he or she "called the shots". This is not constructive empowerment: it subtly robs the child of the needed (now more than ever) awareness that he or she will continue to be taken care of by one or more adults who are strong enough to make the decisions that are needed, as they are needed. Behaviour by an assessor which appears to transfer decision-making capacity from an adult to a child, (however unintentionally), in fact takes away a portion of that needed dependency. This is not the same as demonstrating respect for a child's wishes and opinions. The difference is important, and can be both demonstrated and discussed.

(b) The Matter of Timing

It is just because children are situated in the middle of the parents' dispute that the timing of the assessor's approach to them is so critical. Successful contact with the children is to a large extent a function of their parents' preparation and permission, both verbal and psychological. To the extent that it is possible, you want each parent to refrain from "coaching" the child or from conveying to the child what message they want him or her to project to you. It is probably too much to humanly expect of either parent that they not try to influence in some way the impressions they hope you will gain from talking to their child, but in most cases you can reduce the behaviour significantly through the vehicle of the relationship the parent has established with you. If you see the children too early in the assessment process, before that relationship has begun to build, and some trust in the assessor's capability and (anticipated) fairness has developed, those critical messages to the children (that it is okay to meet with you, and to talk with you in private if they want to, *etc.*) will either not be delivered at all or may be so weakly communicated as to ensure that the child does not really believe them.

It is essential, then, to have moved well into the process before arranging to see the children. You need the parent's help each time: in fact, you are dependent upon their cooperation and good will in preparing the child(ren) for your visit and for creating a climate that facilitates rather than hinders your efforts to really connect. A parent who has connected with you, has built some confidence in you, and has had time to consider your approach, is going to feel safer about arranging for you to talk to their child (an interaction fraught with some potential risk for the parent, in terms of what the child might say). A good contact with the child, then, begins with a good contact with the parent about the process.

(i) *Preparation*

As shown in the earlier discussion of the assessment process, in the very first parental interview you will have touched upon your philosophy and procedures about seeing the child(ren). Reassurance that you do not believe in asking children to choose which parent to live with, and that you will not be asking that question, allays common fears. Somewhere in the course of the second or subsequent interviews the ways in which the parent can facilitate the contact with the child(ren) can be outlined. These can be reviewed later when discussing plans and arranging for the home visit. Whenever you do it, however, explain the following:

- Contact with the child(ren) will be in the context of the home visit.
- The child(ren) need to know that you are coming, who you are, and why you are visiting. Some parents are very fearful of such visits, and want either not to prepare the children at all (leaving the assessor to handle the ensuing situation), or to tell them that you are a friend or relative who hasn't been around for a long time (like never before), who is just "dropping by" for a visit, and wants to meet them.

  Do not allow yourself to be caught in such a charade. Firmly, but nicely, explain that you prefer always to tell children the truth. You will be reviewing who you are and why you are there with the child(ren) when you speak with them. As an introduction, before you even arrive, however, the parent might consider acknowledging the dispute (children always know), and that they have been talking to someone who tries to help when parents cannot arrive at an agreement in these matters by themselves. Because they have been telling this person about them (the children, that is), she is coming to meet them and to visit a bit on such-and-such a date. The parent is pleased about the visit, is looking forward to it. If the child(ren) want to talk with this person, that's fine, and they will not have to tell the parent what they talked about afterwards, if they don't want to.

(ii) *Making the Decision to Speak*

The decision about talking to the children privately, when to do it and where, has to be made on the spot. Some children respond readily to the assessor's presence, and move quickly toward talking privately with her. Others need more time, and may use the first home visit to get acquainted from a safe distance, and will not be ready for a private talk until well into the second visit. Still other children, although old enough to participate in a conversation, are unable to do so, for whatever reason. This latter group is rare but does occur; the unwillingness or inability to risk a private talk has to be respected.

(iii) *When to Tell the Children*

The child(ren) should be told about the upcoming visit close to the date when it will take place. Telling the child(ren) too soon, well before the scheduled date, may create more tension as anxiety builds as they worry about what they may face in questions from this unknown person, and note that parent's anxiety about the visit.

Timing is also a matter of when to make a move to engage a child in a focussed conversation about the parental dispute situation. Although there are no absolute, fail-safe rules about this, a useful guideline is "later rather than sooner". Take your time. Although from time to time one meets a child who is "chomping at the bit", so to speak, and is ready to talk with you at the very first meeting (such a child suggests possible over-preparation by the parent and/or high anxiety in the child or parent), the more usual pattern is that children want some time to look you over and to decide on an opinion about you. Children do not like being rushed; they do very much better if allowed to approach a new adult at their own pace and in their own way. Being guided by the child's timing rather than the adult's pays dividends later, in terms of the child's sense of safety and willingness to talk.

Remember, too, that many children will have been warned repeatedly not to talk to or to accompany adult strangers. Although these warnings will have been enunciated in a totally different context, some carry-over may occur for young children. Sensitivity to this possibility suggests that you sit quietly, watching and waiting, allowing the fact that the parent knows you and approves of your visit, to register. Once children are reassured and comfortable, approach and contact with you becomes possible. Whether the contact and interview occur on the first or second or a subsequent visit is not important: what matters is that the timing of the contact is responsive to the child's readiness and emotional safety, so that the information and impressions gained may be considered useful, and no emotional harm has been done to the child.

(c) Techniques to be Used

Adults rely on a variety of approaches when talking to or with children. These approaches vary with the circumstances, the nature of the relationship, the purpose of the intended conversation, the time available for it, and whether the child's participation is voluntary or otherwise. Every adult who has tried to engage an unwilling child in a conversation knows that "willing is better".

In an assessment, facilitating a useful interview with the child(ren) requires particular attention to technique. Time is limited, the focus is specific rather than general (the difference between an interview and a social conversation), and the subject matter sensitive and upsetting. The assessor must try to establish some trust, show understanding, and facilitate sharing without making promises (which cannot be guaranteed) or manipulating the child into making unwanted revelations. To the degree that it can, the interview should enhance the child's capacity for trust, rather than erode it.

Every assessor longs for a productive interview with the child(ren). The older the child, the more specific the statements, the easier the task may be for an assessor not yet sure about recommendations. But childhood confidences must be earned. No matter the child's age or the parental circumstances and behaviour: no child discusses such matters on demand. Trust must be earned. While some assessors may rely more than others on a variety of tests, specially designed for children, in order to gain insight into their personalities, attitudes, wishes, and preferences, all assessors share the challenge of establishing contact with children and making responsible attempts to elicit information. Some guidelines for undertaking that task follow.

(i) *Location*

While some assessors interview children in their offices, and certainly useful conversations may be conducted there with quite young children as well as with older ones, it is preferable to meet and talk with them while seeing their parents at home. It is, as has been stated earlier, the parent's turf. It may also be the child's home turf, but if it is the home of the non-custodial parent, it is still familiar ground, still "theirs" when they are there. Each home setting is associated with the parent, and as such is (in most cases) perceived as safe. When in the professional's office the setting is not the child's, who may not know where the bathroom is, or how to leave if the interview gets sticky.

In their own homes, children know all these things, as well as where their bedrooms are, where important reassuring possessions are, how to "escape" if they need to, where to stand to look the assessor over for a while in the beginning, and how to get something to eat or drink. Such familiarity allows for more usual behaviour, child/parent, child/child, child/step-parent. Since the assessor is the guest, the demonstrated acceptance by the parent makes it easier for children to accept the stranger's presence, and to begin to share important artifacts such as scrapbooks, paintings, school work books, photographs, special toys, trophies, or things they have made themselves. Such sharing allows for physical closeness which is reassuring to an anxious child, and welcomed by a sad one.

(ii) *First Meeting*

The tone of the first meeting helps to establish the child(ren)'s safety with you. Greeting them pleasantly but not pursuing them, quite literally "sitting put", gives them both space and time before having to interact with you. You are a stranger to them; whatever the parent has said to them about you or however you have been described, each child needs to relate that description to what can now be seen. That is a process, and it takes its own time. Be patient, chat with the parent and/or significant other, admire items pointed out by the parent, talk about the cat, listen to whatever it is that the parent wants you to know about recent events. Smile at and acknowledge the child(ren) as they pass by or through the room, but do not attempt to exploit the proximity: the children are still on an exploratory mission.

Even though unsure or anxious, few children can withstand for long not being part of the action. They will begin to close in by "circling the wagons" more obviously. Efforts may be made to interrupt the adult conversation, to take part in it, or to ask the parent for attention of some kind. Children may begin to add details of a trip taken or an activity participated in at school, or of who said what to whom, and when and what happened next. Conversation that includes them bridges the shyness or anxiety gap, and the assessor is "in".

Some shared activity may follow, from an active game of badminton, to a visit to the playroom where something not-quite-completed is being constructed, to listening while the child plays the piano, to following an explanation of who everybody is in the last set of pictures in a photo album. The activity itself is not important; what is important is the subtle unspoken transfer of the child's attention from the parent to the assessor.

A judgment call is now in order which can only be made by the assessor: do you try for time alone now, or do you wait? Some children cannot safely move beyond this point at this time, and should not be pressured to do so. Others will really begin to relate, and even try to hold the assessor there. Such behaviour may raise a question about the child's emotional condition: grasping on too quickly suggests an insecure, emotionally hungry child. On the other hand, you may remind them of a much loved relative or baby-sitter, and the innocent trust-base is just being transferred to you. This reflects just the opposite of the insecure child: this very young child has been well treated, has had no untoward experiences with adults, and expects to be loved and well-treated by you, too.

As tempting as it is to move quickly, caution is probably advisable. There will be a second home visit, and the behaviour can be reconsidered then. It's important at the same time not to let the child feel rebuffed. Extra time doing something together (colouring, trying to get something to work) will allow for close proximity and communication, both verbal and non-verbal, and help you make up your mind about trying for more or waiting until the second home visit. With very young children the decision may be enhanced or complicated by a determined effort to climb on to your lap or to snuggle closely while you read a story book together.

Touching children, holding them on your lap, or having them sit right close by, must be handled as delicately as the decision to begin to "move in". Allowing touching is the child's prerogative: some indicate very clearly that they will permit it in varying degrees (all the way from a pat on the back right up to a snuggle), while others send a message that such contact is unwelcome. Care must be taken to recognize and respect the signals: there are reasons for any mistrust, whether you know them or not.

For the purposes of this discussion, an assumption is being made that the assessor chooses to wait until the second home visit before seeking private time with the child(ren). If that is the case, it is important to lay some groundwork for the next meeting. This is usually done as part of the process of leaving this home visit and informing them of the next one. Tell the child how pleased you were to meet him or her, and that you will be meeting them soon again, at the other parent's home. Say also that your job is to try to help others make good decisions about them and their parents, and that when you see them the next time perhaps you can take some time together to talk about all that. In the meantime, they can think about any questions they might want to ask you about the situation. That will be easier to do then, because now that you have met, the next time you will recognize each other and be able to say how nice it is to see each other again. This presentation should be made in the parent's presence. It keeps the process up front, keeps the parent an informed participant, reduces (or even prevents) the occasional parental behaviour of resisting other-parent contact.

(iii) *Second Meeting*

The second home visit, to the other parent's home, is a separate experience. While it allows the recognition described above, it has its own emotional and psychological climate. Care must be taken to respect that, and to ensure that adequate time and attention are paid to this parent and any significant other, and that you do not move too quickly to the child(ren). A little time is needed to gauge the emotional "temperature", and if it seems elevated, to decide how to function in the circumstances.

The child(ren) may behave differently during this visit, which may reflect different behavioural standards or tolerance, or simply some initial showing off. Now that they know you a bit, certainly recognize you, understand that you are a part of the parental situation, some brief testing may go on. This may simply reflect an attempt to find out how you treat children, or if you seem to like them or not. This is critical information, if they may be asked to speak with you alone.

As in the previous contact, the operative phrase is "go slow". Ensure that the adults are comfortable with you, and that you have heard any comments or stories they need to tell you. Help the situation become as relaxed as it can; let the child(ren) come to you. Most parents and most children will help, suggesting showing you things or wanting to show you around. This makes it easier for you to move from your location, and to begin to interact with the child(ren). Watching and waiting also are of value, to observe the child/parent interaction. If the parent has remarried or is in a new relationship, the interactions between the adults, the new adult and the children, and if there are any, between the new partner's children and the children you are interested in all merit attention. Allowing them to take the lead in activity may help you to gain some useful information.

Finally, however, the moment comes when you feel it is possible to be alone with the children. A previously considered arrangement with the parent allows that parent to go on a brief errand, leaving you and the child to spend some time together, or to ask directly if you would now like to do that, and suggesting that someone move to another spot in the home to facilitate privacy. Older children often like to choose the location themselves, their bedroom being the usual comfortable spot. But indoors or outdoors, bedroom or kitchen, doesn't matter.

The interview with the child then takes on a procedural quality. Although your external manner is quiet and low key, and appears informal, there should be a clear goal in mind as to hoped-for outcome, and a method of approach as a way to address that goal. The following suggested approach has been useful, and is readily adapted to all ages and stages. The assessor of course gears the language used to the child's age, but the process is the same.

(d) Interviewing Techniques

(i) *Identify Yourself*

Once comfortably situated, open the discussion by asking the child if he or she knows who you are, why you are here, and what your job is. Ensure that the child has the answers to those questions, because everything else that follows exists within that context.

(ii) *Clarify Reality*

Clarify your awareness of the parents' situation and that it is very likely not going to change. Most children need comfort here. Speaking to the feelings you see or can assume are there helps the child to feel understood without having had to tell you. Some children will have maintained right up to this point a sort of "Twinkle-Toes", "Shirley Temple" smiling behaviour. Do not be fooled by this; in many cases it is masking the real feelings which children, especially young children, do not know how to express, or know whether you would understand and accept. If you are to have a really productive contact, you need to help the child let go of that "smiley" behaviour, and to let you see where they are really coming from.

One way to approach this is to ask sympathetically, following the acknowledgement of the parental split, if that makes them sad sometimes. In almost every case, the facade is dropped at once, the child looks sad, and nods in affirmation. A supportive comment then might be that you are sorry that it has to be so, but you can understand why they feel that way. Follow that up with a question, warmly put, about whether when they are all alone in bed at night and nobody can see, they sometimes cry. Again one may see a nod, and body-language that indicates just how hard the situation has been and still is for them. A quiet moment of silence acknowledges your respect for those sad feelings. Small children may come to sit by you at this point, or perhaps you can ask if they need a hug. If they do, they move right in for it, and a quiet moment of comforting helps the child to establish some emotional safety with you, because obviously you understand. Some children will stay close by, some will accept the comfort then move away, and some children will solemnly decline your offer.

(iii) *Clarify Role of Lawyers and Judge*

Clarify the child's understanding of the role of the lawyers (each parent has one, and the child may also) and of a judge. This is important in terms of establishing and reinforcing the message that the decisions (about custody and access) will be made by the adults, not by the child.

(iv) *Define Your Task*

The judge will need to make the very best decision that he can. After all, the decision is really all about the children, so the judge needs to know just as much as possible about them. But since children usually do not go to court in such situations, they need someone to speak for them, to tell the judge if there are any particular things they want to make sure he knows. That is your job: to help the judge. If you are to do that as well as you can, then you need the child to help *you*: are there any particular messages the child wants you to make certain the judge knows? You will see that they are delivered.

Stop at this point, and wait. Many children make excellent use of this opening: the first message in the vast majority of the cases is, "Tell the judge to tell my mother and father to stop fighting".

(v) *Helping Strategies*

Various devices are available to assist at this point. Take out your note pad, and indicate that what they are saying is important, and you want to make sure that you get it down correctly. Many children are pleased with this and cooperate with further "messages" to the judge.

Some children start to talk, then need a breather before resuming. For young children, the suggestion of doing some drawing is useful. Undirected, these children may express on paper their version of life in the present situation, exemplifying the situation or the hostility, or the loneliness they are experiencing. Some children respond well to pretending that you are "Tinker Bell", and they may have three wishes. If that were really so, what would their three wishes be? Those are also carefully written down. Yet another device is an imaginary telephone call — the roles may be reversed, and the child is the grown up: a judge, a lawyer, or the assessor, and they are asking questions of you playing the role of the child.

Older children may not need these devices. Once assured that you can (and do) understand their mixed and confused feelings, they may engage you directly in conversation. It is essential to maintain your same role definition, however, sincerely asking for their opinions or ideas, but avoiding scrupulously asking "the question". It is interesting to note that such discretion often (and even usually) seems to free up the child, and indeed, they do go on to express a wish or preference. If that is the case, then it becomes valid to explore with them their reasons. Some may appear more genuine than others.

Some children will combine talking and using "body language" to communicate their distress or ambivalence. The youngster who has been sitting beside you until now may move away and pointedly change the subject. Roll with it. Pause, wait, engage with the new subject briefly, re-approach the issue. Move to where the child is, or ask a young child to come back and sit with you a bit more. In nice weather, suggest a walk if the location and hour make that practical. Acknowledge again that this is hard work, and that you appreciate their help.

With patience this approach is usually productive and the child returns to the conversation. But there will be the occasional child who simply cannot manage it. Sometimes, as well, the stress of the situation may result in quite aggressive behaviour, ripping up drawings, throwing around toys, being very noisy and assertive with a pet. All of these actions signal a child who cannot risk revealing himself or herself, who cannot trust you enough to talk about feelings or express opinions. It is reasonable to assume that such children are more than aware of the dispute, and of the price to be paid if they really speak up. In such instances, they need to be understood without speech, sympathetically thanked, and allowed to escape. You may not have received all that was hoped for, but their behaviour indicates how toxic the inter-party struggle has become.

(vi) *Respect For Feelings*

If a pause is needed to have a little cry, or to recover poise following a sharing of strong feelings, take it, even temporarily changing the subject for a bit. Your comfort in the presence of strong feelings, and your respect for the child's right to have those feelings, helps to give them legitimacy, and validates the child in his or her own eyes. Some children may have already learned that it is psychologically dangerous to reveal the real depth of their feelings to one or both parents, so seeing your respect for them can be helpful and important.

(vii) *Stopping*

When it is comfortable, go back again to the subject, and ask if there is anything else they can think of, which they would like you to tell the Judge. Note any comments, as before. If there is nothing more, thank the child for his or her help, and for giving you this time, especially when the subject is hard to think and talk about. Rejoin the others, and tell the parent that the child worked really hard and was a lot of help. This acknowledgement is important even with (and perhaps especially with) the child who has been so locked-in that he or she could give you little or no help. That very behaviour, in itself, is of diagnostic value. Assure the child, again in front of the parent, that if he or she wishes to speak to you again at a later time, you would certainly be glad to arrange that. Each parent knows how to reach you, and another meeting could be set up.

(viii) *Siblings: Alone or Together*

In situations where more than one child in the family is the subject of the assessment, the question arises whether you should interview them as a sibling group or individually. The answer is — it depends. There is no hard and fast rule governing this situation; it really is a judgment call. It is often helpful to ask the parents' advice. One or both may be very aware of how the siblings are interacting with each other, and have a real opinion to share with you. In any event, the parents will appreciate your tact in suggesting indirectly that they know their children, and that you need and can use their assistance in setting the interview in place.

Siblings whose parents have separated noisily or whose parents have subsequently continued a quarrelsome, angry or even bitter interaction, often turn to each other for emotional support and reassurance. Observations of one or both parents' behaviour may have led the children to believe that they cannot always rely on the parents to "be there" when needed, or to have the time or inclination to focus on their problems. In such situations, the siblings may lean on each other for mutual emotional support. Such propping up of each other may be termed "tenting relationships" (support from either side meeting in the middle keeps the top on). If such a situation appears to exist, interviewing all the children together may be advisable. The younger child(ren) may need to see and hear the response of their older sibling(s). The older ones, feeling protective of the younger ones, need to be sure that you are not going to upset them unduly. Sometimes, following a group interview, one or more of the children may ask to speak to you privately, then or at another time. Do follow up on the request.

However, when you do not sense that a tenting relationship exists, or where the ages are quite disparate, or where the siblings appear to have a hostile relationship, individual interviews are indicated. It is then important to inform each child that what you are talking to them about is what you talked to the others about, or will be doing so shortly.

(ix) *Confidentiality*

Clarify the issues of confidentiality with each child you interview. This involves explaining your position. If you are going to help the judge, then you need to be able to tell him things in the report. On the other hand, you know they do not want to get into trouble with their parents, so there may be some things they do not want you to tell them or write in the report. You can both understand and respect that, and will do so, with one major exception: if they need to tell you something about things that have been going on about which they are very upset and which they wish would stop, then you will have to tell somebody (another adult) about that. Sometimes we have to tell someone else about things in order for the situation to improve. In other words, one cannot make a blanket promise of confidentiality, and the child needs to know and understand that. It is better to have the youngster be selective in comments to you, than to make a promise you know you may not be able to keep. The seduction of, "Can I tell you a secret?" is great, but is to be avoided.

At the conclusion of the interview, review the points the child has asked to be conveyed to the judge, and confirm that it is all right to do so in the report. Review the wording in the notes and obtain the child's concurrence that it is correct. Accept any gifts of drawings, or so forth, with appropriate appreciation. Identify any item about which you agreed not to tell anyone, if indeed, you did do that. Thank them for their help, and get on your way. Visit briefly with the rest of the family, and leave. Holding the interview with the child(ren) at or near the end of the home visit allows everyone, assessor included, to avoid the awkward moment of a parent not asking how the interview with the child went, and the assessor not replying. But do assure everyone that if any of the children (or parents for that matter) wish to speak with you again, you will be pleased, of course, to arrange that.

8. COLLATERAL INTERVIEWS

The individuals named on each parent's collateral names list may be contacted at any time after completion of the Phase One interviews with the parents or parties. Experience has shown, however, that the value of their comments and opinions is enhanced if the contacts are made later rather than earlier in the assessment process. Previous contact with the school, at least one meeting with the child, and interviews with new spouses or common-law partners, allow you to follow the conversation more effectively and to understand references to persons, places, or events. Some time may have elapsed since the parent asked their permission to give you their name; their recognition of your name and function establishes for you that the conversation did take place.

(a) Purposes

Collateral interviews serve two purposes: to verify and balance the information provided by the parents, and to enable the assessor to consider her response to the parents and possibly modify it. Collateral interviews help to shield the assessor from uncritically accepting a version of the dispute situation presented by one parent which may prove not to have been fully accurate. They also protect each parent from a too-hasty judgment by the assessor.

It is useful to remember that the legislation in Ontario which addresses the ordering and undertaking of an assessment, asserts the primacy of the best interests of the child in evaluating applications for custody and access.[10] It is essential, then, that efforts at verification of each parent's or party's presentations not only be made, but be seen to have been made, thoroughly and fairly. The goal remains: the best interests of the child(ren).

By independently affirming the version of one parent about the marriage breakdown or the current dispute, or conversely, by presenting a different picture of the parties, the child, or the situation, each collateral person adds to your own building fund of information and impressions. Some collaterals will have strong opinions as to the best plan for the child. Others will be reluctant to voice an opinion in that respect at all. Some collaterals may not even know the child, or may not know one of the parties very well. But each conversation adds something.

(b) By Telephone or In Person

Not all collateral interviews need to be in person. You can obtain a clear picture from an employer as to the parent's work performance and reliability just as readily over the telephone. Phone interviews are equally productive when talking to old friends of the parents, or neighbours who knew the couple when they were still living together, or when speaking to other professionals known to a parent or the family.

Personal interviews, at your office or in their home, are particularly valuable with grandparents, babysitters, and close relatives or friends who have been especially noted by the parent when giving you the list. Each of these persons has a view of the family history and an awareness of the parents' behaviour that is unique. Each may have had an active part in the situation, and each now views the outcome of the dispute in a certain way, especially as it will affect the child(ren). Such persons usually welcome an opportunity to speak with you at length. Grandparents usually have strong opinions and equally strong feelings about what has happened. They

10 Children's Law Reform Act, R.S.O. 1980, c. 68 [as amended S.O. 1982, c. 20], s. 24(1).

fear loss of contact with their grandchildren; they may be hurt, sad, and/or angry about the circumstances and behaviour of the parties; they will have much information to share. Babysitters have seen the situation wax and wane, improve or worsen, and at first hand have observed and coped with the child's reactions. As with grandparents, babysitters may become very concerned about the child's future. The same is true for close relatives or friends: they have been, and still are, close to the situation, have genuine concerns about the child, and informed opinions about each parents' capacities.

Personal interviews with such important collaterals allow direct interaction. You can present your need for their help clearly, (this is possible over the phone as well, of course) and note the unspoken language of expression, body movement, eye contact or avoidance, resistance and veiled hostility, sadness, and/or eagerness to be of assistance. During a visit with grandparents or close relatives, information is more comfortably elicited about one of the parties' childhood development and adult adjustment. Tales of their own struggles may flow, adding to your understanding of the factors that shaped their adult child's attitudes and behaviours. Grandparents, babysitters and relatives can confirm their willingness or not to assist with child care in future, and any observations they may have about that. Pauses in the conversation, to regain composure or control anger, are easier to understand when you are there.

(c) Content and Approach

Most collaterals will suggest that you ask them questions about what you want to know. It is better to avoid that approach, as the results will be limited. A more productive approach is to suggest that they just start to talk about the situation: what they know or understand about it, and, of course, if they have any recommendations to make to you concerning the child(ren). You need their help in fleshing out the picture that you have already. It may be useful to add, as well, that you will not be quoting them in the report: you know that life goes on after the assessment.[11] Most persons respond well to this approach, and begin to talk.

Each parent's list may not contain an equal number of names. There is no obligation to speak to exactly the same number of collaterals, but there is the matter of perceived fairness. A report which is clearly over-weighted in one direction may indeed be perceived as unfair by the non-supported parent, and attacked in cross-examination on that basis. Some

11 It may occur that a unique item of information is received from one collateral; if included in the report, the parent(s) may discern the source. This cannot be avoided. Tact and careful wording, and no attribution of source, are indicated in the report.

attempted balance should be reflected in the list of all those spoken to: one or both of the grandparents on either side, for example, if they are available and were listed; balance in terms of contact with friends who knew the parents as a couple, or who now know them only as individuals; balance in terms of those who know the child(ren). Sometimes repeated efforts to make contact with persons on the list prove unsuccessful. If that results in what might be perceived as imbalance, then a comment in the report on the inability to make contact may forestall an allegation of bias.

Take notes during the conversation, whether in person or over the phone. They will be of value when reviewing all the material prior to writing the report. How the collaterals line up viz-à-viz each parent's position, and in what way, will be of use in the process of arriving at the recommendations. For each such collateral interview you will make a judgment as to the person's credibility, wisdom, and fairness in what is shared with you; and the role, if any, those interviewed have played and perhaps continue to play in the unfolding struggle about the child(ren).

(d) Refusal to Be Interviewed

Occasionally, someone whose name was given, and input would be of considerable value, will decline to be interviewed. Often it is the recent, or about to become, common-law partner of one of the parents. If, as you spoke with that parent, you learned of the relationship and of its extent, you will have asked to meet the individual involved. This will be particularly so if the new partner has met the child(ren) in question, and is spending a lot of time with them on weekends. Although not a party to the dispute, the outcome involves the new partner who will be cast in the role of step-parent if the parent with whom he or she is involved gains custody.

Most "significant others" cooperate readily with an interview request. Some feel very strongly about the situation and their place in it, and are not only willing but anxious to talk with you. Others will demur, and choose to remain outside the actual assessment process. Your concern should be expressed to the parent, but the choice and the decision rests with that third person. If the refusal is persistent, and the new partner is absent during the home visit, then you must proceed without their assistance. Make note of the refusal and absence, and take them into account when considering the recommendations. The paucity of information about the new partner's relationship to the child(ren), about their feelings toward the other parent, and about their willingness to take on the added responsibility of the child(ren) should custody go that way, will be a factor in considering that parent's situation.

(e) Guidelines Under the Ontario Children's Law Reform Act

The Ontario Children's Law Reform Act, contains, in section 24(2), seven major factors which the court shall consider "in determining the best interests of a child for the purposes of an application . . . in respect of custody of or access to a child . . . .". Four of these sections require the evaluation of relationships or family functioning:

> (*a*) the love, affection and emotional ties between the child and . . . members of the child's family who reside with the child, and . . . or are involved in the care and upbringing of the child;
>
> . . . .
>
> (*c*) the length of time the child has lived in a stable home environment;
>
> (*d*) the ability and willingness of each person applying for custody of the child to provide the child with guidance and education, the necessaries of life and any special needs of the child;
>
> . . . .
>
> (*f*) the permanence and stability of the family unit with which it is proposed that the child will live . . . .

If the assessment report is to be of genuine assistance to the court, verification of parental claims about family relationships, through observation, interviews, and/or psychological testing is essential. Common-law partners, new spouses, or soon-to-be partners, are included in the overall concept of "family relationships". Absence of a real sense of their role in the family unit to which the child might move, or in which the child might remain, is a significant hole in the picture, and may raise questions for all concerned. If the information vacuum is the result of an omission by the assessor, that can reasonably be considered incompetence, and the report may be invalidated on such grounds. If all reasonable efforts to generate cooperation in interviewing and/or undertaking psychological tests with the "significant other" have been unsuccessful, this fact should be drawn to everyone's attention in the report. Such a statement in the report underscores the assessor's recognition that the best interests of the child must be and do remain paramount. One may be reluctant, indeed, to recommend an arrangement in which a significant amount of the child care would be undertaken by a person unwilling to appear as a *bona fide* part of the life of one of the parents.

On the other hand, the willing participation of such a person will help the assessor understand more fully what a parent's current situation is, and/or what it may be expected to be in and for the foreseeable future. Such information may be strategic in arriving at recommendations.

Collateral interviews, then, serve to demonstrate the assessor's intent to be fair and balanced, and above all, to be child-focussed. Not all the names on a long list (or even a short one) may be interviewed, especially if repeated efforts at contact have been unsuccessful. The absence of such a resource as the collaterals provide from the process, would keep from the assessment a valuable aspect of check-and-balance.

EXHIBIT (**5.1**)

Consent to Release of Information

Audrey Erickson, M.S.W.,C.S.W.
ERICKSON, PIAGET & ASSOCIATES
Child & Family Consultants
Suite 1411, 28 Long Street
Bigtown, Somewhere

Date: ________________

TO WHOM IT MAY CONCERN:

AUTHORIZATION

I HEREBY give my permission for information and records, as required, to be made available to and shared with Audrey Erickson of Erickson, Piaget & Associates, Child and Family Consultants, on behalf of my child(ren):

______________________________ d.o.b. ______________________________
______________________________ d.o.b. ______________________________
______________________________ d.o.b. ______________________________

Signature: ______________________
Address: ________________________
____
____

Relation to Child(ren)

______________________________ .

6

Writing the Report

1. PREPARATION

Now that the data-gathering and impression-gaining are complete, there remains the job of writing the report. This is the document everyone has been waiting for. Now comes the moment of truth: recommendations, and the reasons for them.

The report will have impact, one way or another. The parties may use it as a basis for arriving at an agreement; if not, the court will make use of it as part of the evidence in ensuing litigation. In either eventuality, the report carries weight. It must be thorough, fair, balanced, professional, and practical. The written document carries the assessor's name: that builds reputation. Reputation contributes to credibility, and a willingness, or otherwise, on the part of lawyers and judges to listen to and consider the point of view expressed in that and later assessment reports.

The writing of an assessment report begins with two activities: (1) a thorough re-reading of *all* the materials, including all printed materials and all interview or observation notes; and (2) a period of careful consideration of the issues until clarity about the recommendations has been achieved. Both of these activities take time and are necessary.

Most assessors are busy with other professional activities while conducting the assessment. It is unrealistic to think that they can reliably recall all the bits and pieces in a matter, even if the major incidents are clearly remembered. Refreshing the memory not only focusses the mind, re-reading will often serve to highlight points made early in the process and perhaps forgotten, but now seen as more important information with different implications. Such re-reading is the other side of thoroughness: having been thorough in doing the assessment, it is now time to be thorough in completing the report.

A subsequent advantage of careful re-reading may become clear later. In a meeting with a parent and lawyer to consider the report content, or when giving testimony about it, the details will come more readily to mind. (Of course a review of the file and the report would precede such an activity, but having done a thorough review previously, the second review would be easier.)

Occasionally the matter of what recommendations to make continues to puzzle, even at the point of beginning to write the report. Perhaps either applicant is equally competent to parent but the parenting styles would be very different; or perhaps the deficits seen in both parties are a source of continuing concern about the children's future with either one. The re-reading and thinking would have narrowed the issues, and highlighted the opinions and the comments of the collaterals. Organizing the material as the writing progresses also helps, and usually the scales are tipped as the data unfolds. If serious doubt remains, consultation with a reputable co-professional is indicated.

Writing an assessment report is not easy. Expressing oneself in writing is not the same as verbalizing, where tone, shading, hesitation or emphasis so readily convey meaning. Writing is demanding and time-consuming, but shading, emphasis and nuance are all possible. Some guidelines may assist, in both approach and organization.

2. GUIDELINES FOR WRITING REPORTS

(a) A Caution

Bear in mind that once the report leaves the office, the assessor has no control over its circulation. Thus, the manner of expression and the language used to describe the parties must be tactful and restrained, however clear the report about past or present facts. The report should not damage reputation. As well, be sure to address special factors such as cultural difference, or particular condition, to indicate the steps taken to understand and to ensure fairness. Cultural difference in parenting patterns must be acknowledged and taken into consideration. This is a matter of professional ethics.

(b) Follow An Outline

Follow an outline which clearly directs the reader to each section under discussion. Such an approach appears organized, and conveys professionalism. A report without headings, with no apparent organization, suggests to the reader that the assessor's mind may be well reflected in the rambling disarray. A well-organized report suggests careful work, and therefore reliable content.

Assessors from different professions may use varying outlines for presenting the material.[1] An outline guide which has proven consistently useful is included as Exhibit (6.1) at the end of this chapter and will be discussed later.

(c) What to Include/What to Omit

Consider what material to leave out of a report just as much as you consider what to put in. In the course of any assessment information may be conveyed about a party which has not been heretofore widely or publicly known. Including the information in the report might unnecessarily complicate the situation, or even potentially damage a party's present adjustment. If the information does not materially effect the outcome of the situation, it is better omitted. Remember: the assessor will leave the situation, the parties remain in it. The report and what is said in it is there for them to live with, and perhaps now or later, for children to read. Thoughtful tact is not at all inconsistent with a clear, factual exposition of "what went wrong".

(d) Avoid Jargon

Avoid professional jargon, whether from your own or another professional discipline. Use of jargon does little to enhance credit or reputation. A report which is difficult for others to read or understand is not as useful as it might be, and indeed may create some irritation. Clear expression, somewhat formal usage, and absence of slang and sloppy language are all advisable: "Say what you mean and mean what you say."

---

1 See, for example:
D.C. Day, "Preparing the Assessment" in *Social Work and Family Law* (St. John's: Memorial University, 1987); or
"Custody/Access Assessment Guidelines", Report of the Interdisciplinary Committee for Custody/Access Assessments. The Ontario Psychological Foundation, Toronto, 1988, pp. 11-13; or
D. Skafte, *Child Custody Evaluations, A Practical Guide*, (Beverley Hills: Sage Publications, 1985).

It is advisable, as well, to exercise caution when tempted to use professional terms that are considered to be in the domain of another profession. Avoid using medical (psychiatric) terminology especially. Social workers commonly use such terms as "depression" or "hysterical" when speaking with each other, or with professionals from other disciplines. Such usage is not acceptable in the assessment context. Using such terms, particularly to describe one of the parties' adjustment or emotional status, may provide an avenue of challenge later under cross-examination. The expected query: "Where/when did you receive psychiatric training?", or "Could you remind this court where in your *curriculum vitae* it indicates your graduation from medical school or your qualification as a psychologist?", directed to a social worker, for example, is intended to suggest, at the very least, that that professional over-reached his or her training and area of competence. It is preferable to present information in clear descriptive language. If a specific term or phrase must be used, a statement that this is a term in use by another profession, and perhaps citing the source, acknowledges that you are borrowing.

The assessor's enlightened self-interest provides another reason for caution. Since there is no way to control the distribution of the report, persons unrelated to the dispute may see the particular descriptive or diagnostic term, and perhaps make inappropriate use of it, citing the assessment report as the source. It is surely better to take the time to achieve careful and responsible phrasing when describing behaviour or emotional status, than to risk a civil suit by an angry parent who considers himself or herself to have suffered loss of reputation or other injury because of the language used in the report.

(e) Be Complete/Be Succinct

Present a complete picture, but do it succinctly. Avoid long descriptive passages, quoting conversations at length, expressing personal opinion (*e.g.* "He says she provoked him, but no woman should have to put up with that kind of behaviour.") The opinions expressed must be professional ones only, and if expressed stated as such: "It is my professional opinion that . . . ., *etc.*" Sometimes a situation is so complex that a report of many pages is unavoidable. In that case, a well-organized report which focusses and groups the data under specific headings facilitates understanding, leads readily to the conclusions, and provides the rationale for the recommendations. Then, the reader will find a longish report useful. A lengthy report which is unorganized and full of unnecessary details, irritates the reader, and may appear more "gossipy" than professional.

(f) Function of the Report

Remember that no one is bound by the recommendations. The report is a tool toward understanding, a basis for negotiating, or an item of evidence, the weight and impact of which are at the discretion of the Judge. To be useful, the report must be persuasive and present its position logically and clearly to another profession. It is not etched in stone; it may be as validly met by disagreement as by agreement, in whole or in part. In the last analysis it is a written professional judgment call, reflecting the author's judgment and her professionalism.

3. FOLLOWING THE OUTLINE

As indicated earlier, various professional groups may develop their own favorite assessment report outline. Or individuals may use one they have drawn up for themselves. There is no one "right" outline. Preference is expressed here for the following guide, which has proven consistently useful and which can be adapted to fit various situations or forms of relationships.

Although some assessors present their full *curriculum vitae* within the body of the report, the statement of professional qualifications is not, in itself, a part of the report. In fact, a copy of the assessor's *curriculum vitae* should have been sent to counsel at the beginning of the negotiations to undertake the assignment. If not, the information may be sent along with the report but not attached to it. Some lawyers prefer to keep copies of current *curricula vitae* on file separately so that they are readily available for submission when proposing use of a particular assessor. In such cases, repetition of the professional data is unnecessary at the commencement of the report.

ASSESSMENT REPORT OUTLINE

Date:

Report to:
From:
Concerning:
Persons Concerned:
The Issue:
Persons Interviewed:
I: Background
II: The Mother
III: The Father
IV: The Marriage
V: The Children
VI: Additional Information

VII: Summary/Discussion
VIII: Recommendations

[Signature]
[Professional Designation]

4. CONTENT OF THE REPORT

(a) Addressing Context

"Report To". This would be the registrar or clerk of the court, the Judge who ordered the report, if it was ordered; each lawyer for the parties; and the lawyer appointed for the children, if any.

"From". The assessor's full name, professional designation initials, and professional title (*i.e.*, Jane Smith, M.S.W., C.S.W., Child and Family Consultant, or, John Jones, Ph.D., C.Psych., Registered Clinical Psychologist).

"Concerning". The full name(s) of the child(ren) and their ages.

"Persons Concerned". This is a list of the parties to the dispute, listed separately, with their role and their full address, for example:

> *Mary Jean Quarrel*, the child(ren)'s mother
> 123 Fourth Avenue, Apartment 000
> Anytown, Somewhere
>
> *John Frank Quarrel*, the child(ren)'s father
> 987 Perchance Street
> Anytown, Somewhere

This section also includes listing the child(ren) and where he/she/they are resident at the point of writing, for example:

> Cynthia Penelope Quarrel, x years, y months
> Jonathan Peter Quarrel, x years, y months
> The children in question, presently residing with their father/mother at the above address.

This section lists only those adults who are parties to the action, which may include, for example, grandparents or a stepparent. It does not include anyone who is not a party, even if they are very involved emotionally in the dispute.

"The Issue". This is a succinct, sometimes almost terse statement of the matter at dispute. For example:

"Mary Jean Quarrel has had an interim order of custody of Cynthia and Jonathan since some four months after the separation from John Frank Quarrel. John is now seeking custody for himself of both children. Mary Jean is opposing this action, and is seeking to have custody of both children confirmed to herself."

It does not need further explanation or history, that will come later. Simply identify the dispute. This presents the assessor's terms of reference. If the assessor misunderstood the assignment it will be immediately apparent. As well, it defines the limits of the task, which may prove of value later under cross-examination when the assessor is queried about not having included an in-depth study of a child's learning disability, for example: that was not the assignment.

"Persons Interviewed". There are three aspects to this section:

1. List in sequence, all the persons interviewed during the course of the assessment, and beside their name indicate their place in the scheme of things. For example:

   (1) Mary Jean Quarrel, the child(ren)'s mother.
   (2) Anthony Maybe, mother's common-law partner.
   (3) John Frank Quarrel, the child(ren)'s father.
   (4) Andre Lerigger, father's foreman at "X" industry.
   (5) Susan B. Aude, Principal, "XYZ" school.

   It has proven counter-productive to list beside each name the length of time of the interview. This is an invitation later for an attempt to deflect the impact of the recommendations, by focussing attention on apparent imbalances in the amount of time devoted to interviews. Nor is it necessary to indicate whether the interviews were in person or by phone. The purpose of the section is to show clearly the sources of information upon which the assessor has relied.

2. Add to the list of those interviewed, as a next number, a statement of having met, observed, and spoken with the child(ren) in the home of each party (if, of course, this is so), or in the home of one party, or in the office, if that is the case.

3. List then all written materials read, spelling out each in chronological detail, and the source (*e.g.*, "I read the following materials provided by counsel and father: . . . ."). Such materials may include affidavits, replies, motions, orders, previous assessment reports, school reports, diaries, financial statements, letters, *etc*. Careful itemizing of these materials indicates reliance on more than just the spoken word, a point for thoroughness. It also suggests that the assessor is aware of allegations

made, or denied, and has had an opportunity to consider these in the interviews.

The above categories set out the context of the report. Make sure to insert the date upon which the report is prepared in this section as well. The following headings now guide the presentation of the material about the situation.

(b) I: Background

This section sets out in some detail the story of the history that has led to the present dilemma. A usual place to start is when the parties married, when the children were born, what the circumstances were then, and briefly what began to go wrong. The major dates are useful to include: marriage, births, separations, interim or post-separation or divorce custody/access orders. Bring the story up to date to the present dispute, and the reasons why the assessment was either ordered or agreed upon as needed.

Note: When an assessment has been conducted by a psychologist, the next three sections of her report dealing with each parent and the child(ren) will contain data about the specific standardized tests used by the psychologist in contacts with each party and the child(ren), the results of the tests, and the bases within the test scores for the impressions and conclusions reached by the psychologist. In addition, use of the guidelines below is also advisable.

(c) II: The Mother

A sequential approach is useful. Birth date and place, order in the family's number, some description of what her childhood was like, what her parents' marriage provided by way of example, are all useful. Furthest educational attainment and employment history and present employer are of interest. Describe the impact of the marriage, the pregnancies, or an illness on her, and the way in which the developing difficulties were handled. Point out strengths and weaknesses, how she has handled matters since the separation or divorce, her present adjustment, and the relationship with the children. Indicate the plans she has for caring for them, what her support network is, what her general attitude is toward the other parent, especially concerning the children. If she has established a new relationship, indicate how stable it appears to be, and compare or contrast its potential as against the former one. Add notes about any specific or particular factor about the mother which will assist the reader to understand her present lifestyle and anticipated future adjustment. Indicate how she has responded in the assessment — that is, whether she is very anxious, hostile, resistive, worried, very cooperative, *etc.*

Do not go into detail about what went wrong in the marriage or relationship; that will be handled in a later section.

(d) III: The Father

Follow the same sequential approach as with the mother. (Note: In some situations the parties may not be the usual mother/father dyad. Perhaps they will be stepfather/grandparents. If such is the case, simply alter the heading to accommodate to the facts and provide the same or similar information)

(e) IV: The Marriage

This is the section that should explicate clearly "what went wrong". An historical approach builds the picture. How the couple met, the circumstances surrounding the decision to marry or live together, the timing and impact of the arrival of the children. Dates are useful here; don't worry about being repetitious. Dates give context and clarify the impact of events (e.g., married at 18; first child only six months later, second child 14 months later; second child ill for a long time; discharged from hospital "x" date, *etc.*, serve graphically to illustrate the stress build-up).

There may be differing versions of the incidents that led to the marital breakdown. If so, each needs to be mentioned. If there were repeated separations and reconciliations, these are of interest, with an added indication of how the children were cared for and by whom during those separations. Events leading up to the final break should be included, as well as an indication of the present status (*e.g.*, one parent still seeks a reconciliation, the other resists it, or one parent has now established a steady new relationship or marriage and is anxious to discontinue contact with the former spouse to the extent that that is possible). Presentation of the current situation will lay the groundwork for later recommendations concerning such arrangements as joint custody, frequent overnight access, and so forth.

It is useful not to engage, at this point in a pro/con discussion of the dynamics of the marriage, or where responsibility lies for its failure. That can follow later. This section should be descriptive only, but may carry a statement as to the probability of successful reconciliation.

(f) V: The Children

Each child who is a focus of the assessment should be discussed separately. Again, an historical approach helps, particularly if there were complications (physical or situational, or both) associated with the pregnancy, birth, or early years. Behaviour and personality patterns, developmental problems if any, briefly described, help to individualize each child. School or daycare reports not only flesh out the child as a person, but in the context of the family disruption and the present dispute, provide some index of how the child is coping with all the stress. Indicate the child's general physical appearance, interests, hobbies, general personality make-up. Remember that the description of each child may provide the only real opportunity the Judge (or indeed, the parties' lawyers) may have to see the child as a real person, not as a chattel.

The section should also include descriptions of each child's relationship with each of the parties to the dispute, particularly as observed during home visits, as well as observed or reported relationships with one or both party's "significant other" and that person's children.

If the child has indicated wishes or preferences with respect to the resolution of the dispute, these should be included, perhaps with an additional comment about the child's emotional status, and how these preferences were expressed (drawings, talking, making wishes, *etc.*). Note should also be made of any special needs or problems of each child which should be taken into account in planning for him or her.

(g) VI: Additional Information

This section provides a location for the addition of information which is important to the understanding of the situation, but which is not specifically covered under one of the above headings. In this section information about the "significant others", new spouse or common-law partner, can be presented. Such persons have a stake in the outcome of the case. They are not parties, but they are actually or potentially already involved as persons in a relationship with a parent. They are, or will be, or may be, in some form of parenting interaction with the child(ren). It is important that their views, and the impressions they have conveyed about themselves, their attitudes, and their interest in the child(ren), be presented. Their impact on the situation may be considerable.

The same might be considered advisable about the interaction between grandparents with each other (*e.g.*, ongoing anger and bitterness) that spills over to the parties and the children. Or it might be useful to devote a special section to information provided by medical specialists concerning a potentially disabling illness suffered by one parent (or child). The condition may not now be in particular evidence, but the diagnosis has been made, and in future the capacity to parent may be compromised. In such cases, the assessor will have consulted (with permission) the specialists involved with that parent and/or with that illness, to clarify understanding of the illness and the prognosis, if that can reasonably be ascertained. Such specialists will indicate carefully what can be included in the report and sometimes even dictate a sentence or two directly into the report, in order to assure themselves of accuracy.

(h) VII: Summary and Discussion

This section puts the pieces of the puzzle together to complete the picture. The basic facts are repeated, the pros and cons considered, each parent's position described. Professional opinion may be expressed, presenting a position about, and a suggested understanding of, the parties, their behaviour, the circumstances and factors that were in play in the situation, and the prospective adjustment of each party in the near future. All of these aspects are then considered in the light of the children's needs and wishes, their relationships with each party, and indeed, each party's capacity to meet the children's needs. This formulation should lead directly into the recommendations.

In writing the summary and discussion, it is important to be aware of the relevant statutory guidelines for the determination of custody provided by section 24 of the Children's Law Reform Act[2] (or the Divorce Act, as the case may be, or the applicable statute in the relevant jurisdiction). If counsel has not provided you with a copy of these guidelines, see that you obtain it. Appendix II at the conclusion of the book contains some of the relevant statutory provisions. While the outline of the report does not need to follow these guidelines precisely, your material and the recommendations should enable the lawyers and the Judge to consider the recommendations with the guidelines in mind. Indeed, the court is bound to do so in a matter being heard under that statute.

The guidelines in the Ontario Children's Law Reform Act state specifically:

> 24. (1) The merits of an application under this Part in respect of custody of or access to a child shall be determined on the basis of the best interests of the child.
>
> (2) In determining the best interests of a child for the purposes of an application under this Part in respect of custody of or access to a child, a court shall consider all the needs and circumstances of the child including,
>
> (*a*) the love, affection and emotional ties between the child and,
>
> (i) each person entitled to or claiming custody of or access to the child,
> (ii) other members of the child's family who reside with the child, and
> (iii) persons involved in the care and upbringing of the child;

2 R.S.O. 1980, c. 68 [as amended by S.O. 1982, c. 20].

> (*b*) the views and preferences of the child, where such views and preferences can reasonably be ascertained;
> (*c*) the length of time the child has lived in a stable home environment;
> (*d*) the ability and willingness of each person applying for custody of the child to provide the child with guidance and education, the necessaries of life and any special needs of the child;
> (*e*) any plans proposed for the care and upbringing of the child;
> (*f*) the permanence and stability of the family unit with which it is proposed that the child will live; and
> (*g*) the relationship by blood or through an adoption order between the child and each person who is a party to the application.

It will be useful in this section also to indicate your thinking about the possibility of joint custody in this case, and the reasons why you do or do not favour this form of custody arrangement.

(i) VIII: Framing the Recommendations

(i) *Style and Format*

The concluding sentence of the Summary and Discussion section should lead directly to the recommendations. It is useful to capture that flow by introducing the recommendations in a way that speaks directly to the first guideline noted above: "Therefore, I believe it to be in the best interests of [children's names] for the following to take place, and I recommend . . . .". Clarity of expression is essential.

Begin each recommendation with a capitalized "THAT" which focusses the reader's attention at once to each successive recommendation (*e.g.*, THAT custody remain [or be transferred to . . . .]). List each recommendation separately.

(ii) *Be Specific*

Address the main issue of the dispute first (the matter listed in the report outline as "The Issue") and make your recommendation specific. If you have had reservations about making that recommendation, you can have stated so in the Summary/Discussion section. The point of an assessment, from the lawyers' and parties' point of view, is to gain some guidance toward resolution of the dispute. It is of no help at all to state (as has happened) that the assessor is unable to arrive at recommendations. Be concrete. As has been mentioned earlier in this text, judicial description of general guidelines for an assessor included the statement that,

> He must ensure that any recommendation that he sets forth in his report to the court . . . . has some chance of acceptance especially if it involves some more than usual activity or co-operation by them [the parents].[3]

3 *Boody v. Boody* (1983) 32 R.F.L. (2d) 396, at 399 (Ont. Dist. Ct.).

(iii) *Structure the Implementation*

Spell out in the following recommendations the structure and details you believe to be necessary to a successful implementation of your first recommendation. These items will address such matters as access, shared time (or not) for the major holidays, summer school holidays or vacations, Father's Day, Mother's Day, child and parental birthdays. In some cases it may be necessary to spell out specifics such as who provides transportation for access, or who should pay the cost of public transportation (bus, train, or air travel).

Add, as well, specific recommendations, *as indicated*, which ensure a non-custodial party's entitlement to on-going information about the child(ren)'s health, school performance, and invitations to school or skill recitals, competitions, and so forth in which the children will be participating. It may be advantageous to recommend specifically that the non-custodial parent receive annually a copy of the child(ren)'s school photographs.

(iv) *Avoid Exhortations to Better Behaviour*

Recommendations such as "The parents should stop fighting," may express a fond wish on the assessor's part, but are of little value to the lawyers or the court, who probably wish the same thing. Of much more value will be recommendations directed at *how* that fighting might be at least reasonably curtailed, if not stopped.

(v) *Consider Special Programmes and Activities*

Add specific recommendations, if you believe they are indicated, for special programmes or activities you see as being of assistance in facilitating the main recommendations. Such programmes or activities may include mediation, undertaking or continuing counselling for one or both of the parties, or for one or more of the children, as may have been suggested or recommended by collateral professionals with whom you were in contact.

(vi) *Issues of Religion*

Address the delicate issue of religion within the case from the point of view of the parents' capabilities in meeting the needs of the children. This is a very sensitive area, of course. The guideline to follow is perhaps best expressed by Allan, J.S.C. in *McNeil v. McNeil*:

Religious beliefs and activities are of concern only where the parent's involvement adversely affects the welfare of the children.[4]

(vii) *Practicality*

Review the recommendations to ensure their practicality. Ask yourself if you were on the receiving end of them, instead of the giving end, whether they would make sense, flow as a logical consequence of the material discussed in the body of the report, and if they are manageable within the circumstances and life style of the parties. Do they make sense? Are they as fair as is possible? Are they consistent? Are they child-focussed? Will you be prepared to support and explain them, if called upon in court to do so? If the answer to all these questions is "yes", then your report is concluded.

(viii) *Sign the Report*

Remember to sign each copy of the report.

4 [1989] W.D.F.L. 770 (B.C.S.C.).

7

Post Assessment: The Lawyer/Client Response

1. UNDERSTANDING THE REPORT
2. REVIEWING THE REPORT WITH THE CLIENT
3. DEALING WITH THE UPSET CLIENT
4. MARSHALLING THE DETAILS FOR RESPONSE
5. FORMULATING AN APPROACH
6. USING THE ASSESSMENT IN PRE-TRIAL CONFERENCES

Once the assessment report has been delivered, a new phase of the process begins. Whether or not the bottom line on the assessment favours the client's point of view, the lawyer's task is the same:

- Read and understand the report in its entirety.
- Review the report with the client.
- Together with the client, formulate an approach to the custody/access issues in light of the report.

The assessment is not just a device used to try to win the case. More important, it is a window through which to see the case from a different profession's viewpoint as it affects the children and reveals aspects of the parties and their situation that might not have been readily apparent in lawyer/client and lawyer/lawyer contacts.

1. UNDERSTANDING THE REPORT

First and foremost, read the report. Read the entire report, not just the final paragraphs embodying the recommendations. Read it initially with an open mind, and not through the filter of the mindset, "How can I use this report to win the case?" In a thorough assessment there is often much to learn about one's own client as a person. This is by virtue of the fact that the assessor has had access to more information sources, and has looked at the parties, the children, and the situation from a different professional perspective than the lawyer, and from a child-focussed, rather than a party-focussed perspective. The lawyer may learn about some aspects of the client's behaviour for the first time. Clients are often selective in a self-report to their own lawyers. Information in the opposing party's pleadings and affidavits may be supported by the assessment, having been verified by independent collateral sources unavailable to the lawyer, but interviewed by the assessor.

Pay attention to how your attitude to the client's position and to the client as a person is taking shape. Involvement of the client in the origin of the dispute tends to influence the lawyer's response to the assessment report. Consult the assessor to clarify and amplify any areas of the report that remain unclear or of which further understanding is needed before reviewing the report with the client. Assessors will often go into more detail in conversation than they are prepared to put into writing. Be alert to any parts of the report in which language is used such as, "it would seem fair to suggest that . . . .", or "it seems reasonable to believe that . . . .". Those portions particularly should be discussed with the assessor to learn the unstated information that was relied upon in making those assertions. The assessor will have had reasons for making such statements in the report, but believes it to be imprudent to put all of those reasons in writing.

2. REVIEWING THE REPORT WITH THE CLIENT

The report may have been sent directly to the parties by the assessor. If not, make sure that the client receives a copy of the report, preferably a few days before you meet to discuss it with him or her. Whether the recommendations are supportive of the client's position or not, the report may discuss some painful issues in the client's marriage or childhood. It is considerate to allow the client a day or two of privacy to absorb those and not have to confront any uncomfortable issues for the first time in front of the lawyer. A cooling off period may result in a more constructive discussion of the report.

Even though a competent assessor will have reminded your client that the focus of the custody/access assessment is the future well-being of the children, it can be very difficult for a parent to receive a recommendation contrary to his or her position. Emotional reactions will range from sadness to disbelief, and sometimes anger. Behaviour will range from resignation and acquiescence, to threats of retaliatory treatment of the assessor.

Lawyers influence the client's reaction by their own response to the report recommendations and the client's upset. The lawyer who responds to a negative report with an instantly antagonistic and litigious stance, such as, "We won't take this lying down; we will take this to court", can make things worse and may continue to obscure a real look by the client at the children's well-being. If you stay calmly supportive of the client during the first reactive outburst and help the client to focus concretely on the recommendations, an opportunity is created to examine the situation responsibly.

If the client is very upset and angry, the anger needs to be defused in order for the client to be able to consider and discuss the report constructively. If you avoid dealing with the anger, try to ignore it, and get down to the factual issues immediately, the anger will impede the client's ability to make reasoned decisions and to give informed and coherent instructions about the conduct of the custody/access case.

No lawyer relishes interviews with emotional and angry clients, but the lawyer needs to be part of the client's reaction to the assessment. Too long a delay between delivery of the report and the first post-assessment interview deprives the lawyer of a valuable opportunity to see the client with his or her guard down, and thereby take some measure of whether or not the assessor's version of the client is more accurate than the client's self-report.

If the client vents first, and mainly, to friends and relatives, then the lawyer receives the client's reaction overlaid by the advice of these non-professionals. It becomes harder, rather than easier, to help the client examine his or her position in light of the assessment if the lawyer sidesteps this potentially uncomfortable interview.

3. DEALING WITH THE UPSET CLIENT

The first post-assessment interview with the client provides a context to the client for reaction and response to the assessment in which the lawyer can help the client to manage the emotional reaction through the management and direction of the interview. For the lawyer the task is to differentiate between the client's reactions to the recommendations and to what was said about them and how it was said. If the client feels unfairly treated in the assessment process, he or she may be unable to see even quite sensible recommendations as valid. The lawyer's empathetic listening and confident management of the client's reaction will help the client approach the report more constructively.

(a) The Use of Active Listening

Reacting to the content of the client's comments will not help to calm the client so much as will speaking to the feelings behind the content. Indicate that you hear the client's worry about the implications that the report has for the success of the client's position in negotiations or at trial. Tell the client that you hear his or her fear, anger, disappointment or bewilderment. Sometimes you will need to sit quietly while the client cries, and allow time for that if it is needed. In acknowledging the client's disappointment, or anger, or relief, the lawyer is not there to be the client's therapist, so it is neither the lawyer's responsibility nor appropriate role to devote the whole interview to listening while the client "ventilates". There is a fine decision to be made as to how long to indulge the expression of emotion. Quietly, but firmly, focus the client on the concrete in order to provide the information that helps you to help the client. Tell the client that this is what you are doing.

(b) Remind the Client About the Function of the Assessment

Remind the client that the role of the assessor is to understand the needs of the children and the strengths and weaknesses that the adult parties bring to the task of parenting, and to make a recommendation to the court as to how the needs of the children might best be met by these parties. Remind the client that the assessor is not advocating for either of the adult parties, but for the interests of the children.

(c) Focus on the Reality of the Situation

Using constructive confrontation the lawyer might say: "What I hear you saying is that you are upset that the assessor has said that you used to drink very heavily, and were convicted of impaired driving, and you think that was an unnecessary revelation. But is that the same thing as your reaction to the recommendation that Jonathan keep on living with Bill?" The next query might be, "And is that information in the report in fact true?" If the client responds with a variation on the theme of, "Yes, but . . . ." the lawyer might then respond, "So part of what you are upset at is seeing this in print."

(d) Help the Client Determine What He or She is Upset About

The exercise of constructive confrontation helps the client narrow down the global emotional reaction to concrete objections to the report. If the client feels unfairly treated it will be hard to address details of the report because the client will presume that the recommendations arise from a biased viewpoint. Being unhappy about the recommendations in a well and fairly done assessment is different from the frightened reaction of a client to an unfairly and poorly made assessment.

(e) Reassure the Client that the Assessment is Not the Final Judgment

The lawyer could tell the client: "This is your first chance to respond to the report, and I hear that you are upset and disappointed with the recommendation. Remember that the final result will either be settled between you and the other party, or will be decided by the judge. The report is not a judgment, it is a recommendation, and we can talk about challenging it later if you wish. The issue is not so much what was said in the report, but was it well done, were you fairly treated, are the facts stated in it correct, and how are we going to respond to it?"

This focus for the lawyer's response to the client serves to bring the interview back to the lawyer's function as the client's lawyer.

(f) Have the Client List His or Her Concerns

Often at this point in the post-assessment interview the client is in enough control to state specific concerns about how the assessment was done, and about the particulars of the recommendations. If the client is still very emotional, then the lawyer might wish to consider the following device and say: "We've come as far as we can today. You need some time to absorb this. We'll make another appointment now, and between now and then I need you to make two lists. One is a list of the things you are unhappy about in the way the assessment was done, and the second is a list of the things you are unhappy about in the recommendations themselves. Bring those two lists with you to our next meeting when we will begin to make plans for how we will approach the rest of the case." The next appointment should be set for a date that will give the client enough time to complete the assigned task.

Giving an assignment helps the client focus on his or her response, and this in turn helps the client manage the emotional reaction by channelling it into action. This empowerment technique gives the client a sense that there is something he *can* do in a situation in which he feels powerless.

The lawyer will continually narrow the discussion toward concreteness. Some clients can do this in one session. Some will need two, and a few may need three. It is wise, even if the client can synopsize all of the objections to the methodology and to the recommendations in one meeting, not to take firm instructions at the first post-assessment interview.

Give the client an opportunity to reflect away from the influence of the moment in the lawyer's office, before giving instructions.

4. MARSHALLING THE DETAILS FOR RESPONSE

Eventually it will be possible to determine precisely what parts of the report the client finds upsetting: the nature of all or some of the recommendations; that the assessment was in fact poorly done; that the client is seeing himself in print and not liking the picture, and therefore wanting to blame the assessor for drawing the picture; or that the assessor in fact missed the client's point, or relied upon inaccurate or incomplete information in arriving at the recommendations.

Just because the client is upset does not, and should not, suggest that the role of the client's lawyer is to refuse to consider the recommendations and the reasons behind them, or to support a "litigate-to-win-at-any-costs" approach, or to refuse to negotiate. It does not necessarily mean that the assessor's recommendation was wrong. The lawyer's role goes beyond sympathetic listening. Reality-testing is an important aspect of the lawyer's role in examining the report with the client.

It may be of assistance to lawyer and client alike to review the report with the assessor face to face. Some assessors routinely meet with the parties individually or together at the conclusion of the assessment, either just at, or just before, the delivery of the report. Others prefer a different approach and do not meet the parties again unless requested to do so. Most assessors are prepared to meet after the report has been delivered.

The lawyer's attendance at the meeting is recommended on several grounds: it keeps the meeting from being one in which the party becomes abusive toward the assessor; it allows an opportunity to evaluate objectively the client's complaints about the assessment and the assessor's fairness and thoroughness. It reduces the opportunity for the client later to indulge unchallenged in selective recall about what the assessor did and did not say or do; and it provides an opportunity for the lawyer to evaluate how the assessor handles questioning, and might function as a witness in the case.

The client might say, for example, upon initial review of the report, that the assessor did not interview relevant collateral sources, such as a particular friend or family member. When queried in the meeting on this point the assessor may reply that the collateral was not consulted because in fact the name was never provided by the client, or that the client forbade contact with that collateral, or that the assessor gave up further attempts after four or five unsuccessful ones to contact that person.

Obtain clarification of the points in the report that trouble the client. Inform the assessor of any factual errors and request that they be corrected.

Clarify whether the facts stated incorrectly in the report were relied upon in reaching the conclusions in the recommendation. For instance, a statement that the client was 16 at marriage, instead of the actual age of 26, may have been evidence relied upon by the assessor in drawing conclusions about the effects of a youthful marriage that affected parenting (in which case a factual correction might lead to modification of the recommendations) or it might merely have been a typographical error in the final draft of the report.

If the assessor was fair and thorough, he or she will be able to correct factual mistakes and acknowledge their implications, and discuss the recommendations and the reasons for making them without becoming defensive. The assessor can often be supportive of the client's reaction. The client needs to feel that the lawyer and the assessor are supportive of the client as a *person* whether or not there is uncritical support for the client's point of view.

Even if the assessment recommendation was supportive of the client's stated position, a thorough review of the report with client and assessor is useful, if not crucial. The lawyer has an ongoing responsibility beginning with the first reading of the report to evaluate whether the client has in fact been fairly or unfairly served by the approach and methods of the assessor. Discussion with the assessor, either in the presence of the client or not, can help to evaluate that.

In most cases, no matter what the custody recommendation, the report will advocate that the children continue to have contact with both parents. The client, if still very bitter about the separation, may have great difficulty coming to terms with the access recommendations made concerning the other party. The other party may not acquiesce to a recommendation that the client have custody of the children. In either case, a joint meeting with client and assessor will assist in advising the client as to the strengths and weaknesses of his position should the matter proceed to trial. Even the party whose custodial position has been favoured by the assessment may need to make compromises to arrive at settlement.

It is important to help the client whose custodial position was favoured by the report to avoid the "Hah, hah! We won!" reaction which will only make negotiations more difficult. Recommendations in the report may concern therapy or child services needed. The post-assessment conference is a good time to obtain some guidance and elaboration from the assessor concerning those details so that, if satisfactory to the client, they might be instituted prior to trial.

5. FORMULATING AN APPROACH

Once both lawyer and client understand the basis for the recommendations, the task becomes one of formulating an approach to those issues in light of the data and the recommendations embodied in the report. This is a two-stage process. First of all, evaluate the strength of the client's stated positions on access and the various aspects of custody in light of the report and of the other evidence that has been gathered. Then guide the client through his own evaluation of the desired outcome in light of the report and other evidence. Only then can the client give instructions from a basis of full information, part of which is the lawyer's intelligent prediction of how the client might fare at trial on those issues.

The client may be prepared to settle on the basis of the assessment recommendations or some variation of them. If so, an offer to settle is drafted, or negotiations undertaken with the other party's counsel.

Be cautious of assuming that the client will automatically oppose settlement on some basis similar to recommendations which are contrary to his stated position. Clients usually react negatively to a recommendation that the other party have either custody or more access than is the client's stated position. However, once the client has been helped to hear all that the report is saying about the basis for the recommendations as focussed on the needs of the children, particularly when he or she feels fairly treated, the client may in fact be relieved. If the assessment process was fair and full and competent; if the client feels listened to and respected; if the positive as well as negative aspects of each party's parenting capacities are portrayed fairly; if the report is phrased in a way that preserves the dignity of both parties as people, then the disappointed party may be able to use the report as a way of giving up or modifying his initial stance while saving face:

> Well, if the assessor thinks Sheila can manage Jennifer and Todd even though she is working full time, and if Jennifer is really as settled there as the report says, I guess I can live with Sheila having custody. But I want to see the children often and be able to have real influence on how they grow up.

New, modified positions may emerge. The lawyer's task is to facilitate that process by helping the client identify his real interests behind the positions. "I want custody" may mean, "I want some say in how my children are educated"; "I want to be sure I'll be able to have time with my children to influence the development of their attitudes and values"; "I want my family to be able to see the children often"; and so on.

A statement such as: "I do not want him/her to have access to the children," may mean, "I don't like Dad's new girlfriend"; "I'm afraid Marjorie will use her time with Ricky to turn him against me"; "I worry that Beth will feel neglected if her mom's boyfriend and his kids are always there when Beth visits"; "I can't believe that Dave won't drink and drive with the children in the car"; or, "I get lonesome when the children are away from me".

Helping the client to focus on the real interests behind the stated categorical positions is, of course, an ongoing task with every client from the intake interview onward. Post-assessment is a stage at which to be sure to repeat the process yet again. The exercise may well suggest avenues of negotiation through which it may be possible for the parties to salvage some overlapping common interests and either settle the case or narrow the issues.

Some reports are inadequately framed to assist with the particulars of implementation. Recommendations such as "Margaret and Frank should remain with their father subject to access by their mother", are not specific enough. Comments such as, "The parents must stop fighting about child related issues", state the obvious but are not helpful. A three-way meeting or conference call among both counsel and the assessor may be useful in eliciting concrete suggestions for implementation of the recommendations if settlement appears possible. If, however, the parties are not giving signs of settling the parenting issues, and the recommendations are vague, then one or both lawyers should request the assessor to make the recommendations more specific. Care must be exercised in making such a request (preferably in writing to preserve a record of what was asked of the assessor) not to suggest to the assessor how the lawyer wants the specifics to favour one parent over the other. Vetting such a request for specifics through opposing counsel will forestall them from later alleging that the assessor was influenced to "change the report" and that the entire assessment should therefore be impeached for bias.

Whether or not the stated position of one's own client has been supported by the recommendations, a competent assessment provides useful insights. The professional approach of the assessor is different from that of the lawyer. Lawyers, in their concern to learn about legally relevant facts, may miss out the facts that influence the client's motivation and performance in matters regarding the children. These clinically relevant facts are of significance in the children's future family restructuring and must be taken into account.

If a parent whose custodial position was not supported by the assessment can be helped to give up or modify his or her position to reach a compromise that will meet the parenting needs of the children, while still saving face, then access is less likely to be used as a forum in which to wage an ongoing war.

The reality of a custody dispute is that any agreement, minutes of settlement, or court order reflects two things: first, what will work to reduce or eliminate the conflict now so that people can get on with their lives; second, what is anticipated to be the optimum feasible arrangement for raising the children to adulthood. It will, of necessity, involve compromise, agreed to or imposed from without, as no other solution is likely available.

If one party were to win and take all, the child would be the inevitable loser. The family is in a new situation. The child's parenting needs remain the same, but the parenting will be done differently because the parents live apart. What each parent wants and would like the situation to be, is something each parent cannot have entirely in the reality of the situation. The extent to which the lawyers can help the parents to modify their initial positions is a measure for future healthy functioning of the disrupted and restructured parent/child relationships.

6. USING THE ASSESSMENT IN PRE-TRIAL CONFERENCES

In Ontario, when matters remain unresolved and are noted on the ready list for trial, the court sets a date and time for counsel to meet with a judge of that court to determine whether settlement is possible. A judge who participates in such a pretrial conference, unless in rare instances counsel both consent to the contrary, will not be the judge who conducts the trial of the matter.

The conference is held with the parties usually either present or available to be consulted and involved at an appropriate moment. When an independent custody/access assessment report has been filed with the court the judge will often wish to discuss it as part of that conference.

The actual attendance of the assessor at the pre-trial conference to function as a resource for the judge may be appreciated by the court in cases of intense dispute between the parties. The assessor can assist the court by clarifying and expanding on specifics of the recommendations and reasons for making them. Counsel are usually very frank with the court in such conferences about the strengths and weaknesses of their respective cases.

Suggestions made by the presiding judge as to how he or she would rule if conducting the hearing often form the basis for settlement. The pre-trial conference provides cogent "handwriting on the wall" that can move even stubborn clients in the direction of settlement, and provides the parties with yet another forum in which their views are listened to. If the judge's recommendations build upon those in the assessment report, the parties are often more inclined to compromise.

Of course, if the assessment was not a full, fair and competent one, or if the judge at the pre-trial conference is impatient, gives signs of being uninterested, or has not read and considered the assessment report and the other documents included in the pre-trial brief, then the momentum that the pre-trial conference can provide is reduced. Counsel's own confidence in the pre-trial process, expressed to the client, will influence how the client will be prepared to use any suggestions the judge might put forward.

8

The Assessor as Witness: Notes for Lawyers

1. ATTENDANCE AT TRIAL
2. PREPARATION FOR EXAMINATION-IN-CHIEF
3. EXAMINATION-IN-CHIEF
4. PREPARATION FOR CROSS-EXAMINATION
5. CROSS-EXAMINATION

1. ATTENDANCE AT TRIAL

If settlement of the custody/access dispute proves impossible, the matter will proceed to trial. The lawyer whose client's position most closely accords with the assessment recommendations will have to consider whether to rely upon the report as evidence on its own, or to call the assessor as witness. Counsel for the disappointed party may require the attendance of the assessor at trial to be cross-examined, in any event.

(a) Ontario Statutory Guidelines

Where the assessment was undertaken pursuant to court order under section 30 of the Ontario Children's Law Reform Act[1], the use of the report at hearing and the attendance of the assessor are dealt with therein as follows:

> (7) The person appointed under subsection (1) shall file his report with the clerk or registrar of the court.

---

1 R.S.O. 1980, c. 68 [as amended S.O. 1982, c. 20].

(8) The clerk or registrar of the court shall give a copy of the report to each of the parties and to counsel, if any, representing the child.

(9) The report mentioned in subsection (7) is admissible in evidence in the application.

(10) Any of the parties, and counsel, if any, representing the child, may require the person appointed under subsection (1) to attend as a witness at the hearing of the application.

In order for both parties to be able to cross-examine the assessor, counsel may request the court to order that each party be allowed to cross-examine at trial as in *Hampel v. Hampel*.[2] Such an order might be sought either when the assessor is appointed under subsection 30(1) or at a later stage in the proceedings. Subsection 30(11) provides:

> Upon motion, the court by order may give such directions in respect of the assessment as the court considers appropriate.

Failing such an order for cross-examination, the party who requests the assessor to appear as witness may be limited to direct examination only,[3] even though the assessor's report is directed to the court.

If the assessment was not undertaken pursuant to an order under the Children's Law Reform Act then, as with any expert witness, the party wishing to call the assessor must serve the report and a summary of the assessor's qualifications on the other party prior to trial in accordance with the applicable Evidence Act. The Ontario Legal Aid Plan, if funding one or both parties, will have required the assessment report to be filed as evidence with the court as a condition of granting financing for the assessment, but this does not preclude calling the assessor as a witness.

(b) Utility of *Viva Voce* Testimony

Calling the assessor to testify can be far more useful to the court than simply filing the report in evidence. The court has an opportunity to form an impression of the assessor's credibility that will affect the weight to be attached to the recommendations. Often assessors say less in their reports than appears in their notes, or that they would be able to express in person. On the witness stand, the assessor can expand on the nature and significance of data gathered, observations made, and the results and interpretation of psychological tests, if any. The theoretical foundations for conclusions drawn from the data can be explored. Effective *viva voce* testimony of the assessor can add weight to the report recommendations. By the same token, skillful cross-examination on procedures and theoretical

---

2 *Hampel v. Hampel* (1983), 31 R.F.L. (2d) 462 (Ont. Dist. Ct.).

3 *Sawyer v. Sawyer* (1984), 23 A.C.W.S. (2d) 550 (Ont. Prov. Ct.).

basis can diminish the weight of the recommendations. Requesting the attendance of the assessor as a witness is therefore not without its risks.

(c) Team Assessments — Special Considerations

Sometimes assessments are referred to family court clinics or other such organizations or individuals that conduct assessments using a team approach. Various aspects of the assessment are allocated to different members of the team. All members of the team discuss the case, and the report will carry the signature of the nominal team leader and the other persons primarily involved in the assessment. Because not all team members will have seen all the individual informants, parties, and children, each will likely have some direct knowledge that the other team members do not.

Counsel must decide whether to call all or only one or two members of the assessment team to testify. That decision can only be made after thorough preparation with each member of the team in order to be sure that the assessor who made a vital observation or received an important admission sought to be introduced for "truth of fact" is called as a witness.

Calling all members of the team to testify is expensive, and prolongs the hearing.[4] Cross-examining counsel will be interested to know whether assessment recommendations were unanimous, or opinion was divided.

An assessment team approaches the situation from several different professional perspectives simultaneously. However, responsible individual assessors also use colleagues in the other mental health disciplines on a consultation basis to clarify their own thinking, as needed.

2. PREPARATION FOR EXAMINATION-IN-CHIEF

This chapter is not intended to be a comprehensive text on how to conduct an examination-in-chief of an expert witness. The bibliography lists several useful texts and articles that touch on that subject. This section outlines a few points of particular relevance when the expert witness is a custody/access assessor.

(a) The Factual Basis

Reading the report and learning the facts relied upon by the assessor

---

4 For an overview of the considerations involved in deciding which team member(s) should testify, see G.M. Scarcella "Expert Child Abuse Witnesses: Practical Considerations (An Agency Perspective)," *Family Law In the Provincial Courts (Family Division)* Toronto: Canadian Bar Association, Ontario, Continuing Legal Education, 1986), pp. 20-21.

is the first stage of preparation. The assessor's recommendations are based on data obtained in whole or in part by interviews with the parties, the children, and other collateral informants such as teachers, other involved professionals, friends of the family, and relatives. Each person will have told the assessor about various acts performed and statements made by one or both of the parents, or perhaps the children, which they have themselves observed. The assessor will have arrived at an evaluation of the credibility of each informant, and of each detail of information. This is based, in part, on the consistency of patterns of parenting behaviour and other actions and attitudes of the parties that emerge as diverse information is gathered.

Ascertain the sources of information relied upon by the assessor, and consider calling the informants as witnesses to prove the data independently. Verify the information with the informants. Any discrepancies between the informants' "will-say statements" and the assessor's understanding of their information should be reviewed with the assessor. Significant discrepant testimony by a "collateral" can form the basis for a hypothetical question allowing the assessor to comment on whether the recommendations for custody and access would be different if the facts were other than as noted by the assessor.

Laying the factual foundations for the assessor's recommendations is vital. Although statements made to the assessor are admissible in evidence through the assessor if they form part of the basis for the opinion,[5] failure to prove those facts independently will reduce the weight which the recommendations might otherwise carry. The trier of fact needs to be able to reach his or her own determination of the facts and of the credibility of collateral informants relied upon by the assessor. As John Sopinka states:

> The key to the problem is that the court must be given the substratum of fact upon which the opinion is based. If the substratum is rejected then the opinion is rejected.[6]

In *Boody v. Boody*,[7] Perras D.C.J. said:

> It is not intended that the assessment usurp the trial process where the parties do not agree with the assessor's assessment and recommendations.

---

5 In *Official Solicitor v. K.*, [1965] A.C. 201 at 242 (H.L.), the court held that experts' reports containing or based on hearsay are admissible. Lord Devlin said specifically:

> An inflexible rule against hearsay is quite unsuited to the exercise of a paternal and administrative jurisdiction. The jurisdiction itself is more ancient than the rule against hearsay and I see no reason why that rule should now be introduced into it.

6 J. Sopinka *The Trial of An Action* (Toronto: Butterworths, 1981), p. 70.

7 (1983), 32 R.F.L. (2d) 396, at 400 (Ont. Dist. Ct.).

It is obvious that where assessor's reports are consistent with the facts established at trial and the law pertaining to those facts, they will be given considerable weight. The courts, however, will not routinely accept them. They have been successfully challenged in the past.

(b) Theoretical Basis

Counsel needs to know the theoretical basis for the recommendation. The assessor should be able to suggest reputable articles and texts in current use supporting the theories relied upon in forming her professional opinion. Reference to such sources in chief will add further weight to the recommendations.

If the assessor is also able to alert counsel to current theories, articles and texts contrary to those he or she relies upon, they may be obtained, referred to in chief, and the assessor asked to state why she does not follow them in the case at hand. Cross-examining counsel may either refer to such texts, or call the evidence of another mental health professional as on-side consultant to state that such theories and approaches are to be preferred to the ones adopted by the assessor. Just as contrary facts are better dealt with in chief, so too with contrary theories.

(c) Apparent Weaknesses in the Assessment

Any elements of the assessment process which appear to be missing should be reviewed with the assessor prior to trial, and the assessor prepared to state in evidence why the gaps exist (a collateral may have declined to be interviewed, or a party may have cancelled a home visit, for example). The assessor should clarify what steps were taken to close the gap(s), and be prepared to state as well what, if any, effect the assessor believes these deficiencies had on his or her ability to come to an understanding of the needs of the children and the capacities of the parties to meet those needs. Any apparent weaknesses not covered by examination-in-chief will most certainly be met in cross-examination.

The assessor should be prepared to explain the protocol followed in the assessment indicating why and how each facet was carried out. The assessor should know her position on the issues of custody and access and be able to state clearly why she holds that position instead of any other.

(d) Preparing the Assessor as Witness

No matter how many times a particular assessor has appeared in court in the past, counsel should spend some time with the assessor to review the testimony and determine how it will be presented. Brief the assessor in how to address the court, how to frame answers directly and free from jargon, and how to cope with cross-examination. (See Chapter 9, addressed to assessors, for points to be sure to cover with the assessor prior to trial.)

3. EXAMINATION-IN-CHIEF

(a) Qualifying the Expert Witness

The clinician who has been court-ordered to perform an independent custody/access assessment is essentially already over the hurdle of being accepted by that court as an expert witness. Take the time, however, to establish the assessor's credentials thoroughly at the hearing; the object being to have her give opinion evidence on as broad a front as possible.

An expert witness is one who, by education and experience, is qualified to form his or her own professional opinion in a branch of an art or science in which persons without such special training and experience are unable to form accurate opinions or arrive at valid conclusions.

Lord President Cooper described the role of the expert witness in *Davie v. Magistrates of Edinburgh*,[8] saying:

> Their duty is to furnish the Judge or jury with the necessary scientific criteria for testing the accuracy of their conclusions, so as to enable the Judge or jury to form their own independent judgment by the application of these criteria to the facts proved in evidence.

Ziskin and Faust comment as follows:

> If the subject is one of common knowledge, and the facts can be intelligibly described to the jury, and they can form a reasonable opinion for themselves, the opinion of an expert will be unnecessary. Thus, expert opinion may or may not be admissible, depending upon whether the subject matter is within common experience or whether it is a special field where the opinion of a skilled and experienced expert will assist, and *be of greater validity* than that of the ordinary juryman.
>
> The mere fact that a witness may have more knowledge about the subject of inquiry or may understand it better than the jury, does not necessarily justify his giving opinion instead of fact.[9]

The Supreme Court of Canada dealt with the issue of non-expert opinion evidence in *Graat v. R.*[10] wherein, after a review of the authorities on the issue of non-expert opinions, Dickson J. concluded:

---

8 [1953] S.C. 34, at 40.

9 J. Ziskin and D. Faust, *Coping with Psychiatric and Psychological Testimony*, 4th ed. (Venice, California: Law and Psychology Press, 1988) vol. 1, p. 2

10 [1982] 2 S.C.R. 819, at 835 and 836-37. The issue in this case was whether the

> Except for the sake of convenience there is little, if any, virtue, in any distinction resting on the tenuous, and frequently false, antithesis between fact and opinion. The line between "fact" and "opinion" is not clear.
>
> . . . .
>
> I agree with Professor Cross [citing Sir Rupert Cross, *Evidence*, (5th ed., 1979)] (at p. 443) that "The exclusion of opinion evidence on the ultimate issue can easily become something of a fetish." I can see no reason in principal or in common sense why a lay witness should not be permitted to testify in the form of an opinion if, by doing so, he is able more accurately to express the facts he perceived.
>
> I accept the following passage from Cross as a good statement of the law as to the cases in which non-expert opinion is admissible.
>
>> When, in the words of an American judge, "the facts from which a witness received an impression were too evanescent in their nature to be recollected, or too complicated to be separately and distinctly narrated", a witness may state his opinion or impression. He was better equipped than the jury to form it, and it is impossible for him to convey an adequate idea of the premises on which he acted to the jury. . . .
>>
>> There is nothing in the nature of a closed list of cases in which non-expert opinion evidence is admissible. . . .

File the assessor's *curriculum vitae* with the court as an exhibit, and then lead the assessor/witness through his or her education (both initial professional qualification and continuing education), practical training, length and type of relevant work experience, courses taught, books and articles written, papers delivered at conferences, and memberships in professional societies and organizations. Establish in which subject areas the assessor has testified as an expert witness on prior occasions, and in which courts. If opposing counsel attempts to cut the process short by an admission of expert status, beware. His objective, in the absence of being able to forestall the assessor's qualification as an expert at all, is to define the range of expertise as narrowly as possible.

(b) Counsel's Task

The court is free to accept or reject even uncontradicted opinion evidence because "[t]he parties have invoked the decision of a judicial tribunal and not an oracular pronouncement by an expert".[11] No matter how eminently qualified the assessor; no matter how fair and thorough

---

opinion of laymen (police officers) as opposed to experts (such as medical doctors) was admissible to prove the fact of impairment by alcohol, and the Supreme Court of Canada concluded that it was.

11 *Davie v. Magistrates of Edinburgh*, *supra* note 8, at 40. Closer to home, the British Columbia Court of Appeal held in *Grant v. Grant* (1982), 25 R.F.L. (2d) 386 (B.C. C.A.),

the assessment; the professional opinions expressed in the report and recommendations are persuasive rather than binding. The task for counsel in examination-in-chief is to guide the presentation of the assessor's testimony so as to enhance its persuasion.

(c) Timing of the Assessor's Testimony

Trial judges generally extend great courtesy to assessors and other expert witnesses. Counsel will therefore usually be given wide latitude as to when the assessor's testimony will be received. Assessors should be able to expect the cooperation of counsel in scheduling their testimony to minimize disruption of their office schedules. Attending at court is frustrating for witnesses because it can be hard for counsel to predict with accuracy the hour when testimony will begin and end. Experienced witnesses know to bring a book, knitting, or a brief case with them to fill the unavoidable waiting, but counsel should try to set as firm a starting time as possible. The trial judge will often agree to receive an expert witness's evidence out of sequence, perhaps interrupting the other party's case, or in the middle of the evidence of a lay witness, as necessary.

Scheduling expert evidence first thing in the morning can be a good choice because everyone is fresh and able to deal better with complex evidence. Chambers conferences may delay the start of court for the day, but judges will often keep such meetings brief if advised that an expert witness is standing by. Immediately after the lunch recess can be a good time, in that it gives counsel and the witness an opportunity for last minute preparation and affords a definite time. The advantages may be offset, however, by the torpor that can affect judge and counsel alike following too heavy a lunch. Knowing the lunch habits of the trial judge and opposing counsel can be part of trial planning strategy.

The convenience of witnesses aside, the assessor's testimony may be more effective if it comes later rather than earlier in the case for the party

---

that a trial judge was entitled to weigh the expert's opinion in the light of all the circumstances of the case, and reject some of the opinions if he or she considered that it would be in the best interests of the children to do so. As Anderson J.A. stated at p. 393:

> A trial judge may accept or reject the evidence of any witness in whole or in part. He will not lightly reject the evidence of experts, who, by reason of their training and experience, have specialized knowledge in certain fields. He can, as here, however, consider the opinions given in the light of all the circumstances of the case. The trial judge reviewed all of the facts and reached the conclusion that, in the best interests of the child, he must reject some of the opinions offered by the experts. In my opinion, not only was he entitled to reject those opinions, but he was correct in so doing. . . . he was not bound to accept the evidence of any expert witness.

whose position is supported by the assessment recommendations. Such scheduling will have allowed an opportunity to establish the factual basis for the assessment through the testimony of that party and other witnesses, both lay and professional, who were collateral sources of information for the assessor. Then, if the assessor refers to such sources in testimony, the trial judge has a context in which to evaluate the assessor's reliance upon the information provided by those sources. Counsel has an opportunity to use hypothetical questions as a vehicle for the assessor/witness to indicate how, if at all, the assessment recommendations would be affected if testimony discrepant to the information relied upon by the assessor in forming her professional evaluation were to be accepted as fact by the trial judge.

Hypothetical questions are particularly useful when the assessor testifies at the end of the defendant's case, and counsel can, through such questions put to the assessor, try to minimize the impact of the plaintiff's case. If the assessor is effective as a witness, and the plaintiff has no cross-examination or reply evidence that dislodges the points gained, the assessor's testimony provides a strong closing to the case.

(d) Elements of the Assessor's Testimony

Every lawyer will develop his own style and preferred order of approach to the examination-in-chief of an assessor. But ensure that the testimony establishes the facts relied upon, explains the application of theories, and expands on the recommendations. Points to be covered include:

- When and how the assessor became involved.
- The assessor's method.
- The sources of information used by the assessor.
- Where, when, and under what circumstances the assessor met each of the parties and the children.
- The kinds of tests, if any, administered.
- What the tests administered purport to measure.
- How the reliability of the tests is gauged.
- The wishes of the children, if any, and how they were taken into account in arriving at the recommendations.
- The strengths and weaknesses of each party as potential custodial parent.
- Whether the assessor was, as a result of the investigation, able to reach definite conclusions regarding custody of and access to the children.
- What the conclusions were.

- How the conclusions were derived from the available data, and how the data in turn support the conclusions.
- The theoretical basis for the conclusions, and why that theory and not another applies in the case before the court.
- What other accepted contemporary authorities would hold the same theoretical approach, and which would not.
- How the opinion of the assessor might be modified if any of the disputed facts were other than the assessor believed them to be (using hypothetical questions).
- Why the custody/access arrangement recommended would meet the children's needs better than the arrangements proposed by the other parent, or any other potential arrangements.

4. PREPARATION FOR CROSS-EXAMINATION

This section is not intended to be a complete guide to the cross-examination of expert witnesses. The bibliography lists several helpful articles and texts that deal with cross-examination generally, the cross-examination of experts, in particular, and some concerns peculiar to custody and other child-related litigation. To date, such works have largely been concerned with the evidence of on-side consultants, but the same ideas and techniques are relevant to the evidence of independent custody/access assessors.

The assessor's independence does not ensure infallibility. Assessors are human beings engaged in a predictive, if not speculative, endeavour by the light of inexact sciences. Their recommendations, although helpful, are not binding; their evidence is open to challenge. This part of the chapter addresses concerns about fairness, thoroughness and expertise that are common to cross-examinations of all assessors of all professional backgrounds.

(a) Reading the Report

A thorough critical reading of the report is the first stage in preparing for cross-examination of the assessor. It can be very helpful to engage the services of a mental health professional skilled in assessment as an on-side consultant to review the report and suggest avenues of challenge. Such a consultant should be able to suggest cogent articles and texts for use in the cross-examination and alert you to theoretical approaches which differ from that adopted by the assessor. The consultant could testify at trial as to the weaknesses of the assessor's method and approach; and to the wide credence given to articles and texts which take a different approach than the assessor does.

When reading the report preparing to challenge it, the questions to keep in mind are:

- Was the investigation thorough? Or are there gaps in the data?
- Is the assessment fair? Or is there demonstrable bias in method, conclusions, or expression?
- Does the data support the recommendations? Or are other recommendations equally supportable by the data?

Where the answers to these questions cannot be determined from the report itself, consult the assessor. Sometimes counsel may consider examining the assessor for discovery prior to trial.[12] Usually assessors are prepared to discuss their methods and conclusions with all counsel, making discovery unnecessary. Counsel who ask, rather than demand or attack, will find assessors very cooperative.

An exception to this will be the assessor's reluctance to quote either the children or collaterals word for word. Information which is highly inflammatory, if it was not able to be confirmed, will certainly not be attributed

12 Rule 31.10(1) of the Rules of Civil Procedure of Ontario provides as follows:

> The court may grant leave, on such terms respecting costs and other matters as are just, to examine for discovery any person who there is reason to believe has information relevant to a material issue in the action, other than an expert engaged by or on behalf of a party in preparation for contemplated or pending litigation.

The rule continues in Rule 31.10(2) as follows:

> An order under subrule (1) shall not be made unless the court is satisfied that,
> (a) the moving party has been unable to obtain the information from other persons whom the moving party is entitled to examine for discovery, or from the person he or she seeks to examine;
> (b) it would be unfair to require the moving party to proceed to trial without having the opportunity of examining the person; and
> (c) the examination will not,
> (i) unduly delay the commencement of the trial of the action,
> (ii) entail unreasonable expense for the other parties, or
> (iii) result in unfairness to the person the moving party seeks to examine.

The rest of this rule goes on to provide that the party examining the person orally under that rule will serve every other party who attended with a copy of the transcript free of charge, unless the court orders to the contrary, and the examining party is not entitled to recover any costs of the examination, unless the court expressly orders otherwise. According to Rule 31.10(5) the evidence of a person examined under this rule may not be read into evidence at trial under subrule 31.11(1).

The assessor appointed to perform an independent custody/access assessment is not an expert engaged by or on behalf of a party to prepare for the pending litigation.

It is of interest to note that subsection 2(a) of Rule 31.10 would seem to require that the lawyer seeking the information from the assessor first approach the assessor directly for the information sought. Then, if the assessor were to refuse that information, the court would be more inclined to make the order granting leave.

by the assessor to any specific collateral or party. In short, the assessor will attempt to avoid prolonging name-calling, but will acknowledge awareness of the existence of such accusations or unverified statements.

(b) Challenging Thoroughness

Courts have given little weight to assessment recommendations in instances in which the assessment was demonstrated to lack thoroughness.[13] Likewise, the evidence of a mental health professional who has made recommendations as to custody and access, when her role has actually been that of onside consultant having contact with only one party to the dispute, will not carry as much weight as that of the assessor who performs a thorough independent assessment involving both parents, the children, and other collateral information sources.[14]

(i) *Breadth of Information*

Who was interviewed? Was each parent interviewed more than once?

---

13 In *Gauci v. Gauci* (1972), 9 R.F.L. 189, at 193 (Ont. H.C.) Lacouirer J. stated:

> The Court will, of course, treat the opinion of a highly respected child psychiatrist with great respect; however its delicate function in matters of this kind, as well as in other areas, cannot be surrendered or delegated to any expert however qualified. In the decision-making process, such opinion is considered as a helpful factor, to be weighed and assessed along with all other relevant evidence. After a lengthy trial, and a thorough evaluation of the issues, the decision of the Court on the child's welfare will be based on more complete and reliable information than that available to Dr. Goldstein after an hour-long interview with the plaintiff, her son and her common-law partner.

In *Mason v. Mason* (1985), 7 F.L.R.R. 136 (Ont. H.C.) the court-appointed assessor's recommendation was not followed because the assessor had failed to consider the child's relationship with the mother's new spouse.

In *More v. Primeau*; *Primeau v. More* (1978), 2 R.F.L. (2d) 254 (Ont. C.A.), the court did not follow the recommendation of a child psychiatrist on the basis that the psychiatrist had difficulty relating to one of the parties and her report was found to be partial (that is biased), incomplete, and based on inaccurate premises.

In *Solnik v. Solnik* (1983), 41 O.R. (2d) 427 (H.C.) affirmed (1983), 44 O.R. (2d) 684 (C.A.) the court refused to adopt the conclusions of two psychiatrists testifying as on-side expert witnesses for the mother. Their recommendation that the mother have custody was founded on a diagnosis that the children were suffering a separation-anxiety disorder. The diagnosis was made, the court pointed out, without their having had available to them certain evidence about how the children behaved with their father.

14 In *Olver v. Olver* (1987) 6 R.F.L. (3d) 334 (Ont. C.A.), Grange J.A. overturned a custody decision of the Master, who had relied upon the report of the mother's on-side consultant instead of the report of a representative of the Official Guardian who had considered the matter independently, involving all parties. The mother's on-side consultant had seen only the mother and had never consulted the father, nor seen the father and the children together in the father's home.

Were the children interviewed? Was there a home visit to each home proposed for the children? Were the children observed interacting with each parent? Were the new partners, spouses and significant others of the parents involved? Were other appropriate collateral sources of independent information consulted? Was the school consulted? Was relevant medical information obtained? Did the assessor review the pleadings and affidavits? If the assessor was a psychologist, were appropriate psychometric and projective tests performed to evaluate the proposed care givers and the children? Were such tests scored and interpreted by persons qualified to do so? How long did the assessment take to complete?

Thoroughness has two facets. The obvious one is that both sides of the dispute are evaluated on the basis of as much information as possible, and their plans for parenting are considered in the context of the specific needs of the children. The other facet is that a thorough, reliable custody/access assessment takes time.

(ii) *Time Devoted to Assessment*

A single interview with each parent and one meeting with each child is insufficient. When custody/access assessments begin, all parties are anxious to present the best possible version of themselves and their case to the assessor. Everyone is on his best behaviour. If the assessor arrives at conclusions about a parent or child on the basis of only one meeting, or a number of meetings over too short a time span, the data gathered is unreliable.

On the other hand, if the assessment has been allowed to unfold gradually over a period of several weeks, or even two or three months, the behaviour of the parties begins to revert to normal. They resume living their lives and cannot long remain as frozen tableaux of "ideal parents".

While the assessment that does not take enough time may well be superficial, there can be difficulties as well with the assessment that takes too much time. An assessor who requires several months for the assessment may prolong a placement of the children that is less than beneficial for them, or perhaps even one which maintains a status quo of neglect or emotional or physical abuse. If the assessor allows a significant lapse of time between the completion of the investigative phase and the writing and delivery of the report, then as the parties and children go on with their lives, the assessment may describe and formulate recommendations on the basis of circumstances which no longer exist. If a lengthy time span intervenes between the report and the pre-trial conference or hearing, consider asking the assessor to update the report prior to such proceedings so that it remains relevant. Changed facts and circumstances can result in changed recommendations. The time to discover that is prior to the hearing and not during the assessor's appearance in the court room.

(c) Challenging Fairness

Bias or unfairness are never intentional, nor even conscious, on the part of reputable assessors who will, if aware of a bias concerning the case, refuse the referral. But the possibility of bias should be considered in weighing any assessment report as a possible avenue of challenge.

(i) *Is it Balanced?*

Does the report acknowledge strengths as well as weaknesses of all parties? Is the report expressed in inflammatory or judgmental language? Is one parent described as stubborn, but the other as willing to persevere?[15] Or is the language balanced, contained and fair, even if the report is more critical of one parent than of the other? Does the report take into account all relevant data? Has the assessor considered all the feasible alternatives for custody and access, and weighed the implications of each alternative for the children? Is the information correct and complete? If incomplete, were reasonable steps taken to attempt completeness? Are omissions acknowledged by the assessor? Has approximately equal time been spent with each parent and each set of collaterals suggested by the parents? Are conclusions stated as information with no indication of the factual basis for such conclusions? Was sufficient rapport established to ensure co-operation of the parties on an open and honest basis? Was the assessor's conduct of the assessment consistent with her methodology as explained to the parties and their counsel?

(ii) *Assumptions About Abnormality*

Ziskin and Faust suggest that there is potential for unfairness if behaviours are described in the report as abnormalities when they are, in fact, the expected norm for the abnormal situation in which the parties find themselves. If someone is described as "appearing guarded" in an interview with the assessor, wouldn't anyone in that situation?[16]

---

15 Ziskin and Faust, *supra*, note 9, vol. III, p. 18 suggest a few other examples of language that might be considered judgmental — could "guarded and suspicious" be reframed as "cautious and thoughtful"; "lacks affect" as "stoical" or "cool"; or "over-involved" as "enthusiastic"? Could "litigious paranoia", they ask, be described as old fashioned "stick-to-it-iveness"?

16 Ziskin and Faust, *supra*, note 9, vol. III, p. 17.

Does the report acknowledge that marital discord, custody and access disputes, and undergoing assessments are difficult for people? A party's depression or anxiety observed by the assessor might be a reaction to the party's current difficult experiences. That has a different implication for future parenting abilities than a depression or anxiety that is an enduring feature of that individual's personality. Has the assessor determined whether such emotional states are enduring or reactive? Have unspoken assumptions about the observed mood states biased the interpretation of clinical interviews or tests?

(iii) *Culture and Values Issues*

Is there a possibility that bias has crept in because the culture, value system, lifestyle, or religion of one parent is either closely congruent with, or entirely foreign or antithetical to that of the assessor? The assessor would likely have declined to act in a case in which a party had an antithetical lifestyle or value system about which the assessor was aware in advance and felt strong bias. More subtle is the bias that could arise from identification of assessor with one of the parties and the resultant feeling of being "on the same wave length" with the parent. Even if such congruences between assessor and party are in non-contentious areas, an argument might be made that such identification could result in unconscious bias. Counsel would be on firmer ground with such an argument, however, when other areas of the report are open to challenge and not just congruence of values.[17]

---

17 *More v. Primeau*; *Primeau v. More*, *supra*, note 13, was a custody contest between a natural mother and a stepmother. The parties were assessed by a child psychiatrist who observed the child and both of the parties. The evidence of the child psychiatrist favoured the child's stepmother over the French Canadian natural mother. Blair J.A. stated:

> I conclude that there is little in common between these two ladies, and that, in a realistic sense, one could not easily communicate with the other. Dr. Bijoor is precise and orderly, reflecting her distinctive Anglo-Indian background. It seems clear to me that she would have the greatest difficulty in achieving a rapport with a vivacious French Canadian lady like the defendant. On the other hand, it would be easy to see that she would relate easily, as she obviously did, to the plaintiff. In no sense do I wish to be construed as suggesting that the conclusions of Dr. Bijoor are biased or injudicious, but I have been forced to conclude that she was simply unable to comprehend fully the position of the defendant. (p. 268)
>
> ....
>
> My opinion is not altered by the psychiatrist's report. For reasons already given, I consider it partial, incomplete and based on inaccurate premises. It would be, I think, unsafe to proceed solely upon it. (p. 270)

(iv) *Habits of Attitude*

Inquire of other lawyers who have had assessments done by this clinician whether there are any patterns which they have observed emerging in the recommendations from case to case. Does this assessor consistently favour fathers over mothers as custodial parents? Does this assessor always recommend in favour of the clients of a particular law firm? Does this assessor recommend joint custody in a majority of cases? Does this assessor frequently recommend against the parent of colour in a mixed race marriage breakdown? Does this assessor tend to support the position of adherents to a particular religion in a mixed religion situation?

(d) Does the Data Support the Recommendations?

> We can predict that the adult most likely suited for this role [custodial parent] is the one, if there be one, with whom the child has already had and continues to have an affectionate bond rather than one of otherwise equal potential who is not yet in a primary relationship with the child. Further, we can predict that the younger the child and the more extended the period of uncertainty or separation, the more detrimental it will be to the child's well-being and the more urgent it becomes even without perfect knowledge to place the child permanently.
>
> Beyond these, our capacity to predict is limited. No one — and psychoanalysis creates no exception — can forecast just what experiences, what events, what changes a child, or for that matter his adult custodian, will actually encounter. Nor can anyone predict in detail how the unfolding development of a child and his family will be reflected in the long run in the child's personality and character formation.[18]

Are the facts upon which the assessor relies in arriving at recommendations supportive of those recommendations? Would the same facts support other recommendations? Was this a clear cut decision, or a coin toss? Is the assessor's opinion strongly held or only slightly favoured over another possible custodial arrangement? Would a theory in current professional use which differs from that espoused by the assessor have yielded a different conclusion if applied to the same set of facts? Has the assessor published any books or articles that contradict the theories she currently relies upon? If this is a team assessment, did all members of the team agree on the recommendations? Or was there a difference of opinion? Why was the difference resolved in the way it was?

Upon what specific data does the assessor rely in arriving at her recommendations? Which informants and information did the assessor accept as credible or reject as lacking credibility? The court may not accord

18 J. Goldstein, A. Freud, and A.J.Solnit, *Beyond the Best Interests of the Child* (New York: The Free Press, 1973), p. 51.

the same credit to the informant or credibility of the information as did the assessor. Was there any particular fact upon which the assessor anchored the opinion? Can the assessor hypothesize the effect of its absence on the recommendation? Can other evidence be called to negate that "fact"?

Assessments are predictive. Assessors gather information looking for patterns of parenting and other behaviour that can indicate likely future parenting behaviour and attitudes. In discerning such patterns has the assessor relied upon verified information? Did the assessor consider all the relevant verified data? Did the assessor reserve final judgment until all relevant data was gathered? Or did the assessor make up her mind early in the process and discount or ignore other relevant, verified data discrepant to that viewpoint? Ziskin and Faust, in *Coping with Psychiatric and Psychological Testimony*, comment:

> . . . by the nature of the manner in which a clinician or observer responds to certain kinds of material (often material that seems to support his views) he can inadvertently encourage the patient or person being observed to produce more of that kind of material.[19]

Is the report expressed in jargon borrowed from another professional field? Has the assessor remained within her own field of competence or has a social worker or psychologist expressed a psychiatric diagnosis? Has a social worker or psychiatrist expressed an opinion interpreting a psychometric or projective test within the exclusive domain of the psychologist?

If the assessor has drawn conclusions about the "bonding" between a child and a parent based on observing them together, were factors surrounding place, time and context of that interaction taken into account? A child may behave very differently in a clinician's office or a strange play room behind a one-way window than he would in his own living room at home. Does the assessor know, for instance, that the child was ill, or had missed its nap just before the observed visit?

5. CROSS-EXAMINATION

The first rule in cross-examining any witness is, "Don't", but if you must,[20] then proceed with caution. Expert witnesses are like loaded firearms — in the hands of the careless or inexperienced they may go off at inauspicious moments.

19 Ziskin and Faust, *supra*, note 9, Vol. 1, p. 90.

20 It is suggested that failure to cross-examine may imply acceptance of the witness's evidence. (Sopinka and Lederman, *The Law of Evidence in Civil Cases* (Toronto: Butterworth's, 1974), pp. 515-516).

In his book, *The Trial of An Action*, John Sopinka states:

> Cross-examination must serve one of three purposes,
> (1) obtain helpful admissions or evidence,
> (2) contradict or impeach the witness,
> (3) create an impression or atmosphere for the judge or jury.[21]

In this chapter the segments concerning challenging thoroughness, fairness, expertise and clinical judgment are equally applicable to all assessors of any professional background. Separate segments address avenues of challenge unique to social work, psychiatry and psychology. Even there, overlap of possibility exists.

In designing cross-examination counsel may find it useful to look at Chapter 2 on choosing an assessor to review the specific areas of expertise unique to each profession. Review the guidelines and requirements in legislation, association handbooks or by-laws applicable to the assessor's profession. Has her conduct of the assessment been in keeping with the standards of practice and the code of ethics of her profession? Have the theories and methods unique to the assessor's profession been appropriately applied in the assessment? Has the assessor kept within the bounds of her own professional expertise? Has her performance of the assessment been a diligent application of the skills available to her?

(a) Challenging the Expertise of the Assessor/Witness

The active phase of cross-examination begins when the assessor/witness is being tendered to the court as an expert. The task for cross-examining counsel is to prevent the giving of opinion evidence at all; in the alternative to restrict its scope; and then to minimize its weight.

In the case of *Catholic Children's Aid Society of Hamilton-Wentworth v. J.C.S.*,[22] Steinberg U.F.C.J. ruled that the "children's services worker" from the applicant agency was not allowed to testify as an expert giving opinion evidence concerning, among other issues, the best interests of the child. That case worker's educational background consisted of one year of university that included introductory courses in psychology and sociology, and a two-year diploma in social services from a College of Applied Arts and Technology. She had also had several in-service training courses during her two years of work with the applicant agency.

The assessor may be qualified in some subject areas but not in others. The assessor's *curriculum vitae* can be obtained well in advance of the

21 Sopinka, *supra*, note 6, p. 70.

22 *Catholic Children's Aid Society of Hamilton-Wentworth v. J.C.S.* (April 3, 1986), Doc. No. C1109-84 (Ont. Unified Fam. Ct.).

hearing (it was probably provided when the assessor was initially appointed) and should be studied prior to the hearing for clues as to vulnerability. In challenging the credentials of the assessor/witness on the areas of her expertise, establish the exact education, training and experience that she has had on each issue for which opinion evidence will be sought.

As pointed out in Chapter 2, each of the three main mental health professions lacks some element that one of the others has. Psychiatrists, for instance, receive their formal professional training as medical doctors dealing with the physical aspects of disease. Their training in family dynamics or child development continues within the medical model.

What education and experience has the assessor/witness in human behaviour, family dynamics, child development, the interpretation of psychological tests, interview techniques, the legal criteria of the best interests of the child, and the other areas of skill and knowledge relevant to custody/access disputes? Was that education at a degree-granting level? Has it been kept current by taking formal courses? By reading? By attending workshops or hearing papers at conferences? Was practical training and experience gained in an appropriately monitored setting by internship, residency or supervised field placements? What specific training and experience has the assessor had in the theory and practice of custody/access assessments? Has any of that assessment practice been supervised? Has most of the assessor's clinical practice involved children? Adults? Families? Mentally ill or mentally healthy clients? Is the assessor engaged in clinical practice, or is she an academic? How long has she been performing assessments?

The usual rule of cross-examination applies to questions challenging the expertise of the assessor/witness — ask no questions to which the answers are not already known, or one risks reinforcing the witness's expertise.

If the assessor is, in fact, well qualified and reputable, consider simply admitting expertise as soon as the witness is tendered for qualification as an expert. This may forestall counsel from leading her through the *curriculum vitae* directing the judge's mind to the strong points along the way. If the document is simply filed with the court it may have less impact. The witness must, however, be qualified anew as to expertise each time she appears before a court, and the judge may therefore require the thorough review of the *curriculum vitae* in any event. If the assessor/witness is accepted by the court as an expert on issues where training and experience are insufficient, there may be grounds for appeal if the ultimate decision of the court is anchored by an opinion of the assessor on those issues.

If, on a given issue, the alleged expertise of the assessor/witness is negated, then she may still be able to state an opinion as a layman. Such an opinion will carry far less weight than if expressed by an expert, and will not likely be admissible in evidence on a legal issue such as "best interests" of the child:

> A non-expert witness cannot, of course, give opinion evidence on a legal issue as, for example, whether or not a person was negligent. That is because such an opinion would not qualify as an abbreviated version of the witnesses factual observations. An opinion that someone was negligent is partly factual, but it also involves the application of legal standards.[23]

An assessor will rarely admit that her recommendation is wrong, so that attacking the opinion itself serves only to allow the assessor to restate and expand upon it. Expert evidence is best dealt with by defining its limits tightly, and once the boundaries are established, nibbling away at the edges and underpinnings.

(b) Helpful Admissions

Custody/access assessors are usually at pains to be fair and frank, both in the report and at trial, concerning the strengths as well as the weaknesses of the party whose custodial position was not supported by the recommendations. There are always positive points, and the assessor will acknowledge them unhesitatingly. To do otherwise would open the evidence to impeachment for bias.

Begin from strength, and go after these positive statements early in the cross-examination before concentrating on efforts to minimize the weight of the assessor's recommendation. The positives may be had merely for the asking.

Careful framing of the questions to preclude a "yes, but. . . ." response will help keep the assessor/witness from going on to expound on the negatives. If leading questions can be avoided however, the assessor's testimony about the party's strengths will have more punch coming in the assessor's own words than if in the form of agreement with the statements of counsel.

(c) Challenging Clinical Judgment

(i) *Thoroughness and Fairness*

The weight accorded the testimony of an assessor will be reduced significantly if cross-examining counsel can demonstrate unfairness, bias, lack of thoroughness, or that the data either fails to support the recommendations, or that thc data could support other recommendations equally

---

23 *Graat v. R.* [1982] 2 S.C.R. 819, at 839.

well. These areas of challenge are relevant no matter what the assessor's profession.

(ii) *The Use of Texts and Treatises*

In examination-in-chief, an assessor/witness may have been asked about texts or articles upon which she relies in the application of clinical judgment to data. Portions of those writings relied upon by the assessor may have been read into evidence. During cross-examination, counsel may attempt to off-set the weight which citing such authorities can add to testimony. This is done by demonstrating through the witness that there are other, equally respected, authorities and points of view which could have been adopted by a different assessor, and, in turn possibly have led to different conclusions being drawn from the same data. The court will then feel even more free to arrive at a decision which does not merely "rubber-stamp" the recommendation of the assessor.

Cross-examining counsel might confer with a consulting mental health professional to learn of the texts and treatises expounding different approaches than those relied upon by the assessor. Relevant passages in such texts and articles can be photocopied, marked to stand out from the surrounding text, and carried to court. Make sure to have enough copies ready so that if the text or article can be used, each of the judge, witness and other counsel may receive one. It is a courtesy to provide one as well for the court reporter to facilitate the spelling of names and technical terms.

Theories and approaches in the social sciences come and go over relatively short time spans (decades rather than centuries), appearing to replace the earlier theories. This is in contrast to the hard sciences, such as physics and chemistry, where theories evolve over longer time spans and by means of building upon rather than replacing earlier thinking. Often quite different approaches are deemed acceptable simultaneously within the broader mental health community.

Human behaviour is harder to measure and predict than the behaviour of molecules. Any lump of sodium will react the same way if dropped into distilled water; no two people will exhibit identical behaviour when exposed to the same stress or circumstances. No two people are identical, nor are any two circumstances. No two children in the same family have the same childhood. In their time, all widely held theories in the social sciences were regarded as reliable; used to diagnose and treat; and were relied upon by expert witnesses and courts of law.

When counsel is aware of more theories or approaches in current use than the one followed by the assessor, then illustrate that to the judge. Ask the assessor/witness whether her theoretical point of view is the only one in current use. Take care in framing the question, however, to control the witness and not allow a long expostulation of why the theory adopted by the assessor is the better one.

Texts and treatises contrary to the assessor's point of view cannot simply be read into evidence, for to do so offends the rule against hearsay. Before using the quotation, ask the witness whether that text, article, or author is recognized as authoritative by the assessor's profession, or if she has taken that contrary literature into account in formulating her ideas. If the answer is "yes", the copies of the excerpt from the text or article can be distributed to the judge, witness, and other counsel, then read into evidence and the witness asked to account for the differences of opinion between the text or treatise and her own view.

> If he reads it but does not take it into account, it is obvious that he is ignoring part of the body of knowledge and consequently taking a one-sided view or is asserting greater confidence in his conclusions or statements than would be warranted by the state of controversy that exits in the literature.[24]

This device is similar to the device of impeaching a witness through prior inconsistent statements. The approximation becomes much closer if counsel can use books or articles written by the assessor herself which are at odds with her present approach and conclusions.

The assessor/witness may attempt to avoid the use of this device by refusing to acknowledge that the text or article is authoritative. Even then, so long as it is done without naming the author or text, it is permissible for counsel to read the quotation and ask the witness whether she agrees with it as a valid theory or approach.[25]

If the judge observes counsel picking up and reading from text after text, article after article, repeatedly receiving denials of agreement with the authority of the works and authors and the content of the unattributed quotes, an impression may be formed that the witness' views are not in keeping with the common thread of accepted thought in her profession. The weight to be accorded the witness' opinions may be compromised. If the witness claims not to have read or know of such literature then her ability to defend her own approach is impaired as she is not able to say why her approach is better than that of the contrary literature. If the assessor/witness states that she is familiar with such literature but does not agree with it, then the witness' experience and training are relevant.

(iii) *Clinical Judgment in a Legal Context*

Clinicians who enter the forensic arena also shift from their more familiar

24 Ziskin and Faust, *supra*, note 9, vol. III, p. 34.
25 Sopinka, *supra*, note 6, p. 81.

> role as the patient's helping agent and instead seek to uncover truth, whatever its implications for the person under examination. . . . The forensic role is often less familiar or practiced, the clinician's engrained tendency to support and empathize may cloud objectivity, and the person being examined may be less inclined to disclose information openly and honestly. Clinicians, who usually focus primarily on the patient's subjective reality, must now attempt to determine objective reality, a task for which they may be minimally trained.[26]

Whether the clinical judgment of the assessor/witness is open to or immune from challenge on this basis depends on whether the methods followed in the assessment were balanced and thorough. The assessment prepared on the basis of self-report interviews of relatively brief duration with only the litigating parties is open to such challenge. The assessor's consultation with both sides of the dispute (the essence of assessments as opposed to on-side consultation) over a sufficient time span, and involving verification of information with collateral sources on both sides of the dispute, is an answer to such challenge.

(d) Challenging Social Work Testimony

Approaches unique to social workers are the use of theories about family systems, and about attachment, separation and loss. Systems theories explain the human interaction in families by analogy to social institutions such as business or government. For example, each family has goals, works to acquire resources, and allocates resources within the family to meet those goals. Some goals for the family as a whole or for individuals within it are overtly stated and agreed upon by all members, and some are unstated but operational nonetheless, assisting or subverting the achievement of the goals of other individuals. There are several theoretical approaches to family systems, and the social worker/assessor may be challenged on the basis of texts and treatises on these theories by the method set out earlier in this chapter.

Thorough history-taking and independent verification of the versions of family history given by the parties is an important data-gathering aspect of assessment by a social worker whose conclusions are based on assumptions about family function and dysfunction. Cultural and values biases are relevant areas for cross-examination.

Social workers view attachment, separation, loss, change, and the integration and reintegration of children with parent-figures as processes. A social worker's custody/access assessment report should address the

26 D. Faust and J. Ziskin, "The Expert Witness in Psychology and Psychiatry" (1988) *Science* 241:32.

timing and duration of separation from the child's primary caretaker in terms of the child's tolerance at a given age for such separation, whether for an access visit of short duration, or a move to another community. There are several professional viewpoints on loss, separation, and attachment which provide another area for challenge with texts and treatises. How does the theory relied upon apply to the case at hand?

A fundamental tenet of social work is respect for the individuality of each client and for that client's entitlement to self-determination to the extent that circumstances allow. Has the social worker successfully managed the change in role from counsellor to assessor? Which party's or child's entitlement to self-determination was given priority, and why? The parties' needs and those of the children can often be mutually exclusive in child custody/access disputes.

Was sufficient rapport established with each party to the dispute to elicit cooperation in providing open and uncensored information? If not, then what steps did the assessor take to ensure that she obtained a complete and balanced history of the family upon which to base conclusions about its dynamics? If rapport is insufficient, then the information may be incomplete.

(e) Challenging Psychiatric Testimony

The province of making a diagnosis of mental disorder is unique to the psychiatrist. If a psychiatrist's assessment report contains a psychiatric diagnosis of a party or a child there should be a reference in the report to the three digit diagnostic code from the DSM-III-R[27] for that condition. The omission of the code should be noted. Perhaps the diagnosis is not precise. Does the report disclose the essential elements of the disorder as set out in the DSM-III-R (or as the case may be)? Did the psychiatrist consider the relevant differential diagnosis section that distinguishes between conditions with similar elements and symptoms?

The diagnostic criteria in the DSM-III-R are the only ones officially recognized by North American psychiatrists. However, they can change significantly from edition to edition. M.L. Silverstein published a study in which it was shown that only 55 percent of persons in the study[28] who had originally been classified as suffering from schizophrenia under the

27 *American Psychiatric Association: Diagnostic And Statistical Manual of Mental Disorders*, 4th ed., rev'd (Washington, D.C.: American Psychiatric Association, 1987). This work is revised periodically with a different edition designation being given to each revision. The volume in current use is the one to be consulted. The DSM-IV is anticipated to be published in the early 1990's.

28 M.L. Silverstein *et al.*, "Changes in Diagnosis From DSM-II to the Research Diagnostic Criteria and DSM-III" (1982) *American Journal of Psychiatry* 139, pp. 366-367.

diagnostic criteria of the DSM-II (1968) were still classified as schizophrenic by the light of the DSM-III (1980).

Different conditions are treated differently, and different implications for prognosis apply. The diagnostic criteria in the DSM-III-R (1987) and its predecessor the DSM-III (1980) are described by the authors of those volumes as, "only one still frame in the ongoing process of attempting to better understand mental disorders".[29] It may be that whether someone is mentally ill, or has a specific illness with a particular implication for treatment and outcome depends on when one asks the question.

The diagnosis of a mental disorder is of real relevance only to medical treatment issues. It is a convenient shorthand to allow psychiatrists to communicate about patients. The DSM-III-R includes this "cautionary statement":

> The purpose of DSM-III-R is to provide clear descriptions of diagnostic categories in order to enable clinicians and investigators to diagnose, communicate about, study, and treat the various mental disorders. It is to be understood that inclusion here, for clinical and research purposes, of a diagnostic category such as Pathological Gambling or Pedophilia does not imply that the condition meets legal or other non-medical criteria for what constitutes mental disease, mental disorder, or mental disability. The clinical and scientific considerations involved in categorization of these conditions as mental disorders may not be wholly relevant to legal judgments, for example, that take into account such issues as individual responsibility, disability determination, and competency.[30]

Psychiatric diagnosis can have a values component, and the DSM-III-R itself points out that caution must be exercised by psychiatrists using the criteria to evaluate persons from "an ethnic or cultural group different from that of the clinician's",[31]

> . . . especially when diagnoses are made in a non-western culture, caution should be exercised in the application of DSM-III-R diagnostic criteria to assure that their use is culturally valid. It is important that the clinician not employ DSM-III-R in a mechanical fashion, insensitive to differences in language, values, behavioral norms, and idiomatic expressions of distress . . . when an experience or behaviour is entirely normative for a particular culture . . . it should not be regarded as pathological . . . the DSM-III-R categories are not based on extensive research with non-western populations.[32]

There are large populations of first and second generations of immigrant residents and citizens in North America who still adhere strongly to the cultural values of their countries of origin on issues such as the roles of

29 DSM-III-R, p. xvii.

30 *Ibid.*, p. xxix.

31 *Ibid.*, p. xxvi.

32 *Ibid.*, pp. xxvi-xxvii.

men and women, and child rearing practices. The issue has implications as well for our North American Native populations.[33]

(f) Challenging Psychological Testimony

If the custody/access assessor is a psychologist, she should have employed one or more psychological tests in addition to interviews. Indeed, if a psychologist has *not* used such tests the failure to employ all the means professionally available leaves the assessment open to impeachment for lack of thoroughness. If such tests do provide useful information they should be used. The availability of such tests in the assessor's repertoire of assessment skills is sometimes the reason for choosing a psychologist in a particular case.

(i) *What Psychological Tests Measure*

Depending upon the testing instrument chosen, psychologists can measure such variables as cognitive abilities (intelligence, memory, and perception); skills (*e.g.*, reading comprehension and motor coordination); and personality traits (*e.g.*, tolerance for stress, self-esteem, coping style, thought disorders, and motivation).

Ask the psychologist/witness what she was trying to find out when choosing a particular test or battery of tests. How is that which is being measured relevant to the issues of custody and access, and to determining the best interests of the child(ren)? Can the psychologist/witness demonstrate a logical sequence in the assessment process: deciding what questions to ask; selecting tests to answer the questions; and the interpretation showing how and why the test results substantiate the conclusions drawn?

> Tests used as the basis for expert testimony should be widely used in the profession, the norms should be standardized for the population to whom they are being applied and the tests should be validated for the purposes for which they are used. If a test does not satisfy this three-pronged analysis, the attorney should seek to exclude testimony based on the test or to impeach the weight to be given such testimony.[34]

---

33 This issue is relevant of course for social workers and psychologists as well. A Supreme Court of Alaska decision *Carle v. Carle*, 503 P. 2d 1050 (Alaska 1972) stated the importance of avoiding the biases of the dominant culture to deprive a Haida father living by the norms of his culture of the custody of his son.

34 A. Halarambie, "Experts in Child Custody Cases" in D. Bross and L.F. Michaels, *Foundations of Child Advocacy* (Longmont, Colarado: Bookmakers Guild, Inc., 1987), p. 141

Texts such as Anne Anastasi's, *Psychological Testing*,[35] are a comprehensive source of information on how various psychological tests in widespread use were devised, standardized and normed. There is information concerning administration, scoring and interpretation as well. The assessment report should reveal on its face what tests were administered. If not, contact the assessor and ask for the list, making sure that the edition of the test is specified. Then refer to a text on testing to prepare to cross-examine on specific tests.

There are three basic types of psychological tests that may be encountered. There is the self-report inventory in which the subject answers questions or indicates "true" or "false" to certain statements. The M.M.P.I[36] is one of the most widely used of such inventories. Performance and situational tests pose a task, the purpose of which is disguised, simulating an everyday situation. Projective tests, such as sentence completion tests, picture drawing, and inkblot interpretation tests are based on the assumption that a person will project his or her characteristic modes of response into a relatively unstructured task. Such tests are more or less disguised in their purpose to reduce the likelihood of the subject faking the response to create a specific impression.

> A psychological test is essentially an objective and standardized measure of a sample of behaviour . . . the diagnostic or predictive value of a psychological test depends on the degree to which it serves as an indicator of a relatively broad and significant area of behaviour.
>
> . . . .
>
> No psychological test can do more than measure behaviour. Whether such behaviour can serve as an effective index of other behaviour can be established only by empirical tryout.[37]

Essentially, the test takes a sample of the subject's behaviour — the test answers or response patterns. The scoring and interpretation of the results compare the subject to a standardized population sample, measuring difference, not right or wrong answers.

(ii) *Standardization*

In the process of standardization the test is given to a large sample representative of the type of persons for whom it is designed. The test

35 6th ed. (New York: MacMillan, 1988).

36 S. Hathaway, and J.C. McKinley, *Minnesota Multiphasic Personality Inventory* (Minneapolis: University of Minnesota Press, 1943). This is a 550 question test to which the respondent answers yes or no. The results are plotted on a graph for analysis and interpretation.

37 Anastasi, *supra*, note 35, pp. 23-24; 25.

results for the "standardized sample" serve to establish the norm. Uniformity of procedure is required in administering and scoring psychological tests, and ideally the individual being tested is the only independent variable.

Ask the psychologist/witness how the test was standardized. If the standardized sample is a population nothing like the parties and children being tested, then the weight accorded to conclusions drawn is reduced. Ask whether the testing was administered following the requirements for that test. If not, then the results may be less reliable.

(iii) *Norms*

There are no passing or failing scores on psychological tests. The individual's test scores are compared to those of others who have taken the same test. The "norm" is the average or "normal" performance. Anastasi writes that the norm on a personality test is,

> not necessarily the most desireable or "ideal" performance, any more than a perfect or errorless score is the norm on an aptitude test.[38]

The psychologist/witness should be asked from what population the norms were established. If the witness does not know, or the population was significantly different from the parties or children who were tested as part of the assessment, then the validity of the conclusions drawn on the basis of that test are significantly weakened.

(iv) *Reliability and Validity*

Does the test in fact work to reveal what it purports to measure?

> As used in psychometrics, the term "reliability" always means consistency. Test reliability is the consistency of scores obtained by the same persons when retested with the identical test or with an equivalent form of the test.[39]

One can measure components of a child's personality at age six or younger and compare the child to his contemporaries, but because his or her development is not complete, one cannot reliably derive from a psychological test any ability to predict how the same child would score on the same test when he is older.

> I can tell you that a child is distressed, has a low frustration tolerance, poor self esteem and is very prone to behaviours which are directed by his emotions rather than by rational thought, but I cannot tell you if this situation is

38 Anastasi, *supra*, note 35, p. 26.
39 Anastasi, *supra*, note 35, p. 27.

> permanent. I can, however, describe how these present personality characteristics may interfere with the child's ability to: a) use his intelligence fully; b) benefit from academic instruction; c) interact with others.[40]

Tests that are reliable for adults may be less so for children younger than about 15 years of age.[41]

Validity has to do with how the test really measures what it purports to measure and is useful (or otherwise) in predicting or describing objective reality. Part of ensuring the validity of a psychological test is control over the testing situation.

Was the appropriate test selected to measure the characteristic described? Was the test properly administered and scored? Was the test appropriately interpreted? Were the testing conditions stressful? Had the subject taken this test before and been able to learn what to expect? Was the subject's ability to respond well to the tests affected by his health or the condition of his physical senses such as sight or hearing? Did the testing examiner establish a workable rapport engaging the subject's cooperation so that he or she would respond appropriately to the test? Has the interpretation of the test results differentiated between transient and enduring features of the subject's personality?

(v) *Attempts to "Fake Good"*

The psychologist's objective is to obtain open and honest responses to the testing questions and situations which will reveal the subjects's usual behaviour and attitudes.

Since psychological tests were devised for use in a context of diagnosis and treatment, their interpretation rests in part on the underlying assumption that the subject will be cooperative and honest. This assumption may be inappropriate to child custody/access assessments in which the subject's objective is to look as good as possible. Some lawyers familiar with psychological tests may indeed brief clients on what to expect, although the tests themselves are hard to come by unless supplied by a psychologist. It would be unethical for a psychologist in an on-side consulting role to rehearse a party for psychological testing.

One would query the reliability of psychological tests administered to a psychologist who was himself a party to a custody/access assessment. Presumably he would know how to fake answers through familiarity with the objectives and scoring of most widely used tests.

The disguised purpose of projective tests helps to safeguard against

40 N. Elgie, M.A., C.Psych., "Loss of Future Income Flowing From Personal Injury: What Kind of Help Can You Expect From a Psychologist?" February 1989 (unpublished paper).

41 *Ibid.*

faking. "Faking good" on an intelligence test is virtually impossible and "faking bad" will yield a result at odds with the person's level of actual academic achievement. Children are unlikely to be motivated to try to fake any of their test results. The self report inventories are the most prone to deliberate manipulation, and there is some effort in their design to guard against it. The M.M.P.I., probably the most widely-used self-report inventory, is specifically scored for validation on three separate scales. The "L Scale" (Lies) is a group of items which make the subject look good, but are unlikely to be true if answered in the favourable direction (*e.g.*, I like everyone I know). The "F Scale" (validity) is based on a group of questions that represent less desirable traits but do not make a pattern of abnormality. A high F score might indicate malingering or "faking bad". The "K Scale" (correction score) is another selection of items that measure the subject's attitude to taking the test. A high K score can represent an attempt to "fake good" and a low K score an attempt to "fake bad". If the M.M.P.I, was not scored taking these scales into account, the results will be less persuasive.

> Such [psychological] tests can be attacked on the ground that what they tell about the population used to set the norm cannot be applied to other test-takers. If they are not normed for a minority population, they cannot be applied to minorities.[42]

In fact, some tests were normed against small skewed samples. Some tests were never standardized. Other tests are restandardized from time to time, and in such instances the edition of the test administered may affect its applicability to the individual tested.

The actual test, the subject's answers, and the scoring documents, including any notes made by the psychologist, should be subpoenaed and examined carefully. Actual answers to individual questions on self-report inventories may be at odds with the psychologist's stated conclusions about the subject.

(g) Creating An Atmosphere

The custody/access assessor is not an on-side antagonist, but a professional without personal stake in the outcome of the dispute. The task has been to arrive at an understanding of the situation and to make recommendations to the court on behalf of the child(ren).

The areas of challenge treated in this chapter are all fair game. Counsel's use of assertive cross-examination to test the validity of the

42 Halarambie, *supra*, note 34, p. 142.

assessor's opinion and to advance the client's case is received by experienced assessors as all in a day's work as an expert witness.

Challenge is not the same thing as attack. When cross-examination is couched in rudeness, harassment or personal attack, it antagonizes the assessor/witness who may be less inclined to be forthcoming with helpful evidence. It antagonizes the court, and signals counsel's lack of confidence in his own case. Arguments *ad hominem* fool no one, least of all the judge. The lawyer's adoption of a contemptuous, abusive style of cross-examination reflects badly on that lawyer's client.

When cross-examining the assessor, counsel should strive to set a climate in which the trial judge can feel confident in making a decision contrary to the assessment recommendation. Trial judges are human beings. Their task of maintaining dispassionate rationality is hard enough without their confidence being impaired by counsel's inappropriate demeanour.

(h) A Cautionary Note: Babies and Bathwater

Most of the currently available texts that touch on the cross-examination of expert witnesses do so from the perspective of trying to weaken the evidence of the other party's on-side consultant, and not from the perspective of challenging and testing the evidence of an independent consultant to the court who has interviewed both sides in the dispute.

Any professional point of view is necessarily limited by what is known, factually and theoretically, at any given moment. Tough, assertive cross-examination to challenge the assessor's recommendations is necessary and fair. If the assessor is qualified and reliable, then the independent custody/access assessment provides the best helpful child-focused insight obtainable by both parties. Mental health and social science theories are not so enduring as those of the hard sciences, but to attack those theories and approaches for not being as certain as those of physics is to lose sight of the fact that assessments deal with an imperfect human condition.

In custody/access cases the assessor is never addressing just one issue. There can be no control over the variables, as one can achieve in an experiment in the hard sciences. Authors like Ziskin and Faust[43] castigate psychologists for not being as capable of scientific certainty as physicists, and base their cross-examination strategies upon that theme. The comparison is unfair. A professional judgment call is not necessarily invalid just because it is not and cannot be absolute.

A child custody/access assessor must take into account and apply competing, sometimes mutually exclusive, theoretical approaches and

43 J. Ziskin, and D Faust, *Coping with Psychiatric and Psychological Testimony*, 4th ed. (Venice, California: Law and Psychology Press, 1988).

legislative criteria to contradictory data. The children's tolerances must be matched with the parties' capacities in an effort to reconcile the children's needs with what is feasible and available. Each potential placement represents one of a number of competing relationships, all of which are of some import to the child.

The past must be understood in the service of the future. Absolutes are impossible, but skill and sound clinical judgment can illuminate the court's avenues of choice with the spotlight always on the child.

9

The Assessor as Witness: The Assessor's Perspective

1. INTRODUCTION

Once the assessment report is received, the lawyers and the parties enter into negotiations to consider settlement of the dispute along the lines of the recommendations. Often this becomes possible, with modifications and adjustments on both sides. In other cases, however, the matter goes to court for a trial of the issue. The assessor may be called by either side with respect to the report, to explain and expand upon technique, conclusions, and judgment, or to defend those same components under the challenge of cross-examination.

Attendance at court can be an intimidating experience to those unfamiliar with its procedures and rules. The spectre of cross-examination looms so large for some assessors that they undertake to avoid a court appearance entirely by obtaining a pre-assessment promise that they will not be required to testify post-assessment, regardless of the content or recommendations in their anticipated report.

Such an approach allows the assessor to walk both sides of the street: to influence the decision concerning the future care of children, while avoiding accountability for the process and judgment base that led to the specific recommendations. This is simply not professional. The importance of an assessment report requires the response of scrutiny. A poorly done, biased, or incomplete assessment should be subject to question; a well-done, balanced and thorough report should be given re-enforcing consideration. As well, the matter of check-and-balance is involved. The assessor's position is one of power. Power that is not potentially subject to the restraint of examination is not in responsible control, regardless of the assessor's assurance to everyone concerned of her competence and neutrality. Of the many assessments undertaken, few are challenged in court. For those which do reach this stage, the assessment constitutes a piece of the evidence, and is therefore potentially subject to cross-examination. The judge will arrive at his own conclusion as to the weight to be given to the report recommendations. Observing the demeanour of the assessor/witness, and listening to her answers to questions, assists immeasurably in that process. Clear, thought-out, consistent replies enhance credit and credibility; defensive, wavering, or evasive replies weaken credit and credibility.

Instead of avoiding the court experience, the competent assessor prepares for it, cooperates willingly, and participates graciously in the process. The judge may or may not agree with the report's conclusions and recommendations, but nevertheless will have formed an opinion about that assessor and of the usefulness of assessments. Handling this last part of the assignment well makes a three-fold contribution: to the case itself; to the reputation of the assessor; and to all assessors and the value of assessments generally.

Sometimes the court experience is very trying. Occasionally a lawyer becomes more than assertive in cross-examination. The assessor feels harassed, irritated, and bewildered as to why the judge is allowing the tactic to continue, or why the lawyer on the other side is not objecting to the behaviour. Some background knowledge is of assistance here.

2. THE COURT CONTEXT[1]

Our court system is based on the Socratic idea that the truth of a matter is to be found in a forceful and earnest contest between adversaries. *All* evidence is testable by the other side, and by the judge. Evidence which might mislead (such as hearsay or opinion) is generally to be excluded, even if it is true, because it cannot be tested under cross-examination. There are exceptions: some hearsay may be admitted (*e.g.*, the information given to the assessor about past events, as contained in the assessor's report). Opinion evidence will be admitted from an expert witness whose qualifications of education, training, and experience have been accepted by the court as expert

1 Appreciation is expressed to Professor Bernard Dickens, Faculty of Law, University of Toronto, for assistance in preparing this brief overview.

in relation to the matter at hand, or of an aspect of that matter, prior to any questions having been put to that witness. A person retained to undertake custody/access assessments should have the qualifications necessary to be proposed as, and accepted as, an expert in that area.

Trial of an issue is composed of admissible evidence; questioning of the other side's evidence; and legal argument concerning the applicable portion of the pertinent legislation, and perhaps previous judgments which have addressed the same or similar fact situations. The judge considers all these factors, makes a decision, and composes reasons for judgment setting out his or her conclusions, the facts accepted as established (or rejected), applies relevant legislation, considers precedent judgments (indicating his agreement or otherwise) and finally, the thinking that has led to the conclusions and the orders made.

Lawyers must be loyal to their own client. They must not lie or deceive the court, but they are under no duty to betray their client. They may not ask their own witness (a witness they have called to support or enhance their client's position) leading questions, but they may do so of the other side's witnesses during cross-examination. The procedure is reminiscent of a jousting match: thrust and parry, each medieval knight (the lawyer) trying to knock the opposition off its horse, to penetrate the armour, and strike the telling blow which will be fatal to the other side and carry the day for the victor. As in all battles, skirmishes take place, outright encounters and/or strategic manoeuvers are resorted to. There are rules for the encounter, and one of the functions of the judge is to ensure that they are observed. But the judge may give considerable leeway, perhaps to see how a witness's evidence holds up, perhaps to see whether the lawyer will contain the behaviour or go too far. Sometimes aggressive, harassing behaviour on the part of a lawyer indicates a smoke screen intended to mask a weak case. By letting the behaviour go on for a while the judge may be waiting to see if that is so. Understanding that helps the assessor/witness to cope effectively with the pressure. Not necessarily to like it, mind you, but to cope. The assessor maintains her focus on the original mandate of advising on behalf of the child(ren) and resists the efforts of the cross-examining lawyer to shift that focus to his adult client.

3. GUIDELINES FOR APPEARANCE AS A WITNESS[2]

As with any important activity, good performance is grounded in good preparation and an understanding of what to expect. There are three areas for the assessor to consider, as the date for the court appearance approaches,

---

2 These materials have also been presented in a training video entitled, "Court Preparation for Professionals", prepared in 1987 by the University of Calgary, Department of

or as the reality of being on the witness stand hits home. Guidelines for each of these sections follow.

(a) Guidelines for Preparation

- Be prepared.

Know the five W's: who, what, where, when and why. Have the file up to date, know where the pieces of paper are which you may want to refer to. *Re-read the assessment report.*

- Know your position and why you hold it.

How did you arrive at it? What measures did you take?

- Be familiar with the sources you rely upon.

This includes both pro and con references in the literature, research, or authorities consulted. Be able to name them or refer to them. If needed, write this information down on small file cards to be used at the time.

- Organize and be able to refer to reference material.

This includes your notes, other reports, or pictures.

- Check your *curriculum vitae* ensuring that it is current.

Bring extra copies with you.

- Bring your file with you to court.

All of the file. Do not destroy any notes, for to do so in the face of the sure knowledge of future litigation will be fatal to credibility.

(b) Guidelines for Direct Examination[3]

- Dress comfortably, yet professionally.

You want to convey an impression that you are taking the situation seriously. Proper dress is also a matter of respect for the court.

- Speak up.

A firm voice suggests confidence. Speak clearly. Speak slowly. Remember, the court reporter is trying to follow you.

Communications Media, Calgary, Alberta. The content specialist for the programme was Barbara A. Chisholm, assisted by Dr. Ray Tomlinson, Dean of the Faculty of Social Welfare, University of Calgary.

3 Sometimes referred to as Examination-in-Chief.

- Listen carefully to the wording of each question.

Even in direct examination with a "friendly" lawyer watch out for assumptions you are being asked to agree with. *Do not answer a question you have not understood*; it can be repeated or re-worded.

- Ask permission to refer to notes

Do not always go on memory. If you do not recall a date, or the frequency of interviews, or the length of time of an interview, it is better, and appropriate, to refer to the file. Because checking your notes means looking at materials, copies of which are not in the possession of all counsel, there may be a challenge. Your procedure, if you need to check the file, is to ask permission of the court (the judge) to do so, and then to wait a moment. There may be a challenge from other counsel, who may just want to ensure later access to the file if needed prior to cross-examination. Permission will be granted, and then you open the file to locate the information you need. In fact, having your file there to refer to adds weight to the evidence, rather than just relying on memory.

- Take the time needed to answer a question.

This does not mean unnecessary delay, but rather that you are sure that what you say is what you meant to say. Sometimes a question is confusing or unclear, and too-hasty a reply may lead you into appearing to support a position you did not intend to, or to be appearing to contradict an earlier statement, or a position taken in the report. This error will likely be picked up in cross-examination with the intent of showing you as wavering or inconsistent.

- Always reply to a question.

Do not ever refuse to answer a question. To do so puts you at risk of appearing to be a hostile witness.

- Remember that giving evidence is not the same as having a conversation.

Do not interrupt the lawyer. Do not make amusing asides. Take it seriously.

- Admit you do not know an answer, if that is the case.

Never try to invent a reply. Acknowledging that you cannot answer a question because you do not know the answer or you lack the necessary information, is, in fact, a strengthening of your image, not a weakening of it. Not even expert witnesses can know all there is to know about a matter, or of every piece of literature on the subject that has ever been written. You look a lot worse trying to fudge a reply, and leave yourself open to a hint that maybe you are not as professionally reliable as you want to be considered. If you did not do a certain task in the assessment, admit it, and be prepared to explain why.

- Be humble even while appearing confident.

Acknowledge the limitations of professional knowledge, but clear in your reliance on what *is* known. Do not show off or be arrogant, nor, on the other hand, apologetic about limited experience in a certain area of your profession, or about being a member of a profession that has few, if any, absolutes within its body of knowledge.

(c) Guidelines For Coping With Cross-Examination

This section may be sub-titled "How to Be A Witness and Still Survive", and that is the attitude you want to bring to the experience. It may be difficult, but with attention to handling yourself and the situation, you will come through cross-examination just fine. Remember that the cross-examining lawyer's task is to attempt to weaken or even overturn the points the previous direct examination has established. If you wish to stand behind your assessment process, conclusions, and recommendations, you must be alert to cross-examination strategies, aware of where the questions seem to be leading you, and prepared to withstand the challenge with some strategies of your own. However outrageously you think the lawyer is behaving, you should not reply in kind. Cross-examination is even less a conversation than was examination-in-chief. So be alert, be prepared, and consider the following.

- Use pauses in giving your replies.

You will notice that most lawyers have their questions written out. During examination-in-chief by the other side they will have added more questions, noted your earlier replies, and perhaps even noted the replies they may expect from you in the cross-examination. (Well-prepared lawyers rarely ask a question to which they do not know or believe they know the answer.) Each question is intended to lead to a next question and so on, until the *real*, tough question is reached which they hope will weaken the evidence you gave in examination-in-chief. In moving through the series of questions, counsel sometimes seem to develop a rhythm, an almost metronomic sequence of question-answer, question-answer. The assessor/witness may get caught up in this rhythm too. If the lawyer is paying more attention to his notes than to you as the witness, breaking that metronomc effect can be helpful in ensuring you do not get swept down the garden path to a conclusion you do not want to reach. So take longer between some answers; change the tempo. This changes the atmosphere, and keeps you alert.

- Ask to have questions repeated.

This is essential if you do not understand the question, or if you did not hear the question, or if the lawyer has rolled two or three or four questions into the single one, leaving you bewildered. Indicate your confusion, ask to have the question repeated, or ask which one of the four questions he or she would like you to answer first. Request for repetition also interrupts the flow, and may disconcert the lawyer who is in too much of a hurry to get to the "important" questions.

- If the question is personal, rather than directed at your professional self, consider one or two possible strategies.

Sometimes when the expert witness' evidence is strong and the cross-examining lawyer's case is not, he may shift the challenge target from the report to the assessor. This is an echo of the adage heard in other trial situations that suggests that, "if you can't attack the evidence, attack the witness" — that is, their credibility. Sometimes it helps to go along with one or two questions in this tactic (recognizing the change in tactic should reassure you, rather than alarm). So if the assessor/witness is unmarried, acknowledging that fact is fine; a second or third question as to the number of children the assessor has had (intended probably to embarrass), however, is not. You can see where the lawyer intends to lead you: if you are not married, or have not had children, how can you expect to recommend how other people (especially their not-recommended-for client) should manage parenting? In such a situation, asking for repetition of the question, once or even twice, should suffice to alert the other lawyer or the judge to what is going on, and to intervene. If this does not take place, you may consider requesting to address the court (the judge) and with permission, indicate your wish for assistance. Since you are here in your professional capacity, how would the judge direct you to reply to personal questions, as you are confused by them. Judges are, of course, aware of the games of the joust, and may suggest that particular warrior go after a different target.

- Ask assistance from the judge as you feel the need for it.

If the pressure of cross-examination is getting to you, you may arrange a breather for yourself by certain requests to the judge. These may include asking for a chair if you have been standing for a long time; asking for water; asking for a brief recess for a comfort break. The court will always be considerate of an expert witness. The interruption may be all you require to re-charge your batteries or cool your growing irritation. Fatigue or anger can interfere with alert attention to what is really going on.

- Keep your temper.

Even though personal questions may be attempted, cross-examination is not a personal matter. This is sometimes difficult to believe when your judgment and your skill are being attacked. In 99.9 percent of the instances, the challenge is simply tough cross-examination within the context of a trial. In the .001 percent situation, you are free subsequently to decline to work with that lawyer again.

- Take something to drop into the witness box with you.

Paper clips, a pen, a small elastic band, something like that, is useful. If you find yourself getting testy with the questioning, dropping something on the floor and bending over to locate and retrieve it, allows a small "breather". Apologize for the interruption and ask nicely if counsel could please repeat the last question.

- Don't allow eye contact by a harassing cross-examining lawyer.

Eye contact is a behaviour that acknowledges some form of interaction or relationship. As a way to hold the assessor/witness "in thrall", so to speak, as the lawyer comes close to the "clinch" question, he or she may seek to approach the witness closely and pin him or her in place by establishing direct, intense eye contact. Such eye contact is, in this context, a power behaviour which seems to convey the message that the witness (you) must now answer this next question (in a way that is wanted). It is effective in neutralizing this power play to simply deny the lawyer the behaviour. Cast your eyes down and/or perhaps even close them, suggesting that you are listening very carefully, indeed, to their question. Or perhaps you can choose a picture on the court wall and appear to be studying it, for the same reason. Breaking the "control connection" by not allowing eye contact keeps you, as witness, free of this additional stress, and therefore freer to pay attention to what is being asked.

4. SUMMARY POINTS

While preparing for, or coping with being a witness in court, there are points to consider, about which to remind yourself:

- A court hearing is *not* a case conference. The behaviour and rules are different. Nor is it a form of conversation between equals. Being a witness is a very vertical experience: the lawyer is in charge, and always directs the exchange.

- The lawyers are doing their job. The challenge in cross-examination is not directed at you personally, but at your evidence and its weight.

- The purpose of the hearing is to arrive at a decision in the matter, not at the whole (elusive) truth.
- The assessor is but one witness whose evidence is to be taken into consideration.
- The best way to give your report, your evidence, and your opinions the greatest weight is to present all that professionally and well.

10

Getting Paid: Notes for Assessors

Getting paid a reasonable fee in a timely way is an essential element of any professional practice. Establishing and maintaining an appropriate fee structure, billing process, and collection protocol is the subject of this chapter, addressed to assessors.

By its very nature, custody/access assessment work is usually undertaken in the course of ongoing litigation between the parents or would-be parents, and this context affects the climate in which the assessor is attempting to get paid. In Ontario, section 30 of the Children's Law Reform Act is focussed on achieving the ends of the court, *i.e.*, getting the assessment done. Although that legislation provides that the court will assign responsibility for which party or parties will pay, there is little help for the assessor in the implementation of the order when it comes time to collect the account.

Sometimes the party against whose position the assessment report recommends may view the clinician as having taken sides with the other party. The disappointed party may be upset and angry. On such occasions it can be very difficult to collect that party's share of an outstanding account for the assessment. The approaches suggested in this chapter will help eliminate delinquent accounts and reduce the time spent on collecting outstanding receivables.

1. SETTING FEES

Each clinician will, in the course of her practice, have established an hourly rate for professional services reflecting skill, experience, overhead costs, and the local market. Clinicians who undertake custody/access assessments in which one or both of the parties are funded by a legal aid plan will, like the lawyers in such cases, usually find that they are compromising their regular hourly fees. The lower fee scale of the legal aid tariff is, however, viewed by many practitioners as a reasonable trade-off for security of payment.

As with lawyers who accept legal aid cases, assessors in Ontario are not allowed to extra-bill the parties for the difference between the legal aid tariff and their usual, higher, hourly rate.[1] If legal aid cases account for a significant portion of an assessor's practice, establishing a somewhat higher hourly fee for privately paid assessments than might otherwise be the case, will serve to raise the average hourly rate for overall billings.

Charging an all-inclusive, flat fee, the same for each assessment, is not possible at all in legal aid funded cases. It is possible to bill on this basis in situations in which all of the parties are paying privately, but it is arguably unfair to both the assessor, and the parties. Flat fees are practical and fair only in circumstances in which it is possible to have a reasonable idea in advance of the extent of the work entailed. This is difficult to predict in custody/access assessments. The number of collateral persons consulted, the time to be spent in interviews, the time needed to read the affidavits and pleadings, and the time engaged in writing the report or in travel will differ significantly from file to file.

Agreeing in advance to a flat fee may put the assessor in the position of having either to lose money, which is bad business; extra bill above

1 Information Department of the Law Society of Upper Canada, *Legal Aid Letter*, No. 50, December 1988:

> The Legal Aid Committee has learned that some psychiatrists and psychologists preparing custody and access assessments in family law matters are demanding payment from legally-aided clients for the difference between the rates paid by private clients and the rates paid by the Plan. This practice conflicts with legal aid principles and is inconsistent with the Plan's financial assessment procedure. The Legal Aid Committee is of the view that this extra billing practice should not be allowed and believes that members of the profession have the responsibility of ensuring compliance with legal aid policy in this matter.

the flat fee, which is bad public relations; or cut corners on the service rendered, which is unprofessional and unfair to the children concerned.

In preliminary contacts with the lawyers in each case, the matter of fees should be discussed fully. In special needs cases in which legal aid funding has not been available an assessor may have a policy of accepting a lower hourly fee than would normally be required. Whatever the arrangement regarding the hourly rate at which the assessor bills and expects to be paid, the safest course of action is always to confirm the understanding in writing with counsel.

2. THE INITIAL RETAINER

In private-payment cases a retainer is useful. There are two elements in the retainer — money deposited toward future billings to that party, and a memorandum in which the party acknowledges responsibility to pay his or her share of the account for the assessment.

Lawyers use retainers frequently. The lawyer receives money from his or her client and holds it to the credit of that client in a trust bank account. The funds are then used to pay out-of-pocket disbursements made in the conduct of the client's file, and to pay the lawyer's accounts for fees and disbursements as they are issued to the client. As accounts are paid from the retainer, the client provides additional funds as required to maintain a sufficient retainer on deposit with the lawyer. Usually the lawyer maintains only one trust account containing the funds of all clients, and the bookkeeping entries required by the Law Society enable the lawyer to know how much of the trust account is held to the credit of each client at any time. If at the conclusion of that client's business there is more on deposit than is needed to satisfy the final account, the excess is refunded to the client.

Having money on deposit to the credit of a party eliminates waiting to be paid for all or part of an account. It reduces the outstanding balance of the account to be collected by the amount of the retainer to be applied toward it. Such a system is an effective way to manage accounts receivable, particularly in circumstances when one will occasionally meet reluctance or refusal to pay. The use of retainer deposits will necessitate some extra bookkeeping in order to log how much is held to the credit of each party in each file, and makes a trust bank account advisable. There are no regulations or legislation, as yet, that require the detailed bookkeeping demanded of lawyers in such situations. As the mental health professions increasingly adopt this method of protecting their accounts, licensing legislation will doubtless begin to cover the issue of accountability for funds held on deposit. The inconvenience of the extra bookkeeping is offset by the convenience of quick payments of accounts as they are issued.

If the initial deposit is as large or larger than a party's likely share of the final account, then one bill, issued after the report has been completed, will likely be sufficient. If, however, it becomes apparent that the initial retainer is not large enough to cover the entire bill, an additional instalment of the retainer can be requested. Interim bills may be issued from time to time to keep the assessor's cash flow healthy.

3. DISCUSSING FEES WITH THE PARTIES AND LAWYERS

In a preliminary contact with the lawyers in each case the clinician's retainer requirements should be discussed. The clinician should tell the lawyers how much is required for a retainer, whether that should be in cash, certified cheque, lawyer's trust cheque, or whether the clinician is prepared to accept an uncertified cheque from the lawyer's client. Confirm that in writing.

No matter how much detail is furnished to the lawyers about the clinician's fee structure and billing procedures, it is prudent not to assume that this information has been clearly transmitted to the lawyer's client. Unless legal aid is paying a party's share of the assessment account, the party will be paying all or part of the assessment account and the clinician will need to come to a clear understanding with each party about those billing and collection procedures.

Discussing money in the context of the intake interview can feel awkward to many clinicians and the temptation is strong to postpone that moment indefinitely. Appearing to be concerned primarily with getting paid may be off-putting to the often apprehensive, and sometimes defensive, party who may then cooperate less than whole-heartedly in the assessment, to his own detriment. Failure to discuss payment expectations very early on can engender distrust and confusion between the assessor and the parties. Dealing with the issue late in the first interview allows time to establish rapport with the party, but puts the practical details in place before the end of the first session. An alternative would be to deal with the matter mainly in writing with each party's lawyer, or at least arrange to have the lawyers obtain their clients' signatures on the memorandum agreeing to pay the fees. Some assessors require the lawyers' personal undertakings to secure payment of the portion of the account attributable to each lawyer's client. Be direct and open with the party as to how fees are calculated and how they are to be paid. The party expects to pay for the service, and will be more at ease if the assessor raises the issue. Make sure that the payment arrangements are clarified and agreed to *before* the assessment is continued.

4. MEMORANDUM RE FEES AND BILLING PROCEDURES

A copy of the information on fees and billing provided to the lawyers should also be furnished to each party before or during the initial interview. A memorandum explaining the assessor's billing procedures that is given to every party in every assessment can be useful. An example of the form such a letter might take follows as Exhibit (10.1) at the end of this chapter.

The most prudent route is to obtain the party's signature on a memorandum of agreement acknowledging responsibility for payment of his or her share of the account, and setting out how that will be calculated. The use of such a signed agreement prevents the disappointed litigant from disavowing knowledge of, or agreement with, those payment arrangements.

More than one assessor has consumed as many hours again as were involved in the assessment itself trying to collect all or part of an account. A clearly stated memorandum of agreement as to retainer, fee structure, and responsibility for payment signed by the party will ultimately be reassuring both for that party and the assessor. In the rare case in which the assessor must resort to aggressive collection techniques the signed memorandum is excellent evidence. Be sure that it specifies that responsibility for payment is not contingent upon satisfaction with the assessment recommendation.

Exhibit (10.2), at the end of this chapter, is an example of a Retainer/Memorandum of Agreement that might be used as modified to reflect the assessor's own procedures, both to inform the litigating party and to protect the assessor. Once signed, an original is retained by the assessor, one is given to the party who signed it, and a copy should also be furnished to that party's lawyer.

5. STATUTORY AUTHORITY FOR PAYMENT

(a) Orders for Payment

In Ontario, subsections 30(12)-(14) of the Children's Law Reform Act[2] provide as follows:

> (12) The court shall require the parties to pay the fees and expenses of the person appointed under subsection (1).
>
> (13) The court shall specify in the order the proportions or amounts of the fees and expenses that the court requires each party to pay.
>
> (14) The court may relieve a party from responsibility for payment of any of the fees and expenses of the person appointed under subsection (1)

2 R.S.O. 1980, c. 68.

> where the court is satisfied that payment would cause serious financial hardship to the party.

Assessors in Ontario need to be aware of the limitations of the protection of their accounts offered by these three subsections of the Act.

The issue of who pays, and in what proportion, must, by the mandatory wording of subsections 30(12) and (13), be included in orders made pursuant to the Act. Orders made under the inherent jurisdiction of Superior Courts need contain no such provisions, although their insertion would be prudent. The clinician, upon initial contact from the referring lawyer, should request that all the protection available be included in the terms of any court order for assessment. Do not depend upon the lawyer, or the court for that matter, to see that it is done.

The assessor, once appointed, should obtain a copy of the order of appointment, but the wording of the order cannot be relied upon to protect the account. The Children's Law Reform Act in Ontario does not contain a provision entitling the assessor to judgment on the account in the event that any party should fail to honour the payment obligations specified in the order of appointment. The assessor is not a party to that action.

(b) Orders Changing Payment Responsibility

There is a potential problem for assessors in subsection 30(14) of the Children's Law Reform Act which allows the court to relieve a party from responsibility to pay toward the assessor's fees and expenses. The subsection does not expressly prevent a party to the custody/access action from approaching the court on a subsequent occasion after the assessment is under way, or completed, to request relief from obligation to pay which was imposed under subsections 30(12) and (13) at the time the assessor was appointed under subsection (1).

While consent of the clinician to act as assessor is required by subsection 30(4), there is no requirement of notice to the assessor if a party were to move for relief under subsection (14). There is no requirement that the assessor be served with a copy of such order, if made.

If the assessor has not been explicit before beginning the assessment as to how fees are calculated, a party might conceivably be able to argue financial hardship under section 30(14), saying that he or she had no idea at the outset of how high the fees might be. While there may be genuine cases of hardship, there is a duty incumbent upon a clinician to make sure fees are explained in advance in order to determine whether the referral is even one which he or she is willing to accept and whether the parties are, in fact, prepared to pay. Someone will likely be ordered to pay for the assessment under section 30(14), but this process can delay the day of payment, and will necessitate some correspondence and perhaps some negotiation between the assessor and the party with an additional burden of payment, especially if the party required to pay more than the amount anticipated was not favoured in the report recommendations.

The assessor cannot necessarily depend upon either the parties or their lawyers informing her of a reallocation of responsibility of fees and expenses. The model Memorandum of Agreement at Exhibit (10.2) suggests a way to remind the parties that such notice is desirable. A copy of the memorandum sent upon its signing to the party's lawyer will have made him aware of the need to protect the assessor's interest with respect to the work in progress.

6. THE STATEMENT OF ACCOUNT

(a) Activity Records and Billing Formats

Maintaining a steady cash flow is necessary for the responsible fiscal management of any business or professional practice. In therapeutic practice clinicians often bill and collect for effort on behalf of a client or patient on an appointment by appointment basis. Such a billing method is not very practical in custody/access assessments where responsibility for the assessor's fees and expenses is shared by the parties, and it cannot be used to bill for a legal aid funded assessment.

Each clinician will have developed a form for bills that meets the needs of her own clinical practice. In assessment work, however, the bill will have to be drawn in rather more detail than in other aspects of practice. When parents and other parties are dividing responsibility for payment, and especially when legal aid is footing all or part of the cost, the bill needs to be detailed and specific as to the services provided and the expenses incurred.

A time and activity sheet, or docket sheet, (as in Exhibit (10.3)) should be used to note the date and duration of all interviews, telephone conferences, travel time, home visits, report production and also expenses paid. Accounts may be readily drafted from such an activity sheet in the file. Keeping such a record ensures that all time spent on a file will be reflected in the statement of account. Some assessors may wish to purchase a time slip system from a business forms supplier such as used by many lawyers.

Exhibit (10.4) is an example of a statement of account which divides the cost of the assessment equally between two parties, both of whom are paying privately. The example given is addressed to the father, and the mother's bill would be identical but for the name.

(b) Accounts Underwritten by Legal Aid

Exhibit (10.5) shows what the mother's bill would look like in the same case if her share of the assessment was being paid by legal aid. Note that in this instance the bill is sent to the mother's solicitor, and the form is slightly different, with more detail concerning disbursements. It would do no harm to include the date and time of the various services provided as well.

In order to avoid any delay in legal aid payment, particular attention must be paid to the expenses part of the bill. Frequently, the Ontario Legal Aid Plan will wish to see copies of long distance telephone charges; will always want particulars of why mileage expenses were incurred; and, in any event, will expect the total of fees and expenses combined not to exceed any dollar maximum set in its authorization letter. Overhead items such as typing may not be billed as expenses. If that letter was not provided to the assessor at the beginning of the process, she should be sure to obtain a copy from the relevant lawyer and have it available for reference as the bill is drawn up. If the assessor's bill exceeds the authorized dollar amount, or the time limit that was authorized, a letter should be attached explaining as fully as possible why the extra time was essential. The accounts officer at the Ontario Legal Aid Plan may authorize the additional payment. If it is not authorized, the assessor will have to absorb the loss or try to collect it from the lawyer who retained her.[3] This emphasizes the importance of obtaining details of the authorization for time as early in the process as possible so that in appropriate instances additional time authorization may be requested as soon as the need is perceived, and perhaps granted.[4]

The referring lawyer whose client is funded by legal aid is the assessor's conduit to the Ontario Legal Aid Plan. Just as requests for additional time authorization were channelled through him or her, so too is the statement of account. A lawyer is allowed to send interim bills to legal aid, and the assessor need not have to wait until the case is completed before being paid. When the lawyer forwards the assessment account to legal aid for

---

3 The Ontario Legal Aid Plan, *Legal Aid Tariff Manual*, Toronto, 1988, Item 4010-43 states that "The responsibility for choosing and paying an expert is the solicitor's." The Plan will assume no responsibility for unauthorized disbursements (being the fees and expenses of assessors) in circumstances in which authorizations are necessary and have not been obtained. Also relevant are item 4010-41 which states: "Unreasonable or improper bills need not be paid by solicitors and will not be paid by Legal Aid." and item 4010-42 which states "Solicitors have a responsibility to ensure that all disbursements are reasonable and proper and that public funds are not wasted."

4 See Chapter 3, Exhibit (3.9) for a precedent for a letter to a lawyer requesting authorization for more time.

payment, it will take from four to six weeks on average for the legal aid plan to process the account and pay the lawyer who will then transmit the funds to the assessor. Sometimes lawyers will pay the account themselves and wait to be reimbursed by the plan, but such procedure is the exception rather than the rule. It may be necessary to remind the lawyer after about six weeks if payment is still outstanding.

(c) Timing Issues

Some assessors send bills and require payment before the reports are delivered. If this practice is used, be sure to mention it in the memorandum of agreement in order to avoid bad feelings. Some assessors bill the parties directly, and some bill the lawyers and expect payment from the lawyer, who will then bill the client for reimbursement. Whatever arrangement is used, be sure that it is understood and clearly agreed upon at the outset among assessor, the parties and each party's lawyer, if relevant.

Ideally, if the bill is not presented for payment before the report is sent out, then include it with the report. Even the party who is pleased with the outcome of the assessment will be more likely to pay promptly if the account arrives during the first rush of relief at the recommendation. The longer after the event is over that the bill is issued, the longer will likely be the wait for payment.

7. PROBLEM COLLECTIONS

(a) Assistance From the Lawyer

The assessor faced with an account receivable outstanding past the requested payment date should first seek the assistance of the lawyer who acts for the defaulting party. A word in the party's ear from that quarter will likely be sufficient. Even without a formal memorandum of agreement such as suggested earlier in this chapter, most parties eventually pay their bills although reminders (verbal and written) from both the assessor and their own lawyer may be necessary. Occasionally a disappointed party may simply refuse to honour the account. That party may even have dismissed his or her lawyer upon receipt of a report adverse to their position, and the assessor will either have to deal with the party's next lawyer, who may not be overly helpful, or with the debtor party directly.

If payment is not forthcoming within a reasonable time a letter of reminder should be sent to the defaulting party, perhaps adding any agreed penalty interest charge. Exhibit (10.6) suggests a format for a collection letter. Send a copy to the debtor's lawyer.

(b) Suing the Debtor

Not being entitled to judgment for payment of the account under section 30 before the court that made the appointment and the payment order, the assessor will likely have to resort to the use of a collection agency or the court in a separate proceeding if the party ignores reminders and still refuses or neglects to pay. In Ontario, if the amount outstanding is small enough, the court will be the Provincial Court (Civil Division), commonly called the Small Claims Court. In such an instance it can cost as much or more than the claim is worth to retain counsel. Even if the assessor represents herself there will still be time lost in court appearances that cannot be recompensed financially. In Ontario, a Provincial Court (Civil Division) action must be brought in the court in whose jurisdiction the debtor resides. This may be some distance from the assessor's office or place of residence. Sophisticated debtors know that they can often escape payment simply because the assessor cannot afford to throw good money after bad in order to collect, and will find it cheaper to write off the account balance as a bad debt.

Another difficulty in the cases in which the balance sought to be collected is small enough to be within the Provincial Court (Civil Division) jurisdiction is that the matter will come to trial before a court which is unfamiliar with custody/access assessments. Assessors in such instances have been confronted on occasion with judges willing to listen to debtor's defending on the basis that the assessment was deficient and therefore the bill ought not to be paid, even in the face of the order of the higher court, under section 30, that that party is responsible for payment.

If the assessor's collection action comes to court before the custody/access action does, this can result in a Provincial Court (Civil Division) judge, unfamiliar with assessments, ruling that an assessment is or is not deficient. How this would be treated by the judge who hears argument in another court on the weight to be attached to the assessment recommendation in the custody/access case itself can only be imagined.

8. PROFESSIONALISM

The mandate of the assessor is not simply to investigate and prepare a report, but goes further, to be an effective advocate for the interests of the children as professionally determined by the assessor, and to be an informative and reliable resource for the court. The clinician's business practices of billing and collection can affect this role. The clinician's credibility as an assessor might be eroded in the eyes of some judges if she becomes involved in litigation with one of the parties in the custody/access matter. Certainly any ongoing dispute between assessor and one of the parties to the action will complicate rather than simplify the task of the assessor if she is subsequently asked to testify in court in the custody/access matter. Maintaining sound business methods is part of being, and of appearing to be, professional which, in turn, underscores the credibility of the assessment report and recommendations. The use of a clearly stated memorandum of agreement is good business practice, and will simplify the process of being paid.

In practice, most parties do pay their accounts within 30 to 60 days. Clear understandings about how payment will be made, in writing and accompanied by retainers, will assist in keeping bad debts and the time expended in bill collecting to a minimum.

9. EXHIBITS*

(**10.1**) Memorandum of Billing Procedures
(**10.2**) Memorandum of Agreement re Custody/Access Assessment
(**10.3**) Time and Activity and Billing Record
(**10.4**) Statement of Account for Private Payment
(**10.5**) Statement of Account for Legal Aid Payment
(**10.6**) Collection Letter for Overdue Account (30 Days)

* Please Note: All references to names and details in the following exhibits are entirely fictional.

EXHIBIT (**10.1**)

Memorandum of Billing Procedures

MAULDEN, ROBERTS & ASSOCIATES

MEMORANDUM RE BILLING PROCEDURES IN CHILD CUSTODY/ACCESS ASSESSMENTS

Please be advised that our practice in billing procedures is as follows:

1. An initial retainer of $1,000.00 is payable by certified cheque or bank draft prior to the Initial Interview. If more than one party is personally responsible for the assessment fees and expenses, the $1,000.00 will be payable in proportional shares by the parties responsible prior to their respective Initial Interviews, and a copy of the agreement or court order specifying the proportional responsibility will be furnished to this firm prior to the Initial Interview with the first party.
2. A copy of the Legal Aid authorization letter is required for each party whose responsibility is underwritten by the Legal Aid Plan prior to the Initial Interview with that party.
3. Interim accounts may be rendered from time to time, and the retainer will be replenished before further work is undertaken on the assessment.
4. The final account will be rendered when the report is completed, and once payment in full is received the report will be released to the court, the parties and counsel.
5. Professional fees are charged at the rate of ________ per hour, except for travel time which is charged at ________ per hour. Mileage is charged at _____ cents per kilometre. Postage, Fax, courier, and long distance telephone charges incurred will be billed in addition as disbursements.

MAULDEN, ROBERTS
& ASSOCIATES

Per: ____________________________

EXHIBIT (**10.2**)

Memorandum of Agreement re Custody/Access Assessment

Concerning: Father:
Mother:
Child: Born:
Child: Born:
Child: Born:
Child: Born:
Assessor:

---

1. ______________________________, acknowledges having been
(Assessor)
appointed to conduct a child custody/access assessment and hereby undertakes to do so.

2. ______________________________, acknowledges that he/she
(Party)

is responsible to pay for _____% of the accounts rendered for the said custody/access assessment regardless of the nature of the recommendation, and that the accounts will be paid within thirty (30) days. If unpaid within thirty (30) days the account will attract interest at _____% per month which the party agrees to pay.

3. ______________________________, acknowledges having
(Assessor)
received a retainer in the amount of $_____ which will be applied toward the account. The assessor may request, and the party agrees to pay, further retainers, as requested, which will also be applied toward the account. This paragraph will be amended from time to time as required to acknowledge further retainers as follows:

Date	Amount	Assessor's Initials	Party's Initials

If, when the account for fees and expenses is issued at the end of the assessment, there are surplus funds in the retainer, they will be returned with the account without interest.

4. If, ________________________________ at any time seeks to
(Party)
change the allocation of responsibility for the assessor's fees and expenses, as between him/herself and the other party or parties, notice of the change sought will be given to the assessor.

5. ________________________ and ________________________
(Party) (Assessor)
each acknowledge receipt of a copy of this memorandum, and each agrees to be bound by it.

DATED at ____________________ this _____ day of _____, 19 ___.

________________________ ________________________
(Party) (Assessor)

EXHIBIT (**10.3**)

Time and Activity and Billing Record

TIME AND ACTIVITY AND BILLING RECORD

Private Pay [ ] Legal Aid [ ] Hourly Rate $_____

File Name: **Quarrel vs Quarrel** Page: 1

Fee Rate: Mother: $______/hour Father: $______/hour

DATE	**ACTIVITY**	**DURATION**	**FEE**
1989			
June			
04	Inquiry phone call from father's lawyer	15 min.	
26	Receive and review father's pleadings and affidavits and order appointing and referral letter	½ hour	
28	Receive and review mother's pleadings and affidavits and referral letter	¾ hour	
July			
02	Telephone call from mother arranging appointment	15 min.	
13	Intake Interview — mother	1½ hour	
13	Telephone call to father's lawyer	5 min.	
14	Telephone call from father arranging appointment	15 min.	
19	Intake Interview — father	1¾ hour	
20	Second Interview — mother	1¼ hour	
23	Second Interview — father	1½ hour	
30	Collateral Interview: children's babysitter	25 min.	

August		
03	Home visit with children at mother's/commonlaw spouse present	1½ hour
	Travel Time	1 hour
08	Collateral Interview: Paternal grandparents — Alice & George Quarrel	1 hour
13	Home visit with children at father's	1 hour
	Travel Time	½ hour
18	Collateral Interviews: P. R_____, Neighbour	¼ hour
	J. D_____, friend of father	¼ hour
	C. D_____, mother's sister	½ hour
27	Interview with father	½ hour
28	Telephone conversation with mother	¼ hour
September		
06	Review children's school records	¼ hour
12	School visit:	
	Principal	½ hour
	Current teachers	¼ hour
	Last year's teachers	¾ hour
October		
03	Re-reading file and notes	1 hour
04	Writing report	4 hours
08	Typing of report *	3½ hours
08	Proofreading and revising and mailing report *	½ hour

* These items are not billable on legal aid funded files but will be on privately paid files.

EXHIBIT (**10.4**)

Statement of Account for Private Payment

ERICKSON, PIAGET & ASSOCIATES
Child and Family Consultants
523 Breezeway Avenue, Suite 305
Bigtown, Somewhere M4S 3L7

Date: ________________

To: Mr. John R. S_____
987 Perchance Avenue
Anytown, Somewhere
M2T 7L3

STATEMENT

TO ASSESSMENT REPORT concerning Nicholas S_____, born January 3, 1979, and Natalie S_____, born May 17, 1982.

Time Re Assessment:

1.	Interviews with John Robert S_____.	3.75 hours
2.	Interviews with Evelyn Marie S_____.	3.00 hours
3.	Interviews with collaterals including: Margaret R_____, the maternal grandmother; Fred J_____, friend of the father; Todd B_____, the mother's Commonlaw partner; Sherry H_____, the father's Commonlaw partner.	5.00 hours
4.	School visit to meet with Nicholas and Natalie's teachers.	.75 hours
5.	Home visit to meet the children at the father's home	1.50 hours
6.	Home visit to meet the children at the mother's home.	2.00 hours
7.	Telephone conversations with Nicholas' therapist, Dr. Muriel D_____.	.50 hours
8.	Telephone conversations with counsel for the mother and for the father.	1.00 hour
9.	Reading the materials provided by counsel.	1.00 hour
10.	Preparation of report	6.00 hours
	TOTAL TIME ENGAGED:	24.50 hours

	TO MY FEE HEREIN:	
24.5 hours @ $100.00 per hour		$2,450.00
Disbursements:		
11.	Long distance telephone calls	$22.78
12.	Mileage: 204 km. @ .275	56.10
13.	Photocopying: 144 pages @ .10	14.40
	TOTAL DISBURSEMENTS:	$ 93.28
	ASSESSMENT TOTAL ACCOUNT:	$2,543.28
Your share, being ½ of $2,543.28 =		$1,271.64
	LESS RETAINER PAID BY YOU:	$1,000.00
	BALANCE DUE AND OWING:	$ 271.64

Please Note: A penalty of 1% per month is added to all accounts outstanding over thirty (30) days.

ERICKSON, PIAGET
& ASSOCIATES
Per:

____

Audrey Erickson, M.S.W., C.S.W.

EXHIBIT (**10.5**)

Statement of Account for Legal Aid Payment

ERICKSON, PIAGET & ASSOCIATES
Child and Family Consultants
523 Breezeway Avenue, Suite 305
Bigtown, Somewhere M4S 3L7

To: DUGUID & PROFITT
Barristers & Solicitors
75 Chancery Lane
Anytown, Somewhere
M2S 4B2

Date: ________________

Re: Mrs. Eveyln M. S_____
22 Redding Avenue
Anytown, Somewhere
M3B 4W6

STATEMENT

TO ASSESSMENT REPORT concerning Nicholas S_____, born January 3, 1979, and Natalie S_____, born May 17, 1982.

Time Re Assessment:

1.	Interviews with John Robert S_____.	3.75 hours
2.	Interviews with Evelyn Marie S_____.	3.00 hours
3.	Interviews with collaterals including: Margaret R_____, the maternal grandmother; Fred J_____, friend of the father; Todd B_____, the mother's commonlaw partner; Sherry H_____, the father's commonlaw partner.	5.25 hours
4.	School visit to meet with Nicholas and Natalie's teachers.	.75 hours
5.	Home visit to meet the children at the father's home.	1.50 hours
6.	Home visit to meet the children at the mother's home.	2.00 hours
7.	Telephone conversations with Nicholas' therapist, Dr. Muriel D_____.	.50 hours

8.	Telephone conversations with counsel for the mother and for the father.	1.00 hour
9.	Reading the materials provided by counsel.	1.00 hour
10.	Preparation of report	6.00 hours
	TOTAL TIME ENGAGED:	24.50 hours
	Your ½ of the time: 12.25 hours @ my legal aid hourly rate of $65.00	
	TO MY FEE HEREIN:	$ 796.25

Disbursements:

11.	Long Distance Telephone (Bills available)	$22.78
12.	Mileage: — Home visit at father's home with the children: 44 km — Home visit at mother's home with the children: 160 km — Total: 204 km. @ .275	56.10
13.	Photocopying: 144 pages @ .10	14.40
	TOTAL DISBURSEMENTS:	$ 93.28
	Your client's ½ of disbursements:	$ 46.64
	Your client's share of the account fees:	$796.25
	Disbursements:	46.64
	BALANCE OWED:	$842.89

ERICKSON, PIAGET
& ASSOCIATES

Per:

____

Audrey Erickson, M.S.W., C.S.W.

EXHIBIT (**10.6**)

Collection Letter for Overdue Account (30 Days)

Date: ____________________

Dear ______________________:

Re: Statement of Account Dated ______________________________
for Custody/Access Assessment Dated ____________________

My account to you dated _____ has been outstanding for more than 30 days.

As noted on the account, interest at _____% per month runs from the date of the account onward on accounts outstanding for 30 days. The penalty interest owing now is $ _____, resulting in a total amount due of $ _____.

Your payment within _____ days is requested. If there is a difficulty involved with this account, please contact me.

Yours sincerely,

____

Note: A more strongly worded letter may follow at 60 days. Accounts outstanding beyond 60 days will likely require a lawyer's letter threatening court action if no replies are forthcoming.

11

Ethics and Standards of Practice

1. NOTES FOR LAWYERS
2. NOTES FOR ASSESSORS
3. ESSENTIAL ELEMENTS OF AN ASSESSMENT
4. COMPROMISE OF ASSESSOR'S ROLE
5. AVENUES FOR REDRESS

1. NOTES FOR LAWYERS

(a) The Ethics of Custody Assessments

The Law Society of Upper Canada has not yet published annotations to the Rules of Professional Conduct as they relate to lawyers in procuring, using and challenging custody/access assessment. There are, however, considerations related to ethics and standards of practice.

An issue of good faith is involved for the lawyer whether the assessment is obtained on consent, or has been court ordered after opposition by one parent. The parties are obliged to cooperate with the assessment. The lawyer is obliged not to subvert that cooperation.

While the rights of the client must be protected and respected in negotiations and at trial, and while the client's position must be advocated firmly and effectively, there is the added dimension in custody/access cases that the commitment to the client exists within the shadow of the interest of the children. It is therefore not an unqualified commitment to try to win the case at all costs. This affects the nature of the advice a lawyer will give and the strategies he will be prepared to undertake in representing the wishes and interests of the client.

It might be argued that if the children's interests are represented by counsel for the children, or by the very existence of a custody/access assessment, then the lawyer is freed from that concern and may concentrate on trying to win. Even this view must be modified by realization that the result sought by the client, if achieved, will be acted out in the daily lives of the children. The issue of winning does not exist in a vacuum.

The court is required in a custody/access dispute not simply to determine which party's position will prevail, but also to establish a structure for the children's remaining period of dependency. How this is accomplished, and the attitudes brought to bear within the court action, will affect how that structure will be implemented, perhaps modified, cooperated with, or undermined and sabotaged. Other types of litigation are retrospective, and sometimes retributive, but the custody/access aspects of family litigation are prospective and pro-active.

(b) The Context of a Custody Dispute

Separated husbands and wives can, and indeed must, go their separate ways; fathers and mothers never can entirely. Disputes involving the future of the children, within the context of separation and divorce, can significantly complicate the parties' adjustment to the marriage breakdown. At this point in their lives, the spouses legitimately need to move away from each other's sphere of influence, to allow the pain to subside and the healing to start. Ultimately this leads to getting their individual lives back in control again. The fact that the children need decisions and parents forces the parties constantly to interact and share. For many couples, this forced interaction mitigates against the healing, re-opens the wounds, and keeps the pain high and current. Energy at this point may be directed to self-survival, and having to share parenting with the other person who is seen as the source of the pain is very difficult. This need to move away from each other as husband and wife, while being pulled back to interact as father and mother, has been described as "The Elastic Band Syndrome",[1] and may be illustrated thus:

THE ELASTIC BAND SYNDROME

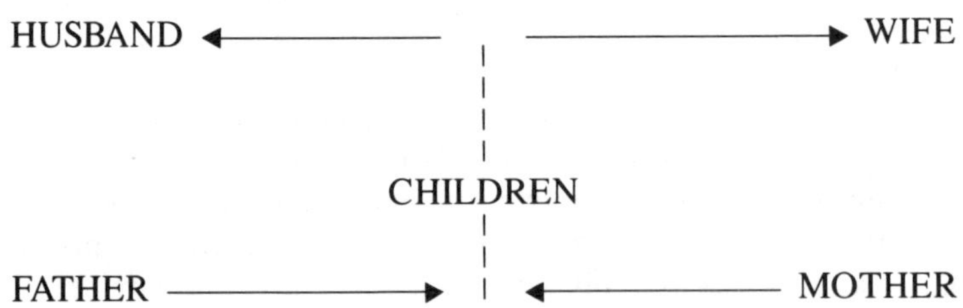

1 B. A. Chisholm, "Preparing Your Client for Assessment or Mediation" (1987) 1 C.F.L.Q. 385.

The children are not the clients of the parents' lawyers, but are totally involved in the outcome. If the actions of either parent's counsel cause an already stressed situation to deteriorate further, future parenting cooperation becomes more difficult or impossible. Remember, the client pays the bill, but the children pay the price.

(c) Tactics that Jeopardize the Assessment

Viewing the assessor as an enemy, or as an obstacle to be overcome, leads some lawyers to indulge in such strategies as proceeding with non-emergency litigation steps during an ongoing assessment. This serves to keep all parties emotionally off balance, and contaminates the assessment by putting the assessor at some risk of noting attitudes and behaviour on the part of either or both parents that are artifacts of the deliberately aggravated situational stress. This is particularly so if the assessor does not know about the additional pressure being put on the parties by such an intervention[2]

It is difficult enough to assess parental behaviour in the best of

---

2 Part of the task of an assessor is to differentiate behaviour and attitudes of the parents or parties that are reactions to specific stresses inherent in the marriage breakdown and custody/access dispute from those which are more enduring features of the parties' personalities and coping styles.

In diagnostic functions psychiatrists are advised by the DSM-III-R (*American Psychiatric Association: Diagnostic and Statistical Manual of Mental Disorders*, 3d ed., Rev'd ed. (Washington, D.C.: American Psychiatric Association, 1987)) in determining etiologically significant psycho-social stressors to consider the following, among other, areas (p. 19-20): marital discord and separation; other discordant personal relations with friends, family and associates; change in residence; change in financial status; persecution; law suits; and trials. All of the foregoing are inherent to some degree in marriage breakdown.

For children and adolescents the list is further expanded (p. 20) to include:

> cold, hostile, intrusive, abusive, conflictual, or confusingly inconsistent relationship between parents or toward child; . . . lack of parental guidance or excessively harsh or inconsistent parental control . . . anomalous family situation, e.g., complex or inconsistent parental custody and visitation arrangements . . . loss of nuclear family members.

The same DSM-III-R on its Severity of Psycho-Social Stressors Scale: Adult (p. 11) notes marital separation as a moderate (code 3) psycho-social stressor, and divorce as severe (code 4). On the child and adolescent scale (p. 11) chronic parental discord is rated moderate (code 3) and divorce of parents as severe (code 4). Both severity codes range from code 1-mild to code 6-catastrophic.

Unnecessary steps in litigation can prolong and increase the overall sensitivities of all family members to the already stressed situation. Because the child's time scale is different from that of adults, an incident or series of incidents which might be an acute stressor of relatively short duration for an adult, may be experienced by a child as being a more enduring circumstance. Citing "chronic parental discord" as an "enduring circumstance" the authors of the DSM-III-R state (p. 19):

circumstances. Continuing to bring procedural motions; requesting a change in custody or access in mid-assessment; initiating discoveries or cross-examinations, even on financial matters, should be avoided. An arms-length, yet cooperative position by all counsel will assist the assessor to complete the process efficiently and fairly.

If a motion or other step in litigation becomes absolutely necessary, counsel should observe the courtesy of informing the assessor and provide copies of pleadings and affidavits being served and filed. Depending on the nature of the proceeding, the assessor may stand aside and wait for the interim matter to be resolved before continuing the assessment.

Foreseeing the possibility that recommendations of the assessor may fail to support their client's position, some lawyers may deliberately set about creating an atmosphere of antagonism with the assessor so that they may later allege that the assessor was biased, or deliberately thwart the flow of information so that they may later allege that the report is based on incomplete information and is therefore of diminished weight.

Such tactics may be as direct as harassing, aggressive phone calls and letters to the assessor; attempts to examine the assessor for discovery before the assessment is completed; or advising clients to falsify information in family history or on answers to psychological tests. More subtle lawyers attempt the same ends with passive-aggressive means such as "forgetting" to send copies of the client's pleadings and affidavits for the assessor to review; "forgetting" to send the retainer or to obtain payment authorization from Legal Aid; "forgetting" to have the client call the assessor for the first appointment, if that has been requested, and so on.

Deliberate delay in implementing an assessment or other interference tactics to increase the anxiety of the other party, or to hinder the assessor, or to prolong a favourable status quo position, are arguably a breach of Rules 10,[3]

> . . . there is evidence that predominantly enduring psychosocial stressors are more likely to predispose children to develop mental disorders than predominantly acute events.

The issue therefore goes beyond the ethics of keeping the pot on the boil to frustrate an assessment, it may entail real harm to the children.

3 The Law Society of Upper Canada's Rules of Professional Conduct, Rule 10 states as follows:

> When acting as an advocate the lawyer, while treating the tribunal with courtesy and respect, must represent his client resolutely and honorably within the limits of the law.

In an independent custody/access assessment the assessor is an investigative delegate of the court. To interfere with the assessment is to interfere with the court.

If the assessor is considered as a witness in the proceeding, Commentary 2 becomes relevant. It states:

> The lawyer has a duty to the client to raise fearlessly every issue, advance every argument, and ask every question, however distasteful, which the lawyer thinks will

and 14[4] of the Rules of Professional Conduct of the Law Society of Upper Canada. Such conduct may also serve to erode the client's faith in the lawyer and in the court system.

2. NOTES FOR ASSESSORS

Complaints and discipline proceedings arising from alleged professional misconduct and failure to maintain the standards of practice of the clinician's profession are becoming more common in custody/access assessments as they come into wider use. To date, the main causes for complaint to professional accrediting bodies have related to deficiencies in competence, thoroughness and fairness. Compromise of the assessor's role is another area for potential complaint.

Professional competence in an assessor's profession of social work, psychiatry or psychology alone is no guarantee of competence in custody/access assessment work. Education, training, reading, and current practical experience related to children and families, the dynamics of separation and divorce and the role of the assessment as part of the web of evidence used by the court to structure children's futures are basic pre-requisites. There are no bodies that specifically accredit custody/access assessors in Canada. There is no one established, recognized statement of practice standards for assessors. Despite certain divergent viewpoints expressed in various publications, a review of the literature and of available professional discipline proceedings reveals common competence concerns. The Ontario Board of Examiners in Psychology, reviewing its own experience with complaints arising out of custody/access assessments suggested that,

---

> help the client's case .... The lawyer must discharge this duty by fair and honourable means . . . and in a manner consistent with the lawyer's duty to treat the tribunal with candour, fairness, courtesy, and respect.
>
> The lawyer must not, for example:
>
> . . .
>
> (k) needlessly abuse, hector, or harass a witness;
> (l) needlessly inconvenience a witness.

Commentary 5 to Rule 10 of the Rules of Professional Conduct states:

> The lawyer should never waive or abandon the client's legal rights . . . without the client's informed consent. In civil matters it is desirable that the lawyer should avoid and discourage the client from resorting to . . . tactics which will merely delay or harass the other side. Such practices can readily bring the administration of justice and the legal profession into disrepute.

4 The Law Society of Upper Canada's Rules of Professional Conduct, Rule 14, states that "The lawyer's conduct toward other lawyers should be characterized by courtesy and good faith." Opposing counsel has a right to expect the full cooperation of the lawyer regarding the assessment.

a special caution be issued to registrants undertaking this type of work, together with some suggestions as to relevant literature and remarks as to some particular hazards observed by the board.[5]

3. ESSENTIAL ELEMENTS OF AN ASSESSMENT

Some commonly recognized essential elements of a competent assessment may be summarized as follows:

- The assessor shall demonstrate acceptable competence in the theory and practice of her profession as applied to the specific task of assessment.
- The assessor shall obtain sufficient information, including relevant documents, to acquire a broadly-based understanding of the history and nature of the dispute and of the parties.
- The assessor shall have personal contact with all parties seeking custody or access.
- The assessor shall verify the information received from the parties by obtaining sufficient information from independent collateral sources and/or the results of psychological testing, to evaluate the assertions of the interested parties.
- The assessor shall meet and visit the children (in the home of each parent, if possible, and if consistent with the tenets of the clinician's discipline). In any event, the assessor shall afford each child sufficient privacy for a personal interview.
- The assessor shall obtain each child's wishes and point of view in an appropriate way and shall express the child's wishes and preferences responsibly and fairly in the report.
- The assessor shall meet and evaluate the impact on the child of all potential care givers, including significant others in the life of each parent or party.
- The assessor shall reveal to the parties and the court all received and verified information relied upon in arriving at the recommendations as to the best interests of the children.
- The assessor shall deal with the parties to the dispute in a fair and even-handed way not only in the investigative and valuative stages,

5 B. Quarrington, "Custody and Access Assessments", *The Bulletin*, The Ontario Board of Examiners in Psychology, Vol. 11, No. 1, April 1988.

but also in framing the report, acknowledging the strengths as well as weaknesses of all parties.

- The assessor shall consider all reasonably viable custody and access options, and present fairly the implications for the children inherent in each.
- The assessor shall use all relevant data gathered in a way consistent with sound practice of her profession in order to formulate recommendations reflecting expert professional opinion, which in turn shall be derived from and supported by the data.
- The assessor shall refuse cases which are beyond her competence, and seek supervision and professional consultation as appropriate.

In January 1987, a discipline tribunal of the Ontario Board of Examiners in Psychology heard evidence on a charge of professional misconduct against a psychologist who was found guilty of professional misconduct under the Psychologists Registration Act,[6] in that he failed to maintain the Standards of Practice of the profession in his psychological assessment of, and 1984 report concerning, a child.[7] He was found guilty, reprimanded, and required to refrain from practice in the area of custody assessment without first providing evidence of being qualified in that area of practice that was satisfactory to the Board. It is instructive to examine the allegations in the Notice of Hearing, all of which were admitted by the psychologist:

1. He failed to interview the child's mother or stepfather and failed to seek independent information and verification before making recommendations and drawing conclusions concerning custody of and access to A;
2. He relied upon statements made by the father of the child about the mother and the stepfather of the child without seeking independent verification of the truth of those statements, and without obtaining information and responses from the mother and stepfather;
3. He failed to advise the reader of his report of the limitations which would be inherent in the recommendations made by him because of the limitations of the investigation conducted by him;
4. He failed to conduct adequate tests so as to adequately assess the child psychometrically;
5. He stated conclusions and made recommendations based upon inadequate psychometric testing and not supported by the psychometric tests performed;

6 R.S.O. 1980, c. 404.

7 The Ontario Board of Examiners in Psychology. *The Bulletin*, Vol. 10, No. 3, October 1987.

6. He made recommendations as to custody and access of the child, as contained in his 1984 report, which were based on insufficient investigation of the facts.[8]

The child in question was 10 years of age and had been living with his mother in her legal custody almost since his birth at the time that the psychologist did what purported to be an assessment. The psychologist interviewed the child and his father three times each individually, and once together; he met with the father and his partner; and he "evaluated" a Halloween drawing made by the child. At no time was the mother, as custodial parent, ever informed of the psychologist's intervention, nor was she ever contacted by the psychologist or otherwise requested to participate in the process that gave rise to a report making recommendations as to custody of and access to the child. No psychometric testing was done of the child or adults who were contacted. No other independent collateral information sources were contacted by the psychologist.

On-side consultation, as such, is a valid service which may be provided by mental health professionals. Such on-side consultations must, however, conform to established professional practice standards and cannot go beyond the scope of what they are. An on-side consultation with one parent and child cannot result in custody/access recommendations because to make such recommendations implies that adequate data was obtained to allow comparison with the other parent. Likewise, the mental health professions require that consent of the custodial parent be obtained before becoming involved with a child,[9] unless, of course, an assessment has been agreed to or court-ordered, in which case contact with the child is mandated either specifically or by implication. Occasionally, parents will refuse to cooperate with an assessment, and will not meet with the assessor or provide names of collateral information sources. The failure of a parent to cooperate with an assessment does not convert it into an on-side consultation. Subsection 30(6) of the Ontario Children's Law Reform Act deals with this situation.[10]

---

8 *Ibid.*

9 The first case ever to come before a hearing conducted by the Discipline Committee of the Ontario College of Certified Social Workers in 1985 was one in which a social worker had done an on-side consultation in which the children had been involved without the knowledge or consent of the custodial parent. The social worker was found guilty of professional misconduct and was reprimanded.

10 R.S.O. 1980, c. 68 s. 30(6) [as amended S.O. 1982, c. 20] states:

> Where a person ordered under this section to attend for assessment refuses to attend or undergo the assessment, the court may draw such inferences in respect of the ability and willingness of any person to satisfy the needs of the child as the court considers appropriate.

4. COMPROMISE OF ASSESSOR'S ROLE

Assessment is not therapy, although having participated in assessment may have a therapeutic spin-off effect for some parties. Assessment is not mediation, although the parties may ultimately settle on the basis of the assessor's recommendations or some variation of them.

For the assessor to refer either or both of the parties to herself for counselling during or after an assessment is an abuse of power of the original role. The party may feel that he or she has no choice in the matter, and there can be no valid therapeutic process (which implies confidentiality) under circumstances in which all that is revealed, if in any way relevant to the well-being of the children, will be subject to comment in the assessment report, or to cross-examination if the matter is subsequently litigated. To convert assessment to counselling with one or all of the parties is a breach of the terms of the retainer, and also places the clinician in a position of conflict of interest.

Likewise, the assessor should not refer the couple to herself for mediation mid-assessment. Assessment is not a process which can be whatever the clinician and parties would like to make it from moment to moment. The assessor is an investigative arm of the court whose duty it is to evaluate the situation and make concrete recommendations to the court based upon expert professional opinion. The assessment report is but one part of the evidence which the court will consider in the case.

Attempts by the assessor to mediate during an on-going assessment, even with the most benign of intentions, can be construed by the parties as confusing and potentially coercive, even though presented as an attempt to facilitate the parties' own decision-making. If mediation or negotiation had succeeded, the parties would not now be undergoing an assessment. The parties remain the clients of the lawyers. The assessor has been retained by the lawyers to perform a specific function. For the assessor to change roles arbitrarily mid-assessment is a breach of the retainer.

It may be that in the course of contact with one parent or the other the assessor may be told that one parent could do "X" if the other parent would do "Y". Or the two parents may independently define similar situations if asked to tell the assessor about child care arrangements with which they could cooperate. Instead of negotiating such an arrangement, the assessor should note the information in the report either as data or as a recommendation. It is then up to the parties and their lawyers to negotiate settlement, or proceed to trial.

While the court system has its limitations, it exists for a purpose. As commendable as attempts to settle disputes without resort to a trial may be, it is not the assessor's prerogative to assume the management of the case. Once a matter is before the courts case management is the prerogative of the clients through the agency of their counsel. Not all family legal disputes can be settled. There are some persons for whom the experience of a hearing is a useful catharsis, and others for whom the salutary experience of a hearing and court judgment is necessary before they understand that they must respect and abide by specific directions regarding custody and access.

5. AVENUES FOR REDRESS

Assessors are on the whole drawn from three main professions — social work, psychiatry and psychology. One reason for lawyers to retain as custody/access assessors only those clinicians who are accredited in an established mental health profession is that there is as yet no licensing or accrediting body for "child custody/access assessors" per se in Canada. The professional conduct of clinician *qua* assessor must therefore be examined in the light of her own profession's code of ethics and published standards of practice.

Malpractice complaints concerning social workers in Ontario should be directed to the Ontario College of Certified Social Workers.[11] Until such time as there is legislation in Ontario requiring professional social workers to join, membership in the College is voluntary. The College can only discipline its members. Remedies against non-members must be sought through the Civil Courts. Professional social workers in private practice in Ontario should, but are not yet required to have malpractice insurance.

In Ontario, complaints concerning psychiatrists should be directed to the College of Physicians and Surgeons of Ontario,[12] to which all psychiatrists must belong. All psychiatrists are covered by malpractice insurance.

Complaints concerning psychologists in Ontario should be directed to The Ontario Board of Examiners in Psychology[13] which licenses and regulates all registered clinical psychologists. Clinical psychologists may have malpractice insurance, but are not required to do so.

Ontario lawyers are licensed to practice by the Law Society of Upper Canada[14] to which complaints of unprofessional conduct should be

11 The Ontario College of Certified Social Workers, 517 College Street, Suite 315, Toronto, Ontario, M6G 4A2. Telephone: (416) 923-7875

12 The College of Physicians and Surgeons of Ontario, 80 College Street, Toronto, Ontario, M5G 2E2. Telephone: (416) 961-1711.

13 The Ontario Board of Examiners in Psychology, 101 Davenport Road, Toronto, Ontario, M5R 1H5. Telephone: (416) 961-8817.

14 The Law Society of Upper Canada, Osgoode Hall, 130 Queen Street West, Toronto, Ontario, M5H 2N6. Telephone: (416) 947-3300.

directed. All lawyers are required to maintain errors and omissions insurance.

For law and the mental health professions alike, complaints are submitted in writing for the consideration of a Complaints Committee. Those matters unresolved in the complaints phase, and deemed serious enough by that committee, are referred to the Discipline Committee. In all cases, sanctions available include reprimand; a requirement to submit to therapy or other treatment (e.g., for alcoholism); the requirement to practise under supervision for a stipulated period of time; and temporary suspension or permanent revocation of membership or licence to practise.

APPENDIX I

Legislation Mandating Assessments in Child Custody and Access Actions

YUKON

Children's Act, R.S.Y. 1986, c. 22 [as amended]

Request for investigation

43. (1) In an application under this Part in respect of a child, the court may request the director of family and children's services appointed under section 108 to cause an investigation to be made and to report to the court upon all matters relating to the custody, support and education of the child.

[**Obligation of director**]

(2) The director shall have no obligation to prepare a report or to prepare a report within a stipulated period unless he consents to or has given a prior written report.

BRITISH COLUMBIA

Family Relations Act, R.S.B.C. 1979, c. 121 [as amended S.B.C. 1984, c. 30]

Expert witness provisions respecting family matters

15. (1) In a proceeding under this Act, the court may, on application, including *ex parte* application, direct an investigation into a family matter by a person who

(a) has had no previous connection with the parties to the proceeding or to whom each party consents; and
(b) is a family counsellor, social worker, probation officer or other person approved by the court for the purpose.

[**Reporting results of investigation**]

(2) A person directed to carry out an investigation under subsection (1) shall report, in the manner which the court may direct, the results of the investigation.

[**Copy of report to be served**]

(3) No person shall report to a court the result of an investigation under subsection (1) unless, not less than 24 hours before the report is to be given, he serves a copy of the report on every party to the proceeding.

[Exemption by court]

(4) Where satisfied that circumstances warrant, the court may grant an exemption from subsection (3).

MANITOBA

The Family Maintenance Act, R.S.M. 1987, c. F20 [as amended]

Court may direct investigation

3. (1) In a proceeding under this Act, the court may direct an investigation into any matter by a person who

(a) has had no previous connection with the parties to the proceeding or to whom each party consents; and
(b) is a family investigator, social worker or other person approved by the court for the purpose.

Investigation only to determine best interests

3. (2) A court may direct an investigation under subsection (1) only if satisfied that it is necessary in order to determine the best interests of the child.

Refusal to co-operate

(3) Where a court directs an investigation pursuant to subsection (1) and a party refuses to co-operate with the investigator, the investigator shall so report to the court which may draw any inference therefrom it considers appropriate.

ONTARIO

Children's Law Reform Act, R.S.O. 1980, c. 68 [as amended S.O. 1982, c. 20]

Assessment of needs of child

30. (1) The court before which an application is brought in respect of custody of or access to a child, by order, may appoint a person who has technical or professional skill to assess and report to the court on the needs of the child and the ability and willingness of the parties or any of them to satisfy the needs of the child.

When order may be made

(2) An order may be made under subsection (1) on or before the

hearing of the application in respect of custody of or access to the child and with or without a request by a party to the application.

Agreement by parties

(3) The court shall, if possible, appoint a person agreed upon by the parties, but if the parties do not agree the court shall choose and appoint the person.

Consent to act

(4) The court shall not appoint a person under subsection (1) unless the person has consented to make the assessment and to report to the court within the period of time specified by the court.

Attendance for assessment

(5) In an order under subsection (1), the court may require the parties, the child and any other person who has been given notice of the proposed order, or any of them, to attend for assessment by the person appointed by the court.

Refusal to attend

(6) Where a person ordered under this section to attend for assessment refuses to attend or to undergo the assessment, the court may draw such inferences in respect of the ability and willingness of any person to satisfy the needs of the child as the court considers appropriate.

Report

(7) The person appointed under subsection (1) shall file his report with the clerk or registrar of the court.

Copies of report

(8) The clerk or registrar of the court shall give a copy of the report to each of the parties and to counsel, if any, representing the child.

Admissibility of report

(9) The report mentioned in subsection (7) is admissible in evidence in the application.

Assessor may be witness

(10) Any of the parties, and counsel, if any, representing the child, may require the person appointed under subsection (1) to attend as a witness on the hearing of the application.

Directions

(11) Upon motion, the court by order may give such directions in respect of the assessment as the court considers appropriate.

Fees and expenses

(12) The court shall require the parties to pay the fees and expenses of the person appointed under subsection (1).

Idem, proportions or amounts

(13) The court shall specify in the order the proportions or amounts of the fees and expenses that the court requires each party to pay.

Idem, serious financial hardship

(14) The court may relieve a party from responsibility for payment of any of the fees and expenses of the person appointed under subsection (1) where the court is satisfied that payment would cause serious financial hardship to the party.

Other expert evidence

(15) The appointment of a person under subsection (1) does not prevent the parties or counsel representing the child from submitting other expert evidence as to the needs of the child and the ability and willingness of the parties or any of them to satisfy the needs of the child.

NEW BRUNSWICK

Family Services Act, S.N.B. 1980, c. F-2.2 [as amended]

[**Court may order psychiatric, etc., examination of child and parents**]

8. In any proceedings under this Act that affects a child, the court may, where it determines that it would be in the best interests of the child to do so, require that the child, a parent or any other person living with the child or in such a close relationship with the child as to be in a position to influence the nature of the care and control exercised with respect to the child, undergo a psychiatric, psychological, social, physical or any other examination or evaluation specified by the court, prior to or during the hearing, and in the event of the refusal or failure of any person to participate in an examination or evaluation, or to consent to the examination or evaluation of a child under his care, the court may draw such inferences as appear to the court to be warranted under the circumstances.

PRINCE EDWARD ISLAND

Custody Jurisdiction and Enforcement Act, S.P.E.I. 1984, c. 17

Application for order

4. (1) A parent of a child or any other person may apply to a court for an order respecting custody of or access to the child or determining any aspect of the incidents of custody of the child.

Idem

(2) On an application under this section, the court may require the Director of Child Welfare to cause an investigation to be made and to report to the court on all matters relating to the custody, maintenance and education of the child.

NEWFOUNDLAND

The Unified Family Court Act, S.N. 1977, c. 88 [as amended]

Court may order investigation

16. (1) Upon *ex parte* application, the court may direct a person who

(a) has had no previous connection with the parties to the proceeding, and

(b) is a family counsellor, social worker, probation officer, or other person approved by the court for the purpose,

to make a report on a party to the family matter or any other person who, in the opinion of the court, is associated with the family matter.

[**Presentation of report**]

(2) A person directed to make a report under subsection (1) shall, in such manner as the court may direct, present the report.

[**Service of copy of report**]

(3) No person shall present to a court the report made under subsection (1) unless, not less than twenty-four hours before the report is to be presented, he serves a copy of the report upon every party to the proceeding.

The Children's Law Act, S.N. 1988, c. 61 [as amended S.N. 1989, c. 11, s. 3(6), (7)]

Assessment of needs of child

36. (1) The court before which an application is brought in respect of custody of or access to a child, by order, may appoint a person who has technical or professional skill to investigate, assess and report to the court on the needs of the child and the ability and willingness of the parties to satisfy the needs of the child.

[**Order for assessment**]

(2) An order may be made under subsection (1) on or before the hearing of the application in respect of custody of or access to the child and with or without a request by a party to the application.

[**Appointment of person**]

(3) The court shall, if possible, appoint a person agreed upon by the parties, but if the parties do not agree the court shall choose and appoint an independent person.

[**Consent to appointment**]

(4) The court shall not appoint a person under this section unless the person has consented to make the assessment and to report to the court within the period of time specified by the court.

[**Terms of order**]

(5) In an order under subsection (1), the court may require the parties, the child and any other person who has been given notice of the proposed order, or any of them, to attend for assessment by the person appointed by the order.

[**Refusal to undergo assessment**]

(6) Where a person ordered under this section to attend for assessment refuses to attend or to undergo the assessment, the court may draw those inferences in respect of the ability and willingness of a person to satisfy the needs of the child that the court considers appropriate.

[**Report**]

(7) The person appointed under subsection (1) shall file his or her report with the clerk or registrar of the court.

[Copies]

(8) The clerk or registrar of the court shall give a copy of the report to each of the parties and to counsel, if any, representing the child.

[Admissibility]

(9) The report mentioned in subsection (7) is admissible in evidence in the application.

[Attendance at hearing]

(10) The parties, and counsel, if any, representing the child, may require the person appointed under subsection (1) to attend as a witness at the hearing of the application.

[Directions]

(11) Upon motion, the court by order may give those directions in respect of the assessment that the court considers appropriate.

[Fees and expenses]

(12) The court shall require the parties to pay the fees and expenses of the person appointed under subsection (1) except where that person is on the staff of the court.

[Apportionment of fees and expenses]

(13) The court shall specify in the order the proportions or amounts of the fees and expenses that the court requires each party to pay.

[Idem]

(14) The court may require one party to pay all the fees and expenses of the person appointed under subsection (1) where the court is satisfied that payment would cause the other party serious financial hardship.

[Other expert evidence]

(15) The appointment of a person under subsection (1) does not prevent the parties or counsel representing the child from submitting other expert evidence as to the needs of the child and the ability and willingness of the parties to satisfy the needs of the child.

APPENDIX II

Legislative Guidelines for the Determination of Custody

The generally accepted standard the courts must apply to custody disputes in Canada is "best interests" of the child. Provincial statutes have only begun the task of defining "best interests" in the past few years, and consequently courts must also look to a broad compendium of case law to determine which facts must be weighed in determining "best interest".

Assessors should ensure that they receive, from the referring lawyers, a copy of any relevant legislative sections defining the standards to be used by the court with jurisdiction over the case. Lawyers should ensure that the assessor knows which factors the court must consider, and ask the assessor to bear those in mind while conducting the assessment and framing the report.

It is not the assessor's task to acquire the evidence for the lawyers on the issue of "best interests", but the factors to be considered by the court should be borne in mind and addressed if possible.

CANADA

The Divorce Act, R.S.C. 1985, c. 3 (2nd Supp.) [as amended]

[**Order for custody**]

Factors

16. (8) In making an order under this section, the court shall take into consideration only the best interests of the child of the marriage as determined by reference to the condition, means, needs and other circumstances of the child.

Past conduct

(9) In making an order under this section, the court shall not take into consideration the past conduct of any person unless the conduct is relevant to the ability of that person to act as a parent of a child.

Maximum contact

(10) In making an order under this section, the court shall give effect to the principle that a child of the marriage should have as much contact with each spouse as is consistent with the best interests of the child and, for that purpose, shall take into consideration the willingness of the person for whom custody is going to facilitate such contact.

NORTHWEST TERRITORIES

Domestic Relations Act, R.S.N.W.T. 1974, c. D-9 [as amended S.N.W.T. 1985 (3d) c. 10, s. 52]

[Court considerations]

34. (2) In making an order under subsection (1), the Court shall have regard to

(a) the welfare of the infant,
(b) the conduct of the parents, and
(c) the wishes of the mother as well as of the father.

YUKON

Children's Act, R.S.Y. 1986, c. 22 [as amended]

Best interests of child

30. (1) In determining the best interests of a child for the purposes of an application under this Part in respect of custody of or access to a child, the court shall consider all the needs and circumstances of the child including

(a) the bonding, love, affection and emotional ties between the child and,

(i) each person entitled to or claiming custody of or access to the child,
(ii) other members of the child's family who reside with the child, and
(iii) persons involved in the care and upbringing of the child,

(b) the views and preferences of the child, where such views and preferences can be reasonably ascertained,
(c) the length of time, having regard to the child's sense of time, that the child has lived in a stable home environment.
(d) the ability and willingness of each person applying for custody of the child to provide the child with guidance, education, the necessaries of life and any special needs of the child,
(e) any plans proposed for the care and upbringing of the child,
(f) the permanence and stability of the family unit with which it is proposed that the child will live, and
(g) the effect that awarding custody or care of the child to one party would have on the ability of the other party to have reasonable access to the child.

[Past conduct]

(2) The past conduct of a person is not relevant to a determination of an application under this Part in respect of custody of or access to a child unless the conduct is relevant to the ability of the person to have the care or custody of a child.

[No presumption based on age or sex of child]

(3) There is no presumption of law or fact that the best interests of a child are, solely by virtue of the age or the sex of the child, best served by placing the child in the care or custody of a female person rather than a male person or of a male person rather than a female person.

[Presumption in favour of joint custody]

(4) In any proceedings in respect of custody of a child between the mother and the father of that child, there shall be a rebuttable presumption that the court ought to award the care of the child to one parent or the other and that all other parental rights associated with custody of that child ought to be shared by the mother and the father jointly.

BRITISH COLUMBIA

Family Relations Act, R.S.B.C. 1979, c. 121 [as amended]

Best interests of child are paramount

24. (1) Where making, varying or rescinding an order under this Part, a court shall give paramount consideration to the best interests of the child and, in assessing these interests, shall consider these factors:

(a) the health and emotional well being of the child including any special needs for care and treatment;
(b) where appropriate, the views of the child;
(c) the love, affection and similar ties that exist between the child and other persons;
(d) education and training for the child; and
(e) the capacity of each person to whom guardianship, custody or access rights and duties may be granted to exercise these rights and duties adequately;

and give emphasis to each factor according to the child's needs and circumstances.

. . . .

[Conduct]

(3) Where the conduct of a person does not substantially affect a factor set out in subsection (1) or (2), the court shall not consider that conduct in a proceeding respecting an order under this part.

[How relevant]

(4) Where under subsection (3) the conduct of a person may be considered by a court, the court shall consider the conduct only to the extent that the conduct affects a factor set out in subsection (1) or (2).

ALBERTA

Domestic Relations Act, R.S.A. 1980, c. D-37 [as amended]

[Factors to be considered by Court]

56. (2) In making an order under subsection (1), the Court shall have regard

(a) to the welfare of the minor,
(b) to the conduct of the parents, and
(c) to the wishes as well of the mother as of the father.

SASKATCHEWAN

The Infants' Act, R.S.S. 1978, c. I-9 [as amended]

Orders as to custody, etc. of infants

3. (1) The Court of Queen's Bench may, on the application of a parent or other person having, in the opinion of the court, a sufficient interest, make an order regarding the custody, care and upbringing of an infant.

. . . .

[Welfare of the infant the only consideration]

(3) In making an order under subsection (1), the court shall have regard only for the welfare of the infant and, for that purpose, the court shall consider the physical, psychological, social and economic needs of the infant and in doing so shall take into account:

(a) the quality of the relationships that the infant has with the persons to whom custody, care and upbringing might be entrusted and with any other persons, such as brothers and sisters of the infant, who may have a close connection with the question of the infant's custody, care and upbringing;

(b) the personality and character and the emotional needs of the infant;
(c) the capacity to be a parent of any person to whom the custody, care and upbringing of the infant might be entrusted, the home environment to be provided for the infant and the plans that person has for the future of the infant; and
(d) the preference of the infant, to the extent the court considers appropriate, having regard to the age and maturity of the infant.

MANITOBA

The Family Maintenance Act, R.S.M. 1987, c. F20 [as amended]

Best interests test applies

2. (1) In all proceedings under this Act the best interests of the child shall be the paramount consideration of the court.

Child's views to be considered

(2) Where the court is satisfied that a child is able to understand the nature of the proceedings and the court considers that it would not be harmful to the child, the court may consider the views and preferences of the child.

ONTARIO

The Children's Law Reform Act, R.S.O. 1980, c. 68 [as amended S.O. 1982 c. 20]

Merits of application for custody or access

24. (1) The merits of an application under this Part in respect of custody of or access to a child shall be determined on the basis of the best interests of the child.

Best interests of child

(2) In determining the best interests of a child for the purposes of an application under this Part in respect of custody of or access to a child, a court shall consider all the needs and circumstances of the child including,

(a) the love, affection and emotional ties between the child and,

(i) each person entitled to or claiming custody of or access to the child,
(ii) other members of the child's family who reside with the child, and
(iii) persons involved in the care and upbringing of the child;

(b) the views and preferences of the child, where such views and preferences can reasonably be ascertained;
(c) the length of time the child has lived in a stable home environment;
(d) the ability and willingness of each person applying for custody of the child to provide the child with guidance and education, the necessaries of life and any special needs of the child;
(e) any plans proposed for the care and upbringing of the child;
(f) the permanence and stability of the family unit with which it is proposed that the child will live; and
(g) the relationship by blood or through an adoption order between the child and each person who is a party to the application.

Past conduct

(3) The past conduct of a person is not relevant to a determination of an application under this Part in respect of custody of or access to a child unless the conduct is relevant to the ability of the person to act as a parent of a child.

NOVA SCOTIA

Infants' Custody Act, R.S.N.S. 1967, c. 145 [as amended]

Regard to be had to welfare of infant

2. In making such order the Court or judge shall have regard to the welfare of the infant, and to the conduct or circumstances of the parents, and to the wishes as well of the mother as of the father.

NEW BRUNSWICK

Family Services Act, S.N.B. 1980, c. F-2.2 [as amended]

Definitions

1. In this Act

. . . .

"best interests of the child" means the best interests of the child under the circumstances taking into consideration

(a) the mental, emotional and physical health of the child and his need for appropriate care or treatment, or both;
(b) the views and preferences of the child, where such views and preferences can be reasonably ascertained;
(c) the effect upon the child of any disruption of the child's sense

of continuity;

(d) the love, affection and ties that exist between the child and each person to whom the child's custody is entrusted, each person to whom access to the child is granted and, where appropriate, each sibling of the child;

(e) the merits of any plan proposed by the Minister under which he would be caring for the child, in comparison with the merits of the child returning to or remaining with his parents;

(f) the need to provide a secure environment that would permit the child to become a useful and productive member of society through the achievement of his full potential according to his individual capacity; and

(g) the child's cultural and religious heritage. . . .

NEWFOUNDLAND

The Children's Law Act, S.N. 1988, c. 61

Merits of application for custody or access

31. (1) The merits of an application under this Part in respect of custody of or access to a child shall be determined on the basis of the best interests of the child.

[**Best interests of child**]

(2) In determining the best interests of a child for the purposes of an application under this Part in respect of custody of or access to a child, a court shall consider all the needs and circumstances of the child including

(a) the love, affection and emotional ties between the child and,

(i) each person entitled to or claiming custody of or access to the child,

(ii) other members of the child's family who reside with the child, and

(iii) persons involved in the care and upbringing of the child;

(b) the views and preferences of the child, where the views and preferences can reasonably be ascertained;

(c) the length of time the child has lived in a stable home environment;

(d) the ability and willingness of each person applying for custody of the child to provide the child with guidance and education, the necessaries of life and the special needs of the child;

(e) the ability of each parent seeking the custody or access to act as a parent;
(f) plans proposed for the care and upbringing of the child;
(g) the permanence and stability of the family unit with which it is proposed that the child will live; and
(h) the relationship by blood or through an adoption order between the child and each person who is a party to the application.

[**Past conduct**]

(3) In assessing a person's ability to act as a parent, the court shall consider whether the person has ever acted in a violent manner towards

(a) his or her spouse or child;
(b) his or her child's parent; or
(c) another member of the household,

otherwise a person's past conduct shall only be considered if the court thinks it relevant to the person's ability to act as a parent.

APPENDIX III

Bibliography

Selected Resources re Assessments and Assessment Methodology

Awad, George. "Basic Principles in Custody Assessment." *Journal of the Canadian Psychiatric Association*, Vol. 23, 1978.

Bala, Nicholas. "Assessing The Assessor: Legal Issues." *Assessing The Assessor.* Toronto: Law Society of Upper Canada, 1989.

Blum, D. "The Psychologist as Inexpert Witness" (1980), 15 Reports of Family Law (2d) 24.

Blumall, Donna M. "Child Custody Determination: Issues for Psychological Evaluation." (1980), 12 Reports of Family Law (2d) 18.

Caplan, Paula J. "Preliminary Analysis of the Law Society of Upper Canada's Questionnaire Survey of Mental Health Professionals Who Conduct Child Custody Assessments." *Assessing The Assessor.* Toronto: Law Society of Upper Canada, 1989

Chisholm, Barbara A. "Obtaining and Weighing the Children's Wishes: Private Interviews with a Judge or Assessment by an Expert and Report." (1981), 23 Reports of Family Law (2d) 1.

Chisholm, Barbara A. "Preparing Your Client For Assessment or Mediation." (1987), 1 Canadian Family Law Quarterly 385.

Daley, Timothy T. "Custody, The Social Worker, and The Court." (1981), 18 Reports of Family Law (2d) 14.

Daley, Timothy T. "Negligent Statements and The Social Worker." (1979), 10 Reports of Family Law (2d) 1.

Day, David C. "Preparing The Assessment." Chapter in *Social Work and Family Law.* St. John's, Newfoundland: Memorial University, 1987.

Duquette, Donald N. "Child Custody Decision-Making: The Lawyer-Behavioral Scientist Interface." *Journal of Clinical Child Psychology* Fall 1978, Vol. 7 (3).

Fine, Stuart. "Children in Divorce, Custody, and Access Situations: The Contribution of the Mental Health Professional." *Journal of Child Psychology and Psychiatry and Allied Disciplines,* October 1980, Vol. 21 (4).

Gardner, Richard. *Family Evaluation in Child Custody Litigation.* New Jersey: Creative Therapeutics, 1982.

Gardner, Richard. "My Involvement in Child Custody Litigation: Past, Present and Future." *Family and Conciliation Courts Review*, July 1989, Vol. 27(2).

Gardner, Richard. *Family Evaluation in Child Custody Mediation, Arbitration, and Litigation.* New Jersey: Creative Therapeutics, 1989.

Goldzband, Melvin G. *Consulting in Child Custody: An Introduction to the Ugliest Litigation for Mental Health Professionals.* Toronto: Heath, 1982.

Haller, L.H. "Before the Judge: The Child Custody Evaluation." *Adolescent Psychiatry* Vol. 9, 1981.

Jackson, Anna M., *et. al.* "Beyond the Best Interests of The Child Revisited: An Approach to Child Custody Evaluations." *Journal of Divorce*, Spring 1980, Vol. 3 (3).

Kaplan, F.K., B.L. Landau, and R.L. McWhinney. *Custody/Access Assessment Guidelines: Report of the Interdisciplinary Committee for Custody/Access Assessments.*Toronto: The Ontario Psychological Foundation, 1988.

Keeney, B.P., ed. *Diagnosis and Assessment in Family Therapy.* Colorado: Rockville, Aspen Publications, 1983.

Leonoff, A., and M. O'Neill. "Custody Decision: Some Psychological Factors." (1979), 8 Reports of Family Law (2d) 179.

Levy, Alan M. "Child Custody Determination: A Proposed Psychiatric Methodology and its Resultant Case Typology." *Journal of Psychiatry and The Law*, Summer 1978, Vol. 6 (2).

Levy, "Custody Investigations as Evidence in Divorce Cases" (1987), 21 F.L.Q. 149.

Lillesand & Lillesand. "The Role of Psychologists in Child Custody Litigation." Florida B.J., 1989, Vol. 63.

Lytle-Vieiri, Jane E. "Kramer v. Kramer Revisited: The Social Work Role in Child Custody Access." *Social Work*, Jan./Feb. 1987 (5).

Mark, Charles. "The Role and Impact of the Expert in the Resolution of Domestic Disputes." *Families, Children and the Law.* Toronto: Law Society of Upper Canada, 1985.

Mayhew, C., and K. Raiford. "Guidelines for Court Connected Child Custody Evaluations." *Conciliation Courts Review* 1986, Vol. 23.

Menuck, Morton. "Clinical Assessment of Dangerous Behaviour" in M.H. Ben-Aron *et al. Clinical Criminology: The Assessment and Treatment of*

Criminal Behaviour. Clark Institute of Psychiatry. Toronto: University of Toronto, 1985.

Musetto, Andrew P. "Child Custody and Visitation: The Role of the Clinician in Relation to the Family." *Family Therapy* 1978 b, 5, pp. 143-150.

Musetto, Andrew P. "Evaluating Families with Custody or Visitation Problems." *Journal of Marriage and Family Counselling* 1978 a, 4 (4), pp. 59-65.

Parry, Ruth, E. Broder, E.A.F. Schmidt, E. Saunders, and E. Hood. *Custody Disputes Evaluation and Intervention.* Toronto: Lexington Books, 1985.

Pauker, Jerome D. "The Role of Psychological Testing in Custody Assessment." Paper presented at conference of the Ontario Psychological Association, Toronto, 1983.

Quarrington, Bruce. "Custody and Access Assessments." *The Bulletin, The Ontario Board of Examiners in Psychology,* Vol. II No. 1, April 1988.

Seagull, E.A.W. "The Child Psychologist's Role in Family Assessments" in R.E. Helfer and R.S. Kempe, *The Battered Child.* 4th ed. Chicago: University of Chicago Press, 1987.

Skafte, Dianne. *Child Custody Evaluations: A Practical Guide.* California: Sage Publications, 1986.

Steinhauer, Paul D. "Assessing for Parenting Capacity." Paper presented at conference of the Ontario Family Court Clinic, Hamilton, May 1981.

Swann, Bill. "The Dangers in Using Court Appointed Experts in Child Custody Cases." 27 *Judge's Journal* 17, 1988.

Woody, Robert H. "Behavioral Science Criteria in Child Custody Determinations." *Journal of Marriage and Family Counselling,* January 1977, Vol. 3(1).

Selected Resources re Child Custody and Child Advocacy

Amos, Iris E. "Child Advocacy and the Adversary System: Round Peg in a Square Hole?" *Journal of Clinical Child Psychology,* Spring 1981, Vol. 10 (1).

Bross, Donald C. and L.F. Michaels. *Foundations of Child Advocacy.* Colorado: Bookmakers Guild Inc., 1987.

Chisholm, Barbara A. "Children's Rights." *Perception.* Canadian Council on Social Development. Ottawa, Nov./Dec. 1977, Vol. 1 (2).

Felner, R.D., and S.S. Farber. "Social Policy for Child Custody: A Multidisciplinary Framework." *Journal of Orthopsychiatry*, April 1980, Vol. 50 (2).

Fineman and Opie. "The Uses of Social Science Data in Legal Policy Making: Custody Determinations and Divorce." *Wisconsin Law Review*, Vol. 107, 1987.

Fineman, Martha. "Dominant Discourse, Professional Language, and Legal Change in Child Custody Decisionmaking." *Harvard Law Review*, February 1988, Vol. 1(4).

Goldstein, J., A. Freud, and A.J. Solnit. *Before the Best Interests of the Child.* New York: The Free Press, 1979.

Goldstein, J., A. Freud, and A.J. Solnit. *Beyond the Best Interests of the Child.* New York: The Free Press, 1973.

Halarambie, Ann. *Handling Child Custody Cases.* Colorado Springs: McGraw Hill Inc., 1983.

Katz, Sanford, ed. *The Youngest Minority — Lawyers in Defence of Children.* Washington, D.C.: American Bar Association, 1974.

McDermott, J.F., *et al.* "Child Custody Decision-Making: The Search for Improvement." *Journal of American Academy of Child Psychiatry*, Winter 1978, Vol. 17 (1).

Musetto, Andrew P. "Standards for Deciding Contested Child Custody." *Journal of Clinical Child Psychology*, Spring 1981, Vol. 10 (1).

Rutter, Michael. *Maternal Deprivation Reassessed.* 2nd ed. Harmondworth: Penguin, 1981.

Zemans, F.H. "The Issue of Cultural Diversity in Custody Disputes." (1983), 32 Reports of Family Law (2d) 50.

Selected Resources re Evaluation and Advocacy re Child Abuse

Bross, Donald C., ed. *Multidisciplinary Advocacy for Mistreated Children.* Denver, Colorado: National Association of Counsel for Children, 1984.

Burgess, A.W., A.N. Groth, L.L. Holstrom, and S.M. Sgroi. *Sexual Assault of Children and Adolescents.* Toronto: Lexington Books, 1978.

Dickens, Bernard M. "Child Abuse Law in Canada and The United States" in R. Volpe, *et al. The Maltreatment of the School-Aged Child.* Toronto: Lexington Books, 1980.

Finkelhor, David, and Associates. *A Sourcebook on Child Sexual Abuse.* California: Sage Publications, 1986.

Finkelhor, David. *Child Sexual Abuse: New Therapy and Research.* New York: The Free Press, 1984.

Finkelhor, David. *Sexually Victimized Children.* New York: The Free Press, 1979.

Helfer, R.E., and R.S. Kempe. *The Battered Child.* 4th ed. Chicago: University of Chicago Press, 1987.

Kempe, Ruth S., and Henry C. Kempe. *The Common Secret: Sexual Abuse of Children and Adolescents.* New York: W.H. Freeman & Co., 1984.

Ontario Association of Professional Social Workers. *Child Abuse: A Handbook for Social Workers in Ontario.* Toronto: The Ontario Association of Professional Social Workers, 1983.

Sgroi, Suzanne. *Handbook of Clinical Intervention in Child Sexual Abuse.* Toronto: Lexington Books, 1984.

Sgroi, Suzanne. *Vulnerable Populations: Evaluation and Treatment of Sexually Abused Children and Adult Survivors.* Vol. 1, Toronto: Lexington Books, 1988.

Selected Resources re the Assessor as Expert Witness

American Psychiatric Association. *Diagnostic and Statistical Manual of Mental Disorders.* 3d ed., Rev'd. Washington, D.C.: American Psychiatric Association, 1987.

Anastasi, Anne. *Psychological Testing.* 6th ed. New York: MacMillan, 1988.

Blum, Donna M. "The Psychologist as 'Inexpert' Witness." (1980), 15 Reports of Family Law (2d) 24.

Cross, Sir Rupert. *Cross On Evidence.* 6th ed. London: Butterworths, 1985.

Dickens, Bernard M. "The Use of Experts in Child Welfare Proceedings." *Family Law in the Provincial Courts (Family Division).* Toronto: Canadian Bar Association-Ontario, 1982.

Faust, D., and J. Ziskin. "The Expert Witness in Psychology and Psychiatry." *Science* 1988, 241:31.

Goldman. "The Use of Learned Treatises in Canadian and United States Litigation." (1976) 24, University of Toronto, L.J., p. 423.

Goldzband, Melvin G. *Custody Cases and Expert Witnesses: A Manual for Attorneys.* New York: Law and Business, Inc., 1980.

Hatton, Mary Jane "Expert Child Abuse Witnesses: The Parents' Perspective." *Family Law in the Provincial Courts (Family Division).* Toronto: Canadian Bar Association-Ontario, 1986.

Levy, Earl J., Q.C. *The Examination of Witnesses in Criminal Cases.* Toronto: Carswell, 1987.

Lightner, J. "An Attorney's Approach to Psychiatrists in Custody Cases." *The Bulletin — American Academy of Psychiatry and Law,* 1976, Vol. 4 (2).

Moir, Donald. "The Clinician As Witness." Conciliation Courts Review, June 1984, Vol. 21 (1).

Rotenberg, Jerome S. "Cross-Examination Skills." *Family Law in the Provincial Courts (Family Division).* Toronto: Canadian Bar Association-Ontario, 1986.

Salhany, Roger E. *Cross-Examination: The Art of the Advocate.* Toronto: Butterworths, 1988.

Scarcella, G.R. "Expert Child Abuse Witnesses: Practical Considerations (An Agency Perspective)." *Family Law in the Provincial Courts (Family Division).* Toronto: Canadian Bar Association-Ontario, 1986.

Sopinka, John. *The Trial of An Action.* Toronto: Butterworths, 1981.

Ziskin, Jay, and David Faust. *Coping with Psychiatric and Psychological Testimony.* 4th ed. Venice, California: Law and Psychology Press, 1988.

Index

Index of Forms and Precedents

LISTED IN APPROXIMATE ORDER OF USE